D0889908

The Easy Chair

The Easy Chair

by

Bernard DeVoto

Essay Index Reprint Series

BOOKS FOR LIBRARIES PRESS
FREEPORT, NEW YORK

Reprinted 1971 by Arrangement with
Houghton Mifflin Company

INTERNATIONAL STANDARD BOOK NUMBER:
0-8369-2433-9

LIBRARY OF CONGRESS CATALOG CARD NUMBER:
78-167333

PRINTED IN THE UNITED STATES OF AMERICA
BY
NEW WORLD BOOK MANUFACTURING CO., INC.
HALLANDALE, FLORIDA 33009

Dedicated to

the Sixth Floor Front

with love and much gratitude to my classmate

Rose Daly

and indulgently to the young folks

Jack Fischer
John Kouwenhoven
Russell Lynes
Kay Jackson
Eric Larrabee
Catharine Meyer
Anne Freedgood

Preface

WHATEVER ELSE society may have, and whatever it may at times lack, it insists on having priests, doctors, and people who disseminate and interpret the news. The demand for the services which the three professions perform is only increased by social turbulence that may threaten other professions with extinction. Journalism ranks much lower than the other two in public esteem and its practitioners are not granted the ordainment priests receive or the consecration doctors advertise themselves as possessing. But they are more constantly in demand and their field is by far the largest. Between them, the town crier and the pamphleteer pretty well cover that field, but it has many departments and they cover it by many kinds of activity, some of which have only an indirect relation to the news as such. Of many of these activities we may say that they are not important, they are only indispensable.

An assumption presents this book as entitled to a certificate of legitimacy under the statutes governing fair trade: the assumption that the kind of journalism represented by the magazine in which its contents appeared has proved necessary. *Harper's* serves a good many uses, and it serves some of them by means of such articles as those reprinted here.

Courses given at schools of journalism must occasionally, I think, discuss *Harper's*. How would a professor who gives such a course describe it to his class? He would characterize it as a magazine of critical inquiry and appraisal, a forum for the expression and discussion of ideas, and a vehicle for the publication of some kinds of news and of comment on many kinds. He would point out that it is addressed to the best educated audience in the United States. He would say that this audience gives it public influence altogether disproportionate to the size of its circulation. And I believe he would be constrained to add that there is no journalism more expert.

It began with the issue for June 1850 and as *Harper's New Monthly Magazine*. Sixteen months later, in the October 1851 issue, a new department appeared in it, called "The Editor's Easy Chair," though it was not written — indeed it never was to be written — by the editor of *Harper's*. It was a department of personal comment and it has appeared regularly ever since, except for a lapse of eight years.

For two years the new department was written, though not signed, by Donald G. Mitchell, who is known to literary history today only as the author, under his pseudonym Ik Marvel, of a series of sentimental fantasies called *Reveries of a Bachelor*. From 1853 to 1859 the Editor's Easy Chair was written jointly by Mitchell and George William Curtis, the encyclopedist, publicist, and reformer. Mitchell's association with it ended in 1859 and Curtis wrote it from then till his death in 1892, following which the eight-year lapse occurred. The column was revived in 1900 under the authorship of William Dean Howells, who wrote it for twenty years. Edward S. Martin succeeded Howells in 1920, and I succeeded Martin in 1935. At that time the name was abbreviated to The Easy Chair.

Thus the Easy Chair is the oldest editorial feature in American journalism. My four predecessors all had literary careers but they were all working journalists too. All had been reporters and editorial writers; all were expert at a characteristic form of magazine journalism that is neither reportorial nor editorial but expository. And all were that indefinable but highly specific thing, the professional writer. The title, the Easy Chair, was no doubt intended to suggest a lamplit study withdrawn from the bustle of commerce, with an overtone of reflection, of leisure, or at least time, to think beyond surface appearances. It was also meant to have a connotation of urbane informality, of a graceful interplay of thought and personality that used to be more highly regarded as literature than it is now. Yet the Easy Chair has never corresponded entirely to these connotations, which add up to the genteel or familiar essay. It has always had a quality it could not get in the study but only down the street, at the square, and in the city hall. If study and reflection have gone into it, so have legwork, sweat, and the opinion that is based not on research but on experience and participation. The five men who have written it were fairly entitled to more than five literary labels; three or perhaps four were novelists, two were humorists, one was a dramatist, and one a historian. But, I repeat, all have been working journalists and all have been professional writers.

We may say that the professional is a writer who has subdued himself to the job rather than shaped the job to enhance his awareness of himself. If the Easy Chair has served a genuine need, it has done so for that reason. Indeed, since it is a column of personal comment, only a professional writer could write it effectively—only a man who knows that the opinion and the expression of the opinion are everything and that the person who holds it does not, in journalism, count at all. I do not know as much about Mitchell as I ought to but I am sure of my ground with the other three. What they had to say and getting it said were important; they knew that they themselves had no importance for the end in view. As for me, I agree with the character farther along in the book who remarks that you would only snicker if the chore boy proved to be too fastidious a spirit to go on mowing the lawn. But the chores have to be done.

I feel that the title does not misrepresent the book, though seven of the thirty-one items reprinted here did not appear originally in the Easy Chair. Six of them were text articles in *Harper's:* "The Century," "Doctors Along the Boardwalk," "The Smokejumpers," "The West Against Itself," "Sacred Cows and Public Lands," and "Conservation: Down and on the Way Out." The seventh, "The Ex-Communists," appeared in the *Atlantic Monthly*. There is no discrepancy. These pieces and the Easy Chair are all of the same substance, the substance of a *Harper's* article, which I have described several times. Even "The Ex-Communists" expounds a text that was first a single sentence in an Easy Chair, in "But Sometimes They Vote Right Too." My friend Charles W. Morton, the associate editor of the *Atlantic*, spotted a sermon in it and asked me to write the sermon.

I have arranged the contents in groups, only the last of which follows a chronological order. I found one misstatement of fact and have corrected it without calling attention to it. Because of developments following the original publication, I have thought it best to make comments on some of the pieces; these comments are in the "Notes."

I am indebted to Harper and Brothers and The Atlantic Monthly Company for permission to reprint these articles, and to Miss Barbara Elferink for making the preliminary selection, preparing the typescript, and doing many other laborious jobs that the book has involved.

I invite the reader to consider "Number 241" a continuation of this preface.

BERNARD DEVOTO

Cambridge, Massachusetts
April 15, 1955

Contents

IV Editorial Column

V Treatise on a Function of Journalism

I

Masthead

Number 241

(NOVEMBER 1955)

The Nieman Fellows are newspapermen who spend a year studying at Harvard in order, so the grant that finances them reads, "to promote and elevate standards of journalism" in the United States. At intervals writers and editors are invited to talk to them about problems of journalism, and some time ago this election fell on the editor of *Harper's*. He chose to discuss the kind of journalism that *Harper's* publishes. Before he got very far there was a question from the floor: What fees did he pay for contributions? They are not of Hollywood size and another question followed at once, "How do you get anyone to write for *Harper's?*" There was no problem, the editor said; the articles that *Harper's* publishes are written by people who want to write for *Harper's*. The magazine pays as much as it can afford to but for the *Harper's* writer the fee is not the first consideration, it is not even an important one. He wants to bring something to the attention of the public.

For many *Harper's* pieces there is only one other possible outlet, the *Atlantic*. I cite the articles about the struggle over the public lands that I have been running periodically in the Easy Chair and the body of the magazine ever since January 1947. Some have been straight news stories, some have been editorial comment, some have been primarily polemic; but whatever their nature, they have given the subject the only adequate coverage it has had anywhere. No newspaper has covered it well, and that goes for the *New York*

Times. Apart from *Harper's* no magazine has more than glanced at it. Presumably I could have published most of my pieces in the *Atlantic* — but where else? Several magazines for sportsmen ran occasional articles about isolated parts of the struggle. In the first year after the story of the landgrab broke — after I broke the story — *Collier's* ran two pieces about it. No other mass-circulation magazine would touch it. The weeklies never got past the fringe. But *Harper's* ran my articles; to run such articles is one of its functions.

Harper's and the *Atlantic* are the only survivors of what was called the Quality Group when I was in college. The phrase carries no implication that there is not journalism as expert in other magazines; it does imply that much quality group journalism is different in kind, context, or treatment from other journalism, and that it has some forms of its own. All the other original members of the group have died and only two magazines that can be considered to belong to it have been established, *Fortune* and the *New Yorker.* Some *Harper's* articles might well appear in one or the other of them; some others might appear in such magazines as the *New Republic* or the *Reporter.* None of these magazines, however, shares more than a part of the *Harper's* field. In the Easy Chair of the Centennial Issue I described that field, and I explained that *Harper's* has survived because it assumed some functions that American journalism at large has either relinquished voluntarily or proved unable to perform. The "people who want to write for *Harper's*" perform those functions.

I appear to be the person who wants most to write for *Harper's.* I have kept a file of my publications but I know that it is not complete and so I cannot say exactly how many pieces I have published in this magazine. There must have been at least thirty text articles and I began writing the Easy Chair twenty years ago this month, with the issue of November 1935. The total must be at least eight hundred thousand words, and more likely it is nine hundred thousand — the equivalent of half a dozen long books. As my twentieth anniversary approached, it occurred to me with some force that I have written more for *Harper's* than anyone else now living.

Number 241 (November 1955)

When my turn to address the Niemans came, I reminded them that the Easy Chair is the oldest editorial feature in American journalism. It is subject to the conditions of monthly journalism but only one limitation is set on it, that of length. I used to work three weeks ahead of publication, but the breath-taking advance in technology that is called American knowhow spread to printing establishments and for some years I have had to work seven weeks ahead. The limitation of length and the long time lapse are a monthly test of a writer's professional judgment, not to speak of his luck. (My luck has been good; in twenty years I have had to make only one stop-press change because a situation had developed otherwise than I had judged it would.) Also, I have a deadline. The editors will tell you that I have never missed it, and I can tell you that I am scrupulous not to anticipate it. One of the satisfactions of being a *Harper's* writer is that you remain your own writer; your work is not taken down, reassembled, and rewritten by a committee; you are expected to provide your own structure, verification, and who-he. But even the writers who edit *Harper's* are editors; their fingers may be counted on to twitch if given time.

When the Niemans pressed me for a label that would describe the Easy Chair I could do no better than "cultural criticism," which is unsatisfactory. I have never formulated any principles for writing it but I have probably observed some. Such a column as this could not easily be pretentious and I have tried to keep it from being pompous. I have tried to avoid repeating myself, at short intervals anyway, and to keep the subject matter so varied that a reader would not know what to expect when he turned to the column. I have ranged so widely that I found I could not represent the full scope of the Easy Chair in this volume of selections. I have assumed that there was no public demand for me to write about anything at all but that if I was interested in something, some readers would be interested in it too. But also I have written about a good many subjects not primarily because I wanted to write about them but because it seemed likely that no one else would. *Harper's* does some chores because it believes that journalism must not leave them undone; so does the Easy Chair.

Some implications of my job were obvious from the beginning; others became apparent to me only gradually. Fact pieces in the *New Yorker* have a formula which is intended to preserve the convention that Mr. Tilley's interest in anything is strictly dilettante. "When I met Mr. Chase the next morning, he suggested that I have coffee with Mr. Sanborn while the reports from the whatisits were coming in." For a time after I began writing the Easy Chair I went to equal length to give it an appearance of editorial anonymity. But the personal pronoun is a space-saver and I found myself more and more forced to make use of it. I was surprised to find that readers welcomed it. Not many places where personal journalism can be practiced legitimately remain; there seems to be a use for what is left of it.

Equally surprising is the value attributed to such editorial space as mine by press agents. In the name of our common culture and the American way they call on me to publicize goods, liquors, restaurants, business firms, crusading organizations, crackpot organizations, causes, people who pay to get their names in print, and one columnist whose social engineer keeps demanding that I explain to my readers how the American language has been enriched by the words he invents. These efforts are occasionally subtle but usually high-pressure, frequently elaborate, and sometimes so persistent that it would have been cheaper for the client to buy four pages of display space in *Harper's.* If any has succeeded, then it succeeded brilliantly for I did not know I was being taken. Sometimes a press agent's solicitation has resulted in my abandoning an Easy Chair I had intended to write.

Such eagerness does not inflate my ego, for there are counterirritants. Some of my most enthusiastic readers are people who have been reading someone else, frequently Elmer Davis. Others understand that the Easy Chair is a department of the *Atlantic.* And things happen, as when an apparently sober publisher once thanked me for rescuing a book he had published. The sale was small and had dried up, he said, but following my Easy Chair about it, it revived and ran sixteen thousand copies. This was a flattering story but it had a hole in it, for I hadn't written anything about the book. And I get a lot of letters praising or denouncing pieces which neither I nor anyone else has written.

Readers write to me; newspapers run quotes from the Easy Chair and write editorials about it; other writers use it or refer to it in articles and books. These are the only means I have of judging the response to it. It has had enough supporters to count or I would have been fired. It has had opponents and even enemies, some of them habitual or occupational. I have annoyed quite a lot of people but though I have cost *Harper's* some subscribers there have been no lawsuits. A cheesemaker tried hard to suppress me and a publisher of books to censor me. Neither succeeded.

The Easy Chair is sometimes called controversial, even by Personal and Otherwise, but the adjective is inaccurate. I have deliberately precipitated only one controversy, the one over the public lands I have mentioned, and I precipitated that one as a reporter. It took me some time to understand what the reality behind the inaccurate adjective is and why the Easy Chair has produced so much more heat than it has carried. My job is to write about anything in American life that may interest me, but it is also to arrive at judgments under my own steam, independently of others. With some judgments that is the end of the line; express them and you have nothing more to do. But there are also judgments that require you to commit yourself, to stick your neck out. Expressing them in print obliges you to go on to advocacy. They get home to people's beliefs and feelings about important things, and that makes them inflammable.

I seem most consistently to offend two groups that have in common a love of simplifications and absolutes: writers of advertising copy and contributors to quarterlies that deal with epistemology and, trailing by some lengths, literature. Copy writers always run a mild fever, quite trivial stimuli can send it shooting up, and I am always wounding these poet-patriots without intending to. Commonly they assail me with one or the other of two libels, that only a communist would disparage manufactured goods and that I could have made a fortune, as clearly I have not done, if I had gone into advertising. Often they are rhetorically belligerent and the announced ambition of one is to punch my nose. Still, I was once asked to address a meeting of advertising men, whereas so far as I know no quarterly has ever approved of anything I have written. The accusation here is on different grounds and there is no lament that I once had it in me to become a literary person. Instead there is a twofold anxiety, to establish that I am middlebrow, philistine, superficial, the enemy — in a word, a journalist — and that I have betrayed or subverted literary thinking.

The condescension seems superfluous, a waste of energy. It is fully visible that I respect reality-judgments as requiring more intelligence than fantasy and think them a better instrument for critical analysis. Just as visibly I distrust the literary approach to experience, preferring direct approaches. The universals of a priori thinking are not for me, large abstractions will not fit my hand, and I work with complexities and tentatives. Certainly, I am a journalist. But who is using all those epithets? Long ago I got used to seeing ideas which were first expressed in this column, or in my books, turn up as the invention and fee-simple property of literary thinkers who scorned and denounced them when I published them.

More than that. When I was preparing this book I found clipped to one Easy Chair an article I had forgotten. The critic who wrote it proved me a fascist, without disclosing that he knew what fascism is but simmering with the same resentment that nowadays represents me as a red, and went on to say, "If Mr. DeVoto is a democrat, then I am not." That may be a true statement but we have no way of knowing, for there is nothing to tell us what he is. I have been reading him for many years and I have yet to see him stick his neck out about anything except the symbol of the peach in "The Love Song of J. Alfred Prufrock." Getting out on that limb may have required courage but not of a kind that would make trouble for him, and I believe that some years later the peach proved to have been eaten by Edward Fitzgerald. Some battles cannot be fought after the fact and in journalism a writer runs into some he does not care to be above.

The first Easy Chair I wrote described some asininities committed by a New Deal agency. (Prophetically, it was a news story, one I had dug out for myself.) Various newspapers promptly admitted Mr. E. S. Martin's successor to the Republican Party. The welcome was premature. I doubt if anyone was ever a 100 per cent New Dealer — obviously Mr. Roosevelt wasn't — but though many New Deal intellectuals had a much higher proof than mine, on the whole I had to go along. I got to that position by studying history, and the study of history has held me to the working principles of American liberalism.

Here, I believe, is where the accusation that I have betrayed literary thinking comes in, for fashions and events have required me, every so often, to show that literary liberalism is something else. I was at odds with the dominant fashions of literary thinking during the nineteen-twenties. Most of those who followed them seemed to me naïve and ignorant, ignorant especially of our history and of politics. During the nineteen-thirties I felt no impulse to seek comfort in Marx and Lenin, and it was again my job to point out that the literary thinkers who did were naïve and ignorant, ignorant especially of American history and of the politics which they told us they had mastered.

And today I feel no impulse to regress to Burke, Hobbes, Mandeville, or personal revelation. It is now high literary fashion to represent the fashionables of the earlier decades as naïve and ignorant, and this fact has a rich flavor but the empirical grounds from which the representation is made seem worse than dubious. The thinkers are still practicing book reviewing. They have mastered politics just as their predecessors did, by making it up while gazing earnestly at their navels. Nothing could astonish a journalist more than the fantasies regularly published in the literary quarterlies about the government of the United States, what its mechanism and energies are, how they are controlled. The practice of journalism has led me not only to work constantly with the reports of committees, commissions, and bureaus, but constantly to study Congress and the federal bureaus in action. I have had to know intimately many Senators, Congressmen, and bureau officials, and I have shared or assisted the work of a good many. I have seen nothing to justify the literary critic's belief that he is more intelligent than the politician. And when I read what the quarterlies say about actions I know empirically — and say with a condescension that would be unbecoming in an archangel — I seldom find any realization at all of what the real energies at work are, or the real issues. I conclude that there is one infrangible virginity: literary criticism is not an approach to politics.

The Chicago *Tribune* put me on its list long ago and invented the word "DeVotoism" to classify one entire order of its phobias. The heaviest mail I have ever received was evoked not by the FBI piece about which McCarthy made libelous statements but by an Easy Chair a year before we entered the war which said that we ought to enter it and predicted that we would. Orders had gone out from the GHQ of America First to work me over. The organization charged its heirs to keep after me and they have been faithful to the trust. A lot of them are too pure in heart to sign their names.

If I have written as readily about disk jockeys as about *The Federalist*, that willingness too can be ascribed to the study of history. Library stacks as well as the town square taught me that no manifestation of American life is trivial to the critic of culture. Such a column as this could not easily avoid politics but no doubt I have felt an additional incentive to write about it because I was practicing history. Also, unlike much writing, political comment is a form of action. Sometimes it runs to prophecy too, and here I am entitled to brag. All but one of my prophecies have been borne out by the event, and if that one was a national-championship flop it originated in a mistake we are all prone to make. I underestimated the stupidity of Republican grand strategy.

My commonest political theme has been the erosion of the Bill of Rights. Before the war, and this is revealing, the Easy Chair was disturbed by such peripheral matters as literary censorship and our home-grown Catos. During the war it was usually suppression of the news, and I was uncomfortable for I had to take potshots at my friend Elmer Davis in order to get at the authorities who were muzzling him. Since the war the attack on our freedoms has come closer to the jugular, and so I have been suspect in the indicated quarters. If I can judge by the quotations adduced by other committees, the file which the Un-American Activities Committee has on me contains little more than the *Daily Worker*'s praise of the Easy Chair on the FBI. But most of the beagles have bayed at me (as their newly arrived imitators in Congress have begun to do) and I have been named on various lists of subversives. Nomination to them is the diagnostic test of decency for anyone who has a public forum. We have fought at Arques: Where were you?

In twenty years I have published eight books and two collections of occasional pieces, I have edited a basic document of American history, and I have supported my family by writing for magazines more affluent than *Harper's*. And I have written the Easy Chair. Always I have written it under pressure of haste and with the morose knowledge that I was not writing it well enough. But in my private assignments it has always come first.

I hope that what I have said has been said gracefully and that sometimes it has been amusing, or informative, or useful. No one has got me to say anything I did not want to say and no one has prevented me from saying anything I wanted to. The Easy Chair has given me a place in the journalism of my time. No one knows better than a journalist that his work is ephemeral. As I have said in my preface, it is not important, it is only indispensable. The life or the half life of an issue of *Harper's* has never been calculated; the magazine has durable covers but even the copies kept in doctors' waiting rooms wear out and are dumped in the bay or ground up for pulp. But a historian knows that a lot of writing which has no caste mark on its forehead gets dumped in the bay too, and that he can count on finding bound files of *Harper's* in library stacks. He has to use them; he cannot write history without them.

The Century

(OCTOBER 1950)

THE PAST, we think, was slower. The United States from 1940 to 1950 is a disk spinning so fast that we can barely cling to it or stay on our feet. But a century seems in retrospect to have moved at a measured, tranquil pace. Change in earlier days was not our master but our servant; season grew to season and the crop came to harvest. This is the visual illusion that makes a body seem to move the more slowly as we get farther away from it. History needs some such device as that by which the movies show a plant growing from slip to leaf to flower in fifty feet of film. It would correct parallax and show that in all ten decades the movements of American society have been close to cataclysmic. We could then see for ourselves that all but one of them have been contained. . . .

East of Lake Ontario, there may have been debatable ground: Which area was truly Canada, which truly the United States? But westward there was not much margin. You could move the boundary a few miles north of the 49th Parallel or a few miles south of it without encountering much difference. But only a few miles: geography, climate, the flow of rivers, the architecture of mountain ranges divided one nation from the other as if by blueprint.

Along the southern edge, as three hundred years of Spain in North America demonstrated, the margin was even narrower: one area was the United States and the other Mexico by the fiat of nature. Earth's creation had surveyed and staked a continental domain between the Atlantic and the Pacific, between Canada and Mexico, for a single people, a single economic system, a single political organization. One determinant of our society is that the United States is a nation which occupies a continental unit. Another one is this: the United States is an empire whose imperial and national boundaries are the same.

A minor but clear-seeing prophet said, "Disunion and Civil War are synonymous terms. The Mississippi, source and mouth, must be controlled by one government." That was in December 1860. In December of 1862 a major prophet repeated what he had said at his inauguration: "Physically speaking we cannot separate. We cannot remove our respective sections from each other nor build an impassable wall between them," and added that the people of the American heartland must forever "find their way to Europe by New York, to South America and Africa by New Orleans, and to Asia by San Francisco." These men were proclaiming the necessity of economic and political unity in a unified geographical system. Thomas Jefferson had anticipated them in 1803, but so had Robert Cavelier, Sieur de la Salle, in 1682.

With an explosive heightening of energy the nation completed the occupation of its continent in a two-year period, 1846–1848. Mexico and Great Britain ceased to be illogical and irrelevant sovereignties in the American geographical system. The event brought to an end the imperial contention for the Great Valley and the Far West that had begun in the seventeenth century, if not indeed in the sixteenth. The Spanish and Russian empires had been merely peripheral forces in this struggle but there had been a full century of conflict between the French and British empires to possess and politically unify the American continent. By the time this struggle ended in victory for the British it had created the American empire. For the people whose representatives met in Philadelphia in 1775 and again in 1787 to make a nation were already an imperial people. As they made the nation they entered a half-century of conflict with Great Britain for the same great stake, the richest area in the world. That conflict settled itself along the lines laid down, leaving only the two illogicalities in the

West that vanished before mid-century.

The attainment of our continental boundaries precipitated the crisis which gave the nation its final shape and pattern, and which made the nation and the empire the same thing. The United States into which Volume I, Number 1, of *Harper's New Monthly Magazine* issued in June of 1850 was already committed to the final testing. A self-governing people had created a democratic republic: Was the system strong enough and flexible enough to maintain itself in a whole continent? Could the conflicting interests, feelings, and beliefs of irrational man in society adapt themselves to the rationality of natural conditions? Was there a self-limiting contradiction within the democratic forms? Could American society govern itself in the single system that the continent demanded, or was that demand too strong for government, which is admittedly man's weakest capacity? Must that weakness falsify the American experience and mock the continental unity by a process of Balkanization that would produce societies smaller and illogical but within man's capacity for government? In that same June of 1850 delegates from nine Southern states met in convention at Nashville to set up an experimental test. By November, convinced that they could predict the outcome, they were proposing to declare the American experience a failure and to dissolve the United States. The proposal was both too early and too late. Between June and November the resources of the political system proved it able, through the compromise of 1850, to preserve the nation and the empire for an undetermined time. Ultimately the period turned out to be ten years. Just long enough.

It was a decade of steadily growing tension, passion, and turbulence. The surface was chaotic but realities beneath the surface were shaping a demand that evasions, ambiguities, and contradictions in the society be faced and resolved. The acquisition of the West revealed the ineluctable fact that the Southern political hegemony would now be extinguished. Political dictation by the minority must end and government must pass to the majority. The Southern hegemony had never had financial dominance; Southern economists were aware that their section was in fact bankrupt and the new territory confirmed their diagnosis. The section's obsolete labor system had managed to keep its economy alive by a process of exhausting soils and then abandoning them for virgin land, but that labor system could not possibly be applied to the virgin land now acquired. Finally, the unresolved contradiction and untreated disease at the core of our social system, Negro slavery, had reached the stage of fatality. Outside the South, an intense moral horror no more to be discounted than that which our generation has felt about forced labor or genocide was now demanding that the spread of slavery be stopped short and some process of eliminating it be invented. The Southern minority responded in the tradition of dying oligarchies, by demanding absolute immunity from control and by convincing itself that financial bankruptcy, political fallacy, and embedded social evil manifested the will of God. Both sections moved toward Lincoln's conclusion that the nation could not exist half slave and half free.

One great American said that God was sifting out the hearts of men before His judgment seat, another that one volume of our history had closed and a new one had opened of which no man could foresee the end, a third that irresistible if unnamable influences had begun to unfold a new destiny. The spinning disk was performing its function of constantly remaking the nation. We see easily enough, today, that the political system was hardening and the cleavage in the social system deepening. But in order to get these motions in focus we need the movies' device to throw on the screen condensed images of other motions. One would show the shaded area on the population map moving constantly westward across the blank area. Another would show a web of railroads being spun east of the Mississippi; others would show the steady multiplication of factory chimneys, the increase of emigration from Europe, the increase of wealth, and the increase of mechanical power. Such images reveal why, in the event, ten years were enough.

The Century (October 1950)

II

Our generation has twice had proved to it that sometimes final decisions have to be reached and that if they cannot be reached in any other way then they must be fought out. "Both parties deprecated war, but one of them would *make* war rather than let the nation survive, and the other would *accept* war rather than let it perish, and the war came." The last four words have the greatest solemnity of our history. Bernard Shaw has said that it "was more clearly than any other war of our time a war for an idea," but it was tragedy to the uttermost. In all history there are no greater ironies than these: that secession belied and repudiated the entire experience of the American people, that the South which forced the war never had a chance to win it, that the Confederacy was an anachronism as society and an unworkable fallacy as government, that if the American system had been broken the European system would have been restored.

The war effected the political decision, "teaching men that what they cannot take by an election, neither can they take it by war." It ended the fatal disease of slavery, though the sequelae, some of them only less evil, have not yet been cured. And it freed the nation forever to develop its empire as a single people in a continental unit. Now there would never be the Balkan States of North America.

No war ends as the same war it was when it began. The lightning of the terrible swift sword revealed again the deepest meaning and the highest aspiration of American life — perhaps they are to be glimpsed only in a lightning flash — and they found their supreme expression in the Gettysburg Address and the Second Inaugural. But if the fires of civil war purified much and forged much into its permanent form, they also destroyed much we should not have lost and they left scars that have proved permanent. But gigantic energies had been loosed. The United States came out of the war with a productive system more diverse, more integrated, and enormously more powerful than it had been in

1860 — and politically entrenched. The expansion of that system, which was without parallel in human experience, was the focus of American history for the next generation.

The continental nation had been freed to develop the resources, natural and human, of the richest geographical entity on earth. The advance of knowledge had provided the necessary instruments, commercial, financial, technological, and scientific. As the disk spins, the energies at work seem to share the impersonality and irresistibility of sidereal forces, and the striking conceit of Henry Adams that they accelerate according to the law of falling bodies almost seems true. Again, we need the condensed motions on a screen. Four years after the end of the war, the diagrammatic railroad track reaches the Pacific. Thereafter it is the weaver's shuttle crossing and crisscrossing the map till the United States has a transportation system previously inconceivable and equaled nowhere else. (To be duplicated by similar lines which show telegraph and telephone systems, roads for automobile transport, and charted flightways for airplane traffic.) The line that measures horsepower per capita shoots steeply upward; it means work done, wealth increased, a constantly accelerating production. The crosshatching on the population map spirals across the West till the only blank spaces left are those which cannot be populated at all. The curve of emigration from Europe is almost as vertical as Jack's beanstalk. There is a jagged oscillation as the areas where great staple crops are grown shift their locations, another one as centers of manufacture do something similar, a third as cities become metropolitan aggregates and the population of rural areas, relatively to them, declines.

Retrospectively, these energies seem uncontrollable and for a time they were, except as some served to limit others. Retrospectively, they seem impersonal and in fact such personality as they found in either individuals or corporations was solely by chance, by the fall of the dice. We misjudge them when we are appalled by such waste as it had been possible for no other people to afford and by the wealth and power that came by accident, luck, ruthlessness, or corruption into hands that were irresponsible and today seem antisocial. For the Cro-Magnon age of American capitalism was both accidental and implicit. We came into it precisely as late fifteenth-century navigators bound for Cathay ran without premonition into the American continent; and for us as for them there was no passage to India except straight on and across.

Nowadays we pronounce derisively such phrases as Empire Builder, Robber Baron, and Captain of Industry; the derision is a judgment of social righteousness on their waste, injustice, and anarchic use of power. Yet they were chance entities in a historical context, points of contact where energies found application or transmission; and if one anonymity had not chanced to serve as such a contact, then of necessity another one must have done so. That an individual acquired fifty million dollars from the public estate, or a corporation collected two hundred million, is in 1950 of no importance considering that both converted the uncapitalized public heritage into public wealth of which their take in profits was an inconsiderable decimal. Most of the Barons' wealth has by now, in one way or another, been returned to the public, and we have spent half a century canalizing the corporate wealth for public usage. Moreover, it is better that there are half a million family houses in Iowa than that the forests of northern Wisconsin should still stand. What was the value of the land granted to the Union Pacific in Nebraska or to the Santa Fe in Kansas? On the books five dollars per section: in fact, zero dollars and zero cents per hundred square miles. It is better that in 1950 these are mature commonwealths, that human society is productive there, that their farms are feeding us and others than that they should be now, say, two-thirds of the way through the frontier stage of an American region, though with no speculative profit in the records.

Include all that can be assessed historically against steel corporations, still it is better that Pittsburgh, Cleveland, Gary and Youngstown are metropolises, that there are skyscrapers in New York and locks in the Panama Canal, and that there have been American battleships in two world wars, than that the Mesabi should be only today coming to the awareness of a nation prepared to manage it more equitably but less rich, less populous, less powerful than the Mesabi has made it. "Fellow countrymen, we cannot escape history." We cannot escape its processes, nor remodel those of the past to accord with changed values. Given the continent of 1850 and given the energies of 1850–1900, it was either a Malefactor of Great Wealth named Smith or one named Jones, it was either Standard Oil or Alias and Otherwise Oil, nor all your tears wash out a word of it.

All this, however, up to a point and from one angle of view. . . . The dynamic equilibrium of a society is unstable. It is forever moving from one phase to another. Its internal forces are always altering in relation to one another and so threatening to destroy it. The genius of the American people . . . no, start that one over. The vigor of our democratic system and the size and richness of our continental empire have enabled American society to contain the internal stresses and, always belatedly but always in time too, to master and redirect their alignment. From where we stand the surface of 1865–1900 looks anarchic but the condensed images show something different.

The industrial system was politically entrenched; for most of a generation the government of the United States was an instrument exquisitely machined to effect the system's will and purpose. A conquered and ruined South dropped into its palm. It came to hold the Middle West under mortgage and to own the West in fee. Nor would our word in 1950 that a man's anguish might be to the ultimate good of his heirs' heirs have comforted a dispossessed Mississippi cotton grower, or a steelworker shot by Pennsylvania militiamen for asserting that he could not live like a human being on two dollars earned in a twelve-hour day, or an Iowa farmer robbed by a manufacturers' tariff, a railroad's freight rates, a bank's crop-note, an elevator-combine's downgrading, and a systematically depressed market for grain. Moreover, a fungus of slums spread over the metropolises and production centers. Mostly they were industrial slums and mostly they were filled with the immigrants, from southern and eastern Europe in the main, whom industry welcomed to keep the labor market overcrowded, now that speculative finance had little free farmland left to hold under mortgage for north Europeans. At least these city slums were no worse than the rural slums that by now had contaminated parts of nearly every state. For if the Negro remained a peon, there were widely distributed poor-white populations — living (in this paradise of agriculture) on exhausted farms, sick with (in this best fed nation) malnutrition and (in this society of universal education) illiteracy and (in this democracy of self-respecting men) mob superstitions and mob hysterias.

So new figures appeared on the screen, long disregarded, long misunderstood, caricatured, at last feared as bomb-throwing anarchists or atheists of the American faith. One might be a soft-spoken scholar looking up from his table of statistics to voice an idea new to Americans, that the continental resources could be exhausted unless more social intelligence were brought to bear on them. Another had many names, individual and collective, Henry George, say, or the Knights of Labor. A third was gaunt, desperate, and terrible, the product of two-cent cotton and ten-cent corn. Their common testimony was that the United States had got out of plumb. They burned their valueless crops to keep their kitchens warm in winter. They derailed Pullmans or floated in barges past locked-out mills to shoot at Pinkertons hired to break their feeble unions. They declaimed in Congress and the state legislatures about a revolution which they knew was under way and were answered with boredom and guffaws. A vestige named Baer told them that they would be protected and cared for "by the Christian men to whom God in His infinite wisdom has given the control of the property interests of the country." He spoke from the system's most powerful battlement, the industrial trust, but he had been a relic for six years when he spoke. Six years earlier the sonorous, fraudulent voice of an eater of wild honey in the hills had quieted a Chicago convention hall. It is easy to grin at him, his drama, and his rhetoric, but not at what the rhetoric meant, "You shall not press down upon the brow of labor this crown of thorns. You shall not crucify mankind upon a cross of gold." That year or another, Bryan or someone else, it must be proclaimed that a turn had been rounded.

In our society a popular reaction eventually asserts itself against concentrations of power that have grown disruptive. Since 1896 one main strand in our history has been our resistance to concentrations of financial power. Its line on the graph is wavy but to see how steadily it has grown stronger one need only contrast Gene Debs's switchmen with Walter Reuther's automobile workers, or the corn-burning Kansas farmers of 1890 with their inheritors in 1950. The democratic society that occupies the vast rich continent has contained the inner stresses. It has braked the disruptive forces well short of the cleavage line. It has kept going.

In their way, both Baer and Bryan signified the same tremendous fact that, whatever its imbalances might be, our continental economy had come of age. The attainment of all majorities is marked by just such confusion as the United States showed at the turn of the century. Our venture in extraterritorial imperialism was impulsive, costly, soon repented, eventually repudiated. Industrial trusts became financial trusts and the collapse of speculative inflations concentrated their power. They presented a mammoth and imperative paradox. They so rationalized the productive system that perhaps gigantic profits were an inconsiderable charge against the economies they effected in the distribution and the price of goods; but they were irresponsible and they must be brought under the public control which it was their nature to defy. Three out of four national administrations labored to get some kind of harness on them, backed by maturing labor organizations, by sectional revolts, and by a groundswell of public awareness which was the ripening of seeds planted by the Grangerites and the Populists long before. The popular historian, forced to compress the first fifteen years of the twentieth century into a single word, at whatever violence to other considerations, has usually ended with the word "reform." And certainly, amid frustrations and failures, the lines were laid down.

In those prewar years another fact was manifest, though but slowly understood: an imperial culture had also come of age. Even the Captains of Industry had helped, for they had pillaged Europe for symbols of what Veblen called conspicuous consumption; and now as they died San Francisco had one of the best medieval libraries in the world and no one could ever again study the history of European art adequately without visiting New York. But institutions that had grown of our own planting in our own soil had ripened unobserved. The land-grant college was developing a test for butter-fat or strains of rust-resistant wheat or an anti-abortion serum, or it was devising such political facilities as the initiative and referendum, or it was spreading skepticism and political enlightenment among a state's electorate. Meanwhile it quietly became a great state university and assumed an additional function as a member of the international community of knowledge, joining the Smithsonian Institution, the Johns Hopkins, President Eliot's Harvard. An old cliché collapsed, the one that held the American scholar to be rare, lonely, inferior, and despised. A westward traffic of European students had begun. They came to a place outlandishly named Flagstaff, say, to study under a scholar who had measured aberrations and found a planet, or to one named Berkeley, where, surprisingly enough, there was a geneticist or a bacteriologist or a physicist who was the best the world had in his field. While our attention was focused on other matters, libraries, museums of natural and applied science, and research foundations had been growing great. It could be seen now that the most various institutions were advancing the frontiers of knowledge: the Bureau of American Ethnology, which had almost unassisted organized a new science; or an astonishing miscellany of learned journals; or the network of historical societies. American hospitals, American medical schools, American research laboratories were dominating twentieth-century medicine. Perhaps grain elevators and steel-frame office buildings were not without cultural significance, and with an understandable wariness explorers began to tolerate the hypothesis that the native arts might express something of the native experience.

Rationalizing the productive system raised the index of horsepower per capita, which had been rising steadily for more than a century; so did the steady development of technology. Now it skyrocketed with an increase in mechanical power from new sources, electricity and internal combustion. Both changed the map, changed industry, changed society, and are still doing so. The interurban railroad has joined the watering trough for horses but there are tractors on the farms and incandescent lights in the farmhouses. Automobiles, hard roads, electric power, telephones began to put an end to hayseed America, closing the gap that had opened between the culture of cities and that of the countryside.

III

Now AN overmastering fact far outran our comprehension of it: we had financed a world war and turned its military stalemate into victory before we realized that our power potentials could be applied internationally. That the United States was a principal member in such a world order as might be said to exist was no news to Europe, though the thunderclap that demonstrated it was not readily taken in. It was much less readily understood by the United States, which repudiated its political power at the moment when it had become decisive, turned back to the domestic market at the moment when the world market had become a necessity to it, and erected the highest tariff wall in its history at the moment when it became a creditor nation and New York displaced London as the financial capital of the world. This was the eighth world war in which the American people had been engaged — it still seemed to them by chance. They came out of it denying that they belonged to a global system and ignorant that there is no way of not using power.

And who were the American people? They were the product of the American continent: a new people in a new world. No one understands them who does not understand that the words mean what they say: this is the New World. They were, for instance, the first people in history who had ever had enough to eat. The first people who were able to build a government and a society from the ground up — and on unencumbered ground. The first people whose society had the dynamics of political equality and political freedom, a class system so flexible that it could not stratify into a caste system, and a common wealth so great that it made economic opportunity a birthright. All this makes a difference. It makes so great a difference that the pattern of their neural paths is radically different from any developed in response to the Old World.

They are hopeful and empirical. In their spring morning, those who made the nation did not doubt that it was the hope of the world. Mankind, they thought, must necessarily come to recognize the superiority of American institutions and, insofar as it could, must adopt or imitate them. They were neither visionaries nor utopians. They were realistic, hardheaded men who understood the dynamics of freedom and saw that if they were loosed in an empty continent an augmentation would follow for which nothing in the past could be an adequate gauge. From then on, not the past but the future has counted in the United States. If it doesn't work, try something else; tomorrow is another day; don't sell America short; the sky is the limit; rags to riches; canal-boat boy to President.

That is what has denied the town dump decisive importance. No one has ever set up Utopia here, our utopian literature has always been clearly understood to be promotional, and the dump is hideous with brutality, exploitation, failure, and human wreckage. The actual line where men meet in society is always a line of blood and struggle. It is perfectly feasible to write American history in terms of blood and struggle, injustice, fraud, desperation. They are on a scale appropriate to the map; they are monstrous. But the difference is that tomorrow is another day. It has always proved to be. No estimate of what the United States could achieve in population, power, comfort, wealth, or living standard has ever proved adequate. When tomorrow came, the expectation proved to have been too moderate, the achievement invariably outran the prophecy.

Europeans came here by the million for a hundred and twenty

years. Their expectation was simple and concrete. They expected a better life than had been open to them at home. More food, more comfort, a job, a farm. Citizenship, a stake in society, acknowledged individual integrity, development according to their capacities, a chance to better themselves, a chance to give their children a still better chance. It sums up not as the kingdom of heaven but as somewhat more favorable odds. The majority vote is that on the whole they got it. They kept on coming.

What kept happening is what made the neural paths different. It is a different consciousness, a different cast of thought. And it is very misleading to Europe. American bumptiousness has always been offensive but the abasement that goes with it is worse, for it has been deceptive. The instinctive generosity of the Americans is curiously linked with rapacity, their kindliness with cruelty, their violence with fear of disorder. They are warm-hearted and cold-blooded, their assertive self-confidence is mingled with self-criticism, and their conservatism is the other lobe of an unparalleled recklessness. Yet the most serious mistake of Europe has always been to misunderstand their romanticism, which is the consequence of having lived a Cinderella story. It has been repeatedly mistaken for softness, gullibility, decadence. Their smile is childlike and bland; they affect an innocence and credulity which the European mind has accepted as real. Yet from Franklin and John Jay on, their negotiators have usually come back not only with all that the adept cynicism of their opponents undertook to take from them by means of a cold deck, but with the scarf pins, cuff links, and pocket watches of the cynical as well. For the romanticism is the thinnest possible veneer. There have been no such realists since the Romans and they are the hardest empiricists of the modern world.

The national experience, that is, has justified the national optimism. The premises on which the hardheaded fathers established the American order were, philosophically, optimistic to the verge of fantasy; but the experience of the nation has been that the fantastic premises pay off. That the rights proclaimed in the Declaration, enacted in the Constitution, and buttressed by the

Bill of Rights make a system which works more efficiently and has a higher potential than any other. That freedom is power, liberates power, generates power. That individual, social, and political freedom are the health of society. That protection of the individual human being's dignity, his freedom of movement, choice, criticism, communication, publication, and participation in government have pragmatically proved their social strength. They enable the organism to resist infections, they give it the equilibrium to develop counterbalances to destructive pressures — and this, the empiricists have found, gets work done, increases power, and can be trusted. They understand their history as proving that the fantastic system works.

IV

When the nation came to its second testing, the terms had changed but it was the same test. Again the United States was out of plumb, but now the world we were enmeshed with was out of plumb too. Again evasions, ambiguities, contradictions, social imbalances, and concentrations of disproportionate power had to be resolved. The illusion of nearness makes the nineteen-thirties seem more desperate than the eighteen-fifties; they would not have seemed so to Lincoln or his electorate. The foreground of our memory is the collapse of values, the spread of panic, the fearful loss of wealth and hope, the millions of unemployed, the Bonus march, farmers wrecking milk trucks as their fathers had wrecked Pullman cars, and arming vigilance committees against forced sales as their grandfathers had forbidden the repossession of fugitive slaves. But the foreground obscures the decisive fact: that the disruptive forces were contained. While other societies splintered, the empirical people held to their experience.

John Adams had said that our first revolution was over when the war which ratified it began; the saying holds for all our revolutions.

We were indeed rounding another decisive turn, closing one volume of our history and opening another one of which no man could foresee the end. But the self-correcting forces of our society were already focused on the reduction of chaos when they found a voice. "We have nothing to fear but fear itself," it said, speaking into the microphone that symbolized so many of the changed conditions of life. Events proved the President right. The continental system was flexible enough as self-government, and rich and powerful enough as a commonwealth, to restore the national health. The empirical faith was justified.

Otherwise there would have been a different outcome when the next decade forced the appeal to "the last argument as well of republics as of kings." The nineteen-thirties had forced us to make final decisions; those we could evade no longer as the nineteen-forties came on must also be final. The necessity stemmed from the fact that we *had* evaded them.

In 1920 the nation had turned away from the oceans that bind the earth's land masses together. It now had learned that the world was not big enough to be withdrawn from. At the midnight of the Civil War Lincoln had speculated about the judgment of God, which seemed to require that every drop of blood drawn with the lash should be paid by another drawn with the sword. Now it seemed that refusal to accept the responsibilities of peace, power, and plenty must be paid a hundredfold, and perhaps by our extinction.

But it was even more ominous than those words say. The United States had been a dynamic revolution from the beginning. Its history meant just what the fathers had said it must: it had been the spearhead of a democratizing process which had been influencing political and social institutions for a century and a half through two-thirds of the world. But our withdrawal from the larger system toward which our whole impetus had carried us was reversing the current of history. As the postwar chaos of Europe became a prewar chaos, old and supposedly dead despotisms were reanimated in new forms: history's basic axiom, that the clock cannot be set back, was on the way to being overturned. There were differences between the two totalitarianisms but both necessarily based their systems on a denial of the dignity of the individual, which we had found to be the pivot on which all else turns; and both destroyed the freedoms which we had proved to be the source of most abundant energy. . . . But that we had moved faster than we supposed was manifested by the swiftness with which we came to understand that we were involved in our ninth world war, though we called it our second one.

The clock was not turned back. And as before, the United States came out of that war more powerful than it was at the beginning and more vigorous too. The productive system had accomplished an expansion whose indexes would seem fantastic if they were not hard fact, and the index of horsepower per capita, always the best gauge of our vitality, had risen enormously. It is on the verge of a quantum jump. As a war measure we developed a new kind of mechanical energy. It has given us, and anyone else who will, the facilities for destroying civilization. It has also put at our disposal power for the enrichment of a peaceful society so great that no previous ways of measuring power can be applied to it.

The fact that dwarfs all others, however, is this: the United States now knows that there is no way of not using power. It is true that no other nation ever came so reluctantly to be the foremost nation of the world, but it is also true that none ever accepted the implications so quickly. Our traditional, no longer humorous quirk makes us present ourselves as bumpkins easily to be outguessed, outmaneuvered, and bilked by the Marxian slickers. Still it was not naïveté that, with the nonchalance of a man who holds four aces, tossed the Marshall Plan into a struggle which seemed more than half lost, or with a calculation of risks superbly vindicated by the outcome, launched the first flight of the Berlin airlift, let the chips fall where they might. The illusion of nearness presents us to ourselves as divided, irresolute, vacillating, and at random — which is the close-up image of any democratic system feeling its way. From the perspective of the eastern shore of the Atlantic we look otherwise. The image of the United States there has always been ogreish, anarchic or revolutionary, and foolish if not mad; but something new has come into it. The Europeans waste no love on us, we give them adequate reason to resent and distrust us, and only the Russians keep the rest of Europe from feeling about us in the twentieth century as it felt about Spain in the sixteenth century or France in the seventeenth. But there is the new ingredient that fulfills quite literally what was laid down: the revolution has gone on and in the awareness of Western Europe we are, however fumbling, however resented, the last, best hope on earth.

There can be no disposition to understate the turbulence, horror, and alarm of the world in which the centennial number of *Harper's* issues. At the moment when man's greatest scientific achievement has unlocked a basic secret of matter, there is no word but Banquo's: fears and scruples shake us, in the great hand of God we stand. It will not be tragedy, it will not even be irony but only farce, if man, mastering nature, fails to govern himself. If he does fail, then the destruction of mankind will cleanse the earth for the convenience of organisms which may learn to create peaceful societies. But to those who have decided that the American people do not understand how desperate their estate is, the answer may be that with death hanging in the balance they trust their experience. They have never seen yesterday win over tomorrow. They believe that history is on their side and that they are on the side of the future.

No one has ever known what the next hour might bring forth but we have always made our bet. There came a moment when Mr. Lincoln quoted scripture: a house divided against itself cannot stand. He went on to say, "I believe this government cannot endure permanently half slave and half free." Either our experience has meaning, as we believe, or else it hasn't. If it has, the world cannot exist permanently half slave and half free.

And mark Lincoln's next words: "I do not expect the Union to be dissolved, I do not expect the house to fall, but I do expect it will cease to be divided." He stood at the height of land between two eras and declared what he understood to be the meaning of history. The empirical people know that, as it turned out, he was right.

The Third Floor

(MARCH 1952)

AT INTERVALS I receive a letter which I have never tried to answer for I am not sure I could tune in on its wave length. I think of it as the same letter for it always says the same things, though various people who do not know each other write it. It begins as a criticism of the Easy Chair but modulates into a complaint about *Harper's* and ends as a lamentation about something entirely different, something for which there is no help.

But let me describe the house I bought a year or so before the war. It is big as, seemingly, houses still capable of being lived in can be big only in New England and ugly as they can be only in Cambridge. It is an Old Cambridge house; it once belonged to a distinguished and celebrated man. His widow lived in it for years after he died and her heirs sold it to me. I could not have afforded to buy it except that real estate was badly depressed that year, and of course in Old Cambridge such an interloper as I would never have aspired to own property on Berkeley Street. But Old Cambridge perished a long time ago.

When I bought the house the only twentieth-century bathroom was on the third floor. It would be thought antiquated now but there had been some effort to make it convenient and comfortable and that was incongruous, for the rest of the floor was stark and dreary. It had been finished only in part and that part parsimoniously. There were only four windows and they were small;

they gave little ventilation and admitted little light. There was just one electric light, the one in the bathroom. Though the flooring elsewhere in the house was of fine oak, much of it parquetry, here it was cheap pine, jagged with splinters and in some places worn through. The heating system had not been extended to the third floor.

In houses the age of mine throughout greater Boston you can see that same floor; usually, in fact, it is cheaper and dingier. It was the servants' floor. In the spacious time nearly a century ago Boston's servants were the surplus virgins of Ireland. They were fortunate girls; by coming here they raised themselves above their station and were privileged to spend their lives among gentle, cultured people and exquisite possessions. They went to work for four dollars a month. It had increased to four dollars a week thirty-five or forty years later when the master, being on the board of trustees, got them a snug place in the Home for the Aged. The mistress taught them neatness, orderliness, obedience, decorum, and virtuous living. She supervised their diversions and their reading, to make sure that they were wholesome. They were free to go to six o'clock Mass on Sunday morning and they had the afternoon hours off one Sunday a month and two Thursdays. They were permitted to receive friends, of the same sex, on evenings when the family did not need their services and the mistress had approved. They received them in the kitchen; they spent their free time in the kitchen after the dishes were washed, the table in the breakfast room set, and the beds on the second floor turned down. They could read by candlelight in their own good warm beds but not for long: the candles were counted. They must be up betimes and too much leisure, too many candles, too much comfort would encourage slackness. That was why the steam pipes were not carried to the third floor; besides, the coal bill would have been bigger. But all day long they could admire the family's furniture and china, the pictures and the books, and could take pride in the carriages that came to the door and the elegant people who got out of them.

But for the last of these maids at 8 Berkeley Street it had been necessary, at some expense, to put in a bathroom.

The latest variant of my periodic letter begins by mentioning "the beautiful dignified English" that Mr. George William Curtis wrote in the Easy Chair. The letter usually does begin with a reference to Mr. Curtis or to Mr. William Dean Howells, who also wrote beautiful dignified English in the Easy Chair as, my correspondent points out, as I do not. He remembers the bound volumes of *Harper's* in his father's study and the boyhood hours he spent reading them. He learned from Mr. Curtis or Mr. Howells the value of chaste prose, prose unmarred by the neologisms, the vulgarisms, the slang, "the crudities like 'OK' and 'sure' for 'surely,'" the bad grammar that he finds everywhere today, even in this once dignified, once chastely written magazine. The language he is forced to read is, in fact, no longer to be called English; it is a debased dialect. He wishes that *Harper's* had been willing to act as "an English Academy, like the French, to pass judgment on any change or addition of new words to our vocabulary." Instead it has basely surrendered to the vulgar. I was therefore, he says, under a greater obligation to preserve in the Easy Chair the fine English that Mr. Curtis and Mr. Howells wrote for it. This, assuredly, I have not done; often the Easy Chair is more offensively written than the rest of *Harper's*. I write the debased dialect, I write vulgarly, I write, as the letter before the latest one put it, like a stable boy.

Yet my correspondent acknowledges that *Harper's* and I are rather signs of our time than debauchers of it. "The truth is," he says, "there are so few cultured people left." I am presumably an "educated" man, nearly everyone is nowadays, nearly everyone has been "to a college of some sort" and has acquired a smattering of new ideas and inventions. But we have no Latin and no Greek, no intellectual discipline, no history and therefore none of the wisdom that history imparts, no reverence for the true or the good, no reasoning power, no ability to perceive the falsity of vulgar errors or the speciousness of popular fallacies. Indeed, though somehow the vulgarization of America is responsible for the disappearance of cultured people, it may also be that their disappearance, which the spread of college education explains, is responsible for the vulgarization.

Here the letter usually turns from the Easy Chair to some article elsewhere in *Harper's*, an article which signalizes the downfall of *Harper's* and of the United States. In the latest variant it was an article that discussed Social Security. This time the letter writer was a woman but her theme is the constant one, "the way we have drifted into socialism," as Social Security shows we have done. She cannot separate that drift from our vulgarity, and she remembers her shock on first perceiving how they were related. That was when, shortly after Inauguration Day in 1933, she went to a reception for U. S. Senators at the Pan American Building, "of all the crude surroundings and crude people!" She was the more shocked in that she had but recently returned from France, which, though a democracy, "gives her functions with dignity and elegance."

Is postwar apathy responsible for our drift into socialism, she wonders, or has some subtler malady made us thoughtless and indifferent? When she was young every county had its Poor House and its Work House, "the latter for those lazy people who would not work to support themselves." So every county could enforce proper behavior on the poor, whereas now Washington just hands out the money without inquiring how it is spent. "I always taught my servants to lay up part of their wages in a savings bank against a rainy day." But now women of the servant class scorn to be thrifty. A waitress will not even save her tips; she regards security in the rainy days of old age as her due.

Since 1933 my correspondent has again traveled much, as she always did. Egypt and Greece are fine places to spend the winter in, South Africa was intensely interesting, South America is always a delight, and the Orient is fascinating. But she always feels a violent shock when she comes home: always we have sunk deeper into the morass. The morass of vulgarity and socialism. Social Security is, as Mr. Curtis might have put it, the payoff. It has killed self-reliance and initiative. It has poisoned us; the United States is "apparently so prosperous but is so rotten at the core. The five-day week and forty-hour week will cause our downfall. To become great we worked all day and six days, and laid by for our old age." But now everyone is recklessly spending money. Everyone has an automobile. Everyone has radio and television, which are turning us into morons. And where, my correspondent asks, where will all this have taken us in another fifty years? This scandalous, appalling idea that people should retire at sixty-five! — "the age should be extended to seventy years."

I need hardly say that this depravity began when Roosevelt, of whom one does not care to speak as President Roosevelt or Mr. Roosevelt, "gave the green light to labor." The unions "have become so strong that they will take over the government unless someone with cold clear judgment and courage gets the Presidency or is put in a leading position." Those last seven words have what Mr. Howells might have called a dying fall and I have heard it before. Not long before Inauguration Day of 1933 various trustees of servants' savings accounts who had embezzled them to trade in the futures of gaseous equities were crying out, not coldly but perhaps courageously, to be saved by someone who might be put in a leading position.

Why, madam, in the Centennial Issue, the editor of *Harper's* and Mr. Elmer Davis and I all addressed ourselves to this matter. All three of us were remembering those bound volumes of *Harper's*. They were in my father's house too, though since he was a poor man the room they were kept in was not called a study. I read Mr. Curtis and Mr. Howells when I was a boy: I cannot plead ignorance of the tradition I have betrayed. But though I wish I could write as well as Mr. Curtis and Mr. Howells I would not care to write like them. They were of their times and wrote for them; and, as you say, their times were not ours, which I must write for. I like the crudities of today's prose that strike your ears so harshly; they are from the living speech. I would hope to get some of the currency of that speech, some of its liveliness, some of its rhythm and accent, into the prose I offer to readers, who for all I know may be having *Harper's* bound for their children. I think that Mr. Curtis and Mr. Howells would not want to act as an Academy for this generation's idiom and would not want their prose to be a mold which their successor's must fit. They would ask him, I think, to write workmanlike prose, as they did. They would ask him, I am certain, to keep the Easy Chair free of vulgarity — the vulgarity not of expressions like "OK" and "sure" but of idea. Such vulgarity as the idea that the United States is rotten at the core because A will not gladly work six twelve-hour days a week so that B can find Egypt a pleasant place to winter in.

If I have betrayed their tradition it is not by writing the vernacular of my time but, conceivably, by failing to wade as deep into the morass as, if they had found themselves in that time, they might have done. My correspondent has forgotten their biographies. Mr. Howells championed uncultivated people, quite poor people in fact, and defended anarchists. He was a professing socialist. Though he had lived in Cambridge (just off Berkeley Street) when it was Old Cambridge, he wrote the Easy Chair in the service of the very drift that has acquainted my correspondent with despair. No one ever respected culture more than he did but in an age when cultured people were much more numerous than they are now he saw some tendencies which, he said with the most violent emphasis, must be reversed. By whatever means.

Mr. Curtis was reared a communist and once solemnly forswore allegiance to the United States on the ground that, though apparently so prosperous, it was rotten at the core. Part of the rot was the educational system: it was turning out morons, especially economic and social morons. Its philosophy was a puritanism very favorable to the cultured class: it taught some people that to labor from the rising up to the going down of the sun was virtuous, and it taught some that to possess the fruit of other people's labor was righteous. The United States of his time, he said, killed self-reliance and initiative, making the poor submissive while those who exploited their submission sold them for a pair of shoes. Looking about him, he found vulgarity on all sides. Uncultured people were vulgar in their willingness to accept so small a fraction of the wealth their labor created. Cultured people were vulgar in exhorting sixty-five-year-old workers to stick it out another five years so that the tax for the Poor House and the Work House would not inconvenience their betters. I do not know what he would have said about the idea that it is reckless to spend money you have earned but admirable to spend money someone else has earned, that a gentlewoman may properly tour the Orient on an inherited income but a waitress is bringing about our downfall if she buys a radio. I do know that year by year in the Easy Chair he told the waitress that her birthright included a radio and much more. Of the system that had her laying by money for someone else's sunny days, he said that it must be changed. By whatever means.

My radical predecessors meant just what they said: by whatever means. If my correspondent will look again at her files of *Harper's*, she will find reported and advocated there the process by which, happily, it was kept from being by whatever means. In her girlhood the magazine was not speaking for the culture she laments as vanished but for another native culture that had self-reliance and initiative of a different kind. For a hundred and two years it has spoken for those who thought American society able and obliged to achieve a very considerable portion of what Mr. Curtis and Mr. Howells desired, thought it could be achieved by implicit means, and foresaw no downfall. That belief was natural to the people whom, like my predecessors, I have called the natural readers of *Harper's*.

They believed that it was no more wrong of the waitress than of the gentlewoman to want a becoming coiffure and a good-looking dress. They believed that leisure and the satisfactions of life were no less good, no less comely, for the unlettered than for the cultured. The seventy-two hour week, they believed, made leisure impossible and stunted one's capacity to enjoy the satisfactions of life. They believed that a shorter work week would increase the satisfactions open to people and their capacity to enjoy them, and that it would also increase the wealth which the hours of work produced. If it did, they believed, not only crude persons but the gentle as well would be better off. Would live in a better country, a United States less likely to rot at the core.

They believed that the rich natural endowment of the United States could be so managed that it would produce a more widespread affluence — and, yes, even a more widespread freedom to spend money. If some people spent money for radios and automobiles, they would not think the expenditure sinful. Perhaps others would take a trip to South America.

They did not profess to foresee how much of this vision could be achieved. They were sure, however, that any part of it would be an improvement on the village Poor House and Work House. If it meant that they must themselves throw in with the vulgar, OK. If it meant disturbing the serenity of the cultured, sure. If it meant the fading out of elegance, too bad but so be it. They believed that what they knew was possible was more desirable than elegance. So they committed themselves, and the United States, to their belief. There was no need to tear the house down, they said, but remodeling was called for and we had better get about it.

It happened just about as they said it would and, madam, if you will look back through *Harper's* you can see it happening. Mr. Curtis was writing the Easy Chair when it began to happen, and his successor tells you that that beginning, which cannot perhaps be precisely dated but which has had much less celebration than it deserves, was one of the decisive turning points in the history of the world. That a very great deal of it had happened by the time Mr. Howells took over the Easy Chair is attested by 8 Berkeley Street, where at just about that time a bathroom was installed for the servants. Mr. Howells' successor tells you that we now have the advantage of hindsight: looking back, we can see as they could not that it was certain to happen. There was bound to come a time when a candle, a tin washbasin, and a chamberpot would not suffice for the third floor.

II

Feature Section

Ninety-Day Venus

(SEPTEMBER 1950)

O BRIGHT ANADYOMENE! Foam-born, at least foam-upborne in a verbena bubble bath, she is as thin-faced as Botticelli's Venus was. We do not know about her hair, whether it be the same dull-red gold and long enough to reach her knees if modesty would free it to, because she has wrapped a towel round it. No, not a towel, this is a turban; she will wear it all day and her hair is soaked in olive oil; tomorrow, docilely indulging a whim manufactured for her, she will change the part in it. Beside her on a stool are a half-emptied cocktail glass and a portable phonograph. Her lips are parted — perhaps they are moving too — and she is reading a book. It is Maurois' *Portrait of a Genius.* The phonograph is playing Saint-Saëns' "Sonata in D Minor." The genius of Maurois' title is Proust, and with Proust one takes Saint-Saëns, as with the *blanquette* of veal for a family dinner one takes an unpretentious Beaujolais.

So *Vogue* lets us see her, but she was different when *Vogue* itself first saw her. I think her name was Arlene then, though it may have been Thelma. She was sad with girlhood, with a girlhood too dreary, too doleful, too commonplace. Some color was missing from the sunlight. She could not quite make out the syllables which she knew the wind out of the woods was whispering. Though she stood on tiptoe and reached out her hands, they fell short of — well of something which she could not see or feel or name but which she knew was precious. She had no word, either, though in the end she would find one, for her unrest. She knew, however, that this lonely pang would some day break the dull chrysalis that encased her; surely, oh surely, her heart said. We may call it discontent and if it is not divine, at least we know that it can be creative. Poets have it, and advertising agencies, and the little podded grass that aspired to be corn. I do not know how long Arlene had to live in the cocoon. There comes a day when the air is full of butterflies. Say that one day, on tiptoe, she stretched out her hands a full inch farther — a girl's reach should exceed her grasp, or what's *Vogue* for? And that was the moment of triumph, of creation.

It was the moment of rebirth, too, and of rebaptism. Would she be Janice now, or Sandra, or Elise? *Vogue* held its breath and then approved her instinct, and its own in picking her to keep an eye on, when she closed for one that had everything and called her new self Gloria. Gloria's unrest had wings now and they had carried her to the magic casements that must swing open, and that was *Vogue*'s job. She could begin her novitiate right away and the first step was to introduce her to the van Pieters. To Wouter van Pieter and his wife Mimi, and their children, Ten Broek (called Tot) and Leonie (called Marshmallow), and to their Afghans and Bedlingtons, and their friends, and their ways.

It has never been clear where the van Pieters live. At the corner of Sunset Boulevard and Fifth Avenue, and yet where the Main Line passes Newport, and where Long Island or Westchester meets Avalon at the horizon and the lotuses grow just off Washington Square. They are all of us just one step more, one bracket higher. They are as unpretentious as their Beaujolais but as sound as their regional claret, as stout as their Ch. Cos d'Estournel, as noble as their best Burgundy. (Because they live quietly, with the *sancta simplicitas* of twelve servants on one page and the bohemian grace of none at all on the next, they have only a few Burgundies. They have enough, however, so that Wouter can choose among them to discriminate exactly according to the status of their guests.) Simplicity and *la vie chic*, mannerly nonchalance, ease that is yet firm in the code, *délicate, endimanchée.*

Thus when the van Pieters dine (alone) on corned beef and cabbage, the well-chilled beer will be in a large carafe, and a carafe is to be insisted on too for the Tavel — it is rosé, Gloria — for a Supper That May Have to Wait for Hours. For one or two guests, an accommodating light wine, and yet if Sunday night is servantless there may be beer. Cold beer for cold boiled halibut with lobster and shrimp on a very hot night, but a youthful Moselle with the slices of smoked sturgeon for a Garden Luncheon. Dear Gloria, the biggish red Burgundy or red Hermitage with the squab of a mere Dinner Party "can be finished off with the cheese, after the interruption of the Dessert." Sometimes you may have supper with a few loved ones and a friend has given Mimi half a pound of caviar. This is no problem for the butler or, I dare say, for Wouter van Pieter, but there is an implied choice that Gloria will be encountering and she may as well learn now what the overtones are. Given half a pound of caviar (and crab gumbo by the chef) there are those who think a very dry champagne of a good year the right thing. Sound — that is, sound enough; one rung down from ours, it is an impeccable choice; but perhaps, may Wouter say?, perhaps such a wine is too easily come by, whereas *le chic* will be patient to search out the harmonious and superior. So a superior Chablis, very hard to find, "say a Vaudesir or a Valmur of 1945." For a headache, dear, three pellets of awspaireen.

Gloria is to be molded and fitted to this society in ninety days, an ordeal by *chic.* But it would not be fair to hurl her into it without a short period of conditioning. She must first learn the steps, the strokes, the form. These are free spirits, oh, *un peuple à propos,* and so she may begin with the drolleries of madcap whim. Thus she may buy a black velvet belt for her white shorts, for this will show she has the assurance of the well aware. Awareness is the all, awareness of so many things, in so many dimensions. Subtleties are the all too, so Gloria will get up at 5 A.M. to see the secret part of the day, and will serve spritzers at a cocktail party, and will prune back the one branch that screened out a view. (Pruning shears, Hammacher Schlemmer, $12; firm gray cotton denim beach costume, jacket $7, pants $3.50, Best's.) Gloria will free her color sense to caprice, she will fill a green glass bowl with pink shells and put it on a terrace table, and on some wanton morning will heap a blue plate with frosted purple grapes. It would be wrong to ask of her too much gustatory awareness as yet but she may practice the elements of gaiety by putting a flick of curry in the French dressing. The quaint remains, and she will make herself some batiste nightgowns like those that Mimi's *grandmère* wore. Her wings may be a little tired by now and we will impel her but lightly to the printed page, though she must get some conditioning for what lies ahead. Let her read Jane Austen in a hammock (Lewis & Conger?) and for this waggery she will wear something in lemon yellow and robin's egg blue, Onondaga silk shantung by Brigance, $70, and sandals of Allied kidskin by Joyce, $9. Then to severity, but not too fast: "Read Plato's *Critias* (only twelve pages) or the last ten of the *Phaedo*." That must be Tot's Plato, for the one on the van Pieter shelves is royal octavo in plum-colored calf and in the fine edition the *Critias* can hardly run ten pages.

I wonder if Gloria took as long as I did to find out what *découpage* is. None of my dictionaries knew, Larousse unhappily among them, and I had to ask at least twenty people before I found one who could tell me. If it was Mimi who directed her to try something in *découpage*, then Mimi had better reinspect her drolleries for she is trembling on the verge of what she calls old hat — already in the basement preparation-rooms of the Museum of Modern Art they are setting up pyrography and decalcomania. Still, with *découpage* the trial run was about over. When Gloria had washed her pearls in lukewarm water and soap flakes (did Black, Starr & Gorham approve of that?) and had made a bowl of hot, hot chili, the van Pieters nodded yes. She was worthy and she was ready. There was no point in giving her a rest period for she was not breathing hard, but she might devote an evening to quiet meditation and purify herself for the rites that would begin tomorrow: *Vogue*'s 90-Day Plan, June to September. (But she must make a memorandum to remind her of one hushed impulse left over from the preliminaries: on St. John's Eve she would read *Puck of Pook's Hill* to the children, sitting in a meadow.)

Ambience. That is what the van Pieters have, they and their way of life. Again I cannot find it in the dictionaries and apparently the French misspell it besides oddly misconceiving what it is. And ambience was what Gloria would achieve if she stuck the course. Much of it she must get for herself. She had the elements by now and had watched the van Pieters quite a while, and listened to them. No one could give her more than an outline but that much she got, as when an architect sketches a plan for a client on an envelope. She got that plan, and she was told what the end in view was: "a mental mosaic that has form, since every piece completes the picture."

Think of that mosaic in *Vogue*'s format, Coca-Cola on one inside cover and on the other a three-carat marquise-cut diamond in a brooch or bracelet, "feminine and dramatic," from DeBeers Consolidated Mines, Ltd., priced from $4000 to $8000. Ambience, *le chic*, harmony, the foods and the wines, the music and the books, the awarenesses and the allusions. As for the books and the music on records for the portable beside the bath — each has, the impresario says, its own ambience, and the ambiences are linked together. They join and widen out, blend, rise higher, and lead on. We may think of the spectrum, the structure of a fugue, or the flying trapeze.

Sun will be tranquil on the van Pieter lawn this summer, only gentle breezes will stir the lily pads or widen the curve the fountain makes, and yet in this drowsy peace it will be right for Gloria to have an awareness of regret. So she is to read a biography of Scott Fitzgerald, and this will naturally take her to Fitzgerald's own story of his fall, *The Crack-Up*. Now mark the soaring wings for the autobiography in turn leads, "only a short walk up the garden path" the impressario says, to the so droll *Is Sex Necessary?* A tucked shirt and a wide skirt of apricot cotton broadcloth will be right for this smooth glide from the agony of human loss to a belly laugh, and play "*Le Boeuf sur le Toit*" on the phonograph for it will remind Gloria of Fitzgerald and mirth and food. Meanwhile Dusharme, the Pearl of Hair Cremes, and for the note that makes not a fourth sound but a star shall today be a Garden Buffet Luncheon with ramequins of sweetbreads and mushrooms?

One of the designs in the mosaic of awarenesses will be spun round the spirit. So Henry Morton Robinson's *The Cardinal*, which will be a fine hair shirt for Gloria to wear beneath the "quick breath of a brief dinner-jacket" of her peach-blossom evening dress. Thence to the Rt. Rev. Msgr. Ronald Knox's translations of the Bible, most new and therefore *chic*, and these are sonorous names and titles for Gloria to mention with casual charm at an Outdoor Seated Luncheon, which is where a young Trainer fits in. From that height she may drift down to Msgr. Knox's detective stories but the ambient mind must not list toward any single creed and so will go on to Dr. Schweitzer's book about Bach, a Protestant composer, and Wanda Landowska playing eight preludes and fugues from *Das wohl-temperierte Klavier*. Listen compliantly, for a harpsichord is *pour le chic* and later on there will be songs from *Gentlemen Prefer Blondes*. Until then, Lanvin's Arpège, white silk crepe spattered with leaf green, and aspic of shellfish with a Pouilly-Fuissé. The Ettrick Sheperd harmonizes with this, for he has become a new awareness, a very new one. The mosaic needs an awareness of nature too; make it *The Voyage of the Beagle*, with the adjective "enchanting" annexed to it, surely for the first time in history. It calls for a spritzer and so Gloria will read Will Cuppy's *How to Attract the Wombat*.

Gloria dear, you do not have to attract the wombat but only mention him. . . . So many awarenesses can be piled up in ninety days that a girl can scatter allusions to them as she scatters smiles, and all rich, all knowing, all glossy with patine: Rouault, Ravel, Edward Bellamy, *The God That Failed*, Charles Williams, René Dubos, *The Medieval Mind*, Mary Barron, Château Montrose, Berlioz, buttered pumpernickel with chopped dill, Marchette Chute, Lady Norelco for a daintier underarm, and again Proust. They are fine words. They have the music and the rainbows of the fountain. Or call them rings that can be tossed in the soft summer air and kept in play, all of the same size, the same depth, the same value. And all meaning Sesame, the corn that will open the cave where the jewels are.

One thinks of Arlene in Brookville, all the Arlenes in all the Brookvilles. She has managed to get an hour squeezed free, this hottest July afternoon, to spend under a dryer at the Bon Ton Beauty Box. She was able to get that free hour because the day *is* hot, and so she will get cold cuts from the delicatessen for dinner, and one of the neighbors has taken little Joe with her own children to the wading pool in the park. "Learn to darn socks as well as you do *gros point*," she reads, one of the madcap whims that Gloria was to have, and she is off to the van Pieters' where there will be *coquille* of shellfish in mayonnaise and pan-broiled guinea hen, and Arlene having said, "Poof! there goes perspiration," with Stopette, is wearing tucked organdy and lace over pink rayon taffeta. If only, before she has to make fresh mustard for the boiled ham, if only she had read *The Cocktail Party* and knew what Mimi has been saying about Wilenski on Degas.

It is not an ignoble wish that urges a tired woman toward the fantasy land where everyone has read or seen Mr. Eliot's play or heard the records of it. It is the wish that gave every folklore the legend about the enchanted wood. What is pathetic is that it should be twinned so credulously with our own cheap fairy tales: the lotion that will make your skin beautiful if you apply it every night, the cream that will take the wrinkles out of it. And with much sorrier self-delusions: that an unattractive woman becomes attractive with perfume behind her ears, that a piece of cantilevered wire will make her breast *seem* youthful. But it is pandered to with an infinitely worse cheapness, the fantasy land it is channeled into is unspeakably ignominious and vulgar.

You can find, you can be led to, an exact formula, to books, music, ideas, dresses, and underarm deodorants that will give you personality. Efficiently, with no lost effort, with no process of weathering, with no seed-time-to-harvest, you can take them from a contrived selection and mix them to an engineered result. Worse still: if you do not know or understand the *St. Matthew*

Passion, or the meaning of treason in American history, or the principles of a reducing diet you can in ninety days qualify yourself if not to understand them at least to allude knowingly to them in the presence of others who are alluding to them, who may even know them. Worst of all, the knowing allusion will do as well as knowledge or understanding, indeed better since it is the end in view. Art and thought are a smartness, a chic, a conversation. You may wear Pablo Casals as you would flowered rayon crepe and add a few sprigs of Charles Waterton to your mind as you would add chives to cream cheese. The assured air of one who serves two wines a day makes the counterfeit better than the reality, the falsies better than Diana's breasts, an allusion to a new often-mentioned book better than the experience of art or thought. Conversational awareness. It is the worst grossness of the phony.

When Gloria was halfway through her course, the weekly magazines began to print pictures of a kind we have not seen for some years. There were a few changes — the planes were jets, the bombs had a new shape — but they were all too familiar. A tank blew up. A plane crashed. Boys' faces were contorted at a dressing station or haggard at some halting place on a road. The dead had been laid out in orderly rows and covered with blankets. No bombs fell near the van Pieter place. Gloria looked at the pictures in her verbena bubble bath, then read a few pages farther in *The Paradox of Oscar Wilde,* while the phonograph played Ljuba Welitsch singing Salome. Tomorrow she would rub her heels in the sand — hard — to make them smooth.

Shop Talk

(DECEMBER 1950)

THE BIG RIVER, when we reached it at the mouth of the little one we had been following, looked pretty good to me. At our feet it flowed through willows with a confiding sibilance; the current farther out was manifest power; beyond a flood plain the bluffs of the far bank were softened by lavender mist. In so high a latitude October sunlight is sedate; a cloud bank coming up in the northwest was a token of winter and the pole. But Sam was not pleased. The water, he said, had been used too often; it was dirty. The foreground was nature being frowzy just to demonstrate that you didn't need cans and old automobile fenders to make a dump. The distance was bad composition; a grain elevator would have helped, or even a backhouse.

Sam is a novelist and, we agree, a good one. I knew that he was cold and guessed he was sulking because we would have to drive sixty miles to get dinner and all he could hope for was hard-fried Chicago cut and, for *vin du pays,* the bottle of rye in my bag. Also, the river was poor in literary associations. I could not enrich them but I explained that we were here because a hundred and ninety years ago a Frenchman had reached this confluence as his farthest west; I supplied a touch of elegance by adding that he was a representative of Louis XV. Ah, Sam said, brightening, *l'état c'est moi.* No, that's his great-grandpa, I said; you must keep your tags straight, this Louis is *après moi le déluge.*

One firm support of our friendship is the ability each has to make the other feel superior. Sam justly values his awareness of my spiritual coarseness, upcountry provincialism, and lack of the artist's intuition. Even more precious to him is the conviction that I have no palate or that, if I have, my taste buds are rudimentary compared with the discriminating subtlety he brings to the food and beverages of both hemispheres. And in turn he comforts me by his lifelong, all but absolute resistance to education: this intercontinental nomad has reached an age as advanced as mine without picking up any knowledge not usually possessed by ten-year-olds. Not that he is without intellectual curiosity or satisfactions. No studious ten-year-old could get more delight from the sudden widening of his horizons on learning what a planet is or that Tolstoy too wrote novels or why people are vaccinated. I can move him to admiration by mentioning James Watt or the Crusades or the continental divide.

Sam moved out of the wind to the shelter of a solitary cottonwood while I photographed the site, took its compass bearings, and made several pages of notes. He watched me with a professional's interest in literary methods. But he decided that this was an ungodly waste of time — drive all this distance, eat all that roadside garbage, make all those notes, and you probably won't get more than a paragraph out of it. I may not even get a sentence, I said, but now I've seen it; we ought to hire a plane and fly over it and I should have brought a sextant, or better an astrolabe. He said that, thank God, if he wanted a pine tree with the leaves off it (he was referring to the cottonwood) and fifty square miles of bad modeling in clay, he needn't stir from the desk, he could make them up. I said he unquestionably would, being known for professional economy, and he'd end with the river flowing upstream. Sam said, Nuts, the fact is you don't have to go through this on-the-spot ritual; it's just an alibi; your heel itches as much as mine does and you'll quit work any time to drive anywhere; but your Puritan inheritance makes you pass off your fun as professional duty. I wish you had gone in for European history, he added — then we wouldn't be risking ptomaine tonight. I said that there was a notable lack of Puritans in Ogden and Genoa, where my line originated, a humble line, I would concede, as compared with the king's men, tobacco planters, and refugee counts he had creatively added to his ancestry.

The clouds reached the sun; the river turned the color of putty and began to growl under a rising wind. Let's get out of here before the blizzard, Sam said. But he stood looking at the swift water, I saw him shudder, and he said, It's sinister — they didn't kill Louis Seize here, did they? I said, Make a note, it's Louis Quinze. Did you get that pronunciation in Ogden or Genoa? he asked. . . . In the car, he was morose. Would you want to live beside that historic water route? he demanded. I said no. Well, he said, this mania of yours must have taken you to most of the soundly American rivers — have you seen any you *would* want to live beside? I live beside the Charles. To call it either interesting or beautiful would be grossly libelous; the poet who once owned the land my house stands on said that in a lifetime he had been unable to decide which way it flowed; but it does all right for me. But Sam's question had urgency and I said, You mean for looks? — there's the Gunnison, or the Snake where it turns its own mountains, or the Fox after it comes out of Lake Winnebago, or I'd settle for the upper Susquehanna. Sam said he had seen no river that he wanted to see again, not the Seine or the Tagus or the Nile or the Ouse, no damn river in the world, rivers got him down.

I tried to poultice the wound I did not understand. At that, I said, I've never known what river it is where Elizabeth at last goes out to meet him in the yellow twilight that fades among the weeping birches. Very fine stuff, I said, and that river would content me, all the more so if Elizabeth would meet me with that mood on her. For the first time in my experience Sam failed to glow at an allusion to one of his books. He said, I moved the Wabash over to Brown County but that light effect was purely local — yes, and so long as you don't have to live in it, which is the best state to live in? I told him I once thought Wisconsin and later made it Idaho, but for many years it had been Vermont and, no, I didn't have to live there, or even where I do live. Under strong pressure he said, If you aren't satisfied with any place your peripatetic compulsion takes you to, why don't you go back where you came from? No, I'll tell you, he hurried on before I could say anything — you don't because you can't. As much as five hundred miles before you get there you have an agony in the gut; you don't know whether it's panic or an ulcer but you do know you'll be sunk for good if you cross the city limits. That's me and Brown County. I've started back from New York, Paris, Marrakech, a lot of places, but I can't make it. Tell me why, scholar. And tell me why there's no river I want to look at again.

I thought but didn't say, History has an advantage in that after a hundred and ninety years the surrogate has been inactive for a long time. I did say, Crossing Texas Cabeza de Vaca shed his skin twice a year like a snake. You don't shed yours so often but that's the principle. Brown County, Marrakech, or any of those well-remembered rivers — you know you'd find them cluttered with things you've put behind you or been forced to put away. Debris of old ambitions or old hopes or old griefs or, what's worse, old asininities. The agony in the gut is a way we find of being kind to ourselves at the closing-in, when the radius shortens. It's protective; it's to make sure you won't find out that what you remember as poignancy has turned into a bum joke.

I had the headlights on now and Sam said, God! I hate autumn and I hate dusk. I said that I liked the word "fall" better and that nothing could be done about the autumnal since it was just our time of life, but if he'd think of dusk as the cocktail hour he would be able to bear up. But he was worrying the previous thesis. It's not shed skins, he said, I don't think it's anything more than just light effects. If you could get rid of them, or else if our trade wasn't so squalid. Don't ever get the idea your books mean anything to anyone, pal. You beat your brains out for ten years to get this Henri Quatre riverman in words and maybe with luck somebody will pass his eyes over the result, but he won't hear what you're saying. I bleed my marrow white trying to say what the leaves did to the light beside the water, which is what everything turns on, and before I'm finished with a three-hundred-word paragraph it has had five thousand words in it, but this yap who goggles at it, he can't read it, he doesn't know how to read.

You mean he doesn't believe the twilight was yellow? I said. It was daffodil yellow, Sam said, and it was heavier than gold; it kept coming at you through the trees and up from the river till I thought my ribs would cave in. Look, I've heard that you write — don't you sometimes wake at 3 A.M. wondering if you can put down how the towers never moved in the lake at dusk or just that blackness late at night with the maple tops bending under the sudden rain, and half crazy because you can't remember where the maples or the towers were? (Sycamores probably, in Brown County, I thought.) I never do find out, Sam said heavily, I've got to but I never do — it's some place where I felt at home and sure once, it was a good place to be, but where was it? — I've got to get back there but you know there's no way to go. At 3 A.M. it's clear I couldn't go if I did know a way — but I can get it said and if I do maybe I'll come around the bend and be at home. Then there's that bay. . . . Here Sam snorted so contemptuously that I decided it was only fifty per cent histrionic. That's the writing life for you, he said. Here we are for no reason that makes sense in a scrofulous prairie, a long way from dinner and a wolf howling because he's even hungrier than I am — so I have to start gabbing about that bay.

It wasn't a prairie and the wolf was a ranch dog but I let it ride, being quite clear that there are no bays in Brown County. When he didn't go on, I said, What bay? He said, Do you suppose I'd have this bur in my hair if I knew where it is or how you get there? All I know is I keep running on it, or it's been going along with me for quite a while, or I wake up and sure enough there it is. It's wider than you'd think and there are hills on the far side. On this side it's a beach so long that there isn't any end. Just sand and empty. You can't hear anything and it's so close to dark that you can barely see the hills. The sky is gray, the beach is gray, the water is gray, you can just make out that the hills are gray — all of them, darker than slate. So you practice the same trade I do, it says — well, bring your Louis Philippe *coureur de bois* and his two-fathom birch canoe and his Indians to this beach and see if you can get down how it feels, for I can't.

Are there bell buoys or channel lights in the bay, Sam? I asked. That only made him explode: All right, don't be a writer, be a yap — I tell you about all the heartbreak there is and you want to know if the Coast Guard is on the job. Listen, there isn't anything at all, it's a world full of nothing. There *is* a cloud, a big one; it's still darker gray than the sky and the water. It's half the sky wide where it comes up from beyond the hills but it narrows to a point aimed straight at the center of the beach. It's a desolation, it's emptiness in monotone. Nobody is there or ever was. I'm not there except to feel that I've found a big gray nothing that's like a hole in time. The feel is: forever. The feel is: silence and aloneness. . . . Well, there you've got it, Sam said. It's a light effect.

And dignified at that, I thought. Though I have been talking with writers most of my life, I seldom know the right thing to say to one. They bleed on from wounds healed long ago, which began by seeming mortal but turned out to need only a Band-Aid or five pages of type. I couldn't bring life or grace to his beach for him. Ebb tide or river flowing in the dusk, the snow that sets in after dark, the falling of the wind — tact required me not to say that they didn't matter much. So I said, I'm sure you'll get most of it said, and very well. As a devoted reader of your stuff I'll be watching for it, and as one who knows your thrift I'll expect to see it several times.

Hell, Sam said, don't let it bother you, it's nothing but a light effect. . . . So is a mirage, I thought, so is witch's fire, but the knowledge that that's all it is never kept anyone from chasing it into the desert or the swamp. A hundred years after the fifteenth Louis' *voyageurs* first reached these parts the burly Americans got here too. They had an adjective for the badly wounded animal, they said it had been "gut-shot," and isn't it interesting that he spoke of an agony in the gut? The trivial scratch that proves fatal, and it hurts no less for being a fictitious scratch invented for a literary end. . . . Sam went on, No, I won't get it said. I've taken all the beating I intend to; I won't even try any more. Only, I wish I knew why I come to and find that it has been going along with me, or why when the clock in the steeple strikes three I wake up with that gray water in my mind. It is coming to a place you used to know by heart, a place that meant everything, but now you don't recognize any part of it and you wonder where it was. Pretty silly at that, for it's just a trick of light.

Sam, I said, I've never seen any intelligent reason for writing books, except that a man wants to. . . . Oh, he said, you're one of the enviable and triumphant, you know your books do you great credit, you're well pleased? — how gratifying. . . . Make it that I've sensibly raised the threshold of my indifference to mediocrity, I said. Furthermore, I can tell you what to do about your gray desolation. There must be driftwood on that beach; pile some of it up and get a different light effect with a match. Better still, cut that scene short and go into the one you've done so well so often. You know, harmony and accord, the attuned spirits, serenity in some quiet room. It's in the city and there's a single table lamp that leaves the faces in shadow, and change the gray to blue evening coming up outside the windows, and the sounds of traffic are diminishing. Or it's a shack in the wilds and a gale is blowing that river against the bank, but within all is peace, for roof and fire hold off the storm and this is the strength of shared emotion. You just need a second character, an old friend or a new girl. You'll have to make up the quiet room and the shared peace but you've always found that easy; you made up this fortunate isle whose name you have forgotten. . . . I turned on the car heater and said, This is a snug enclosed space too, not much different from a quiet room or a stormbound shack; if you'll be literary you'll get the light effect and feel how harmonious things are. That also will be made up but there's the solid fact that you can warm your shins at the heater and your hands too, if not your heart. But I agree that it would be injudicious to go back to Brown County.

It's our lousy trade, he said. Here we are, a couple of old crocks, two word-floggers on an errand without meaning, out in what must be God's country for who else would want it, driving in the dark toward nowhere worth getting to. So I tell you a couple of dime-store daydreams and you come right back with some almost negotiable platitudes. If that's the best we've got, we ought to shut up, except writers are the people who won't shut up. . . . You're doing fine, I said — in no time at all you've made it a usable symbol which I'm sure your public will admire. That's what learned people call the philosophy of the porch and it's very sound. It shakes down to a single aphorism: don't kid yourself but if it's more comfortable that way, go ahead.

I expected Sam to rise to a literary allusion but he didn't. Instead he weakened his own definition by falling silent. You can make good time on the north country roads and I drove fast, since I could do nothing to medicine his trifling hurt. While the headlights reached across the plain he settled into a reverie that had yellow twilight in it, blue evening outside the windows, the river he could not bear to see again, and gray cloud and water in a desolation so painful he must not speak its name. I wondered if he named it to himself. Probably not, for an ignominy truth may have is that sometimes it is too unimportant to be borne. If a fineness seems to increase our stature an inch or two, we aren't comfortable till we've cut ourselves back to life size by denying it. A line by a better writer rose in my mind, the one which speaks of the lies men tell themselves to cheat despair. I was going to quote it to Sam but just then a glow appeared ahead of us on the edge of the known world.

There's a light effect, I said; we'll be there in ten minutes and it means dinner.

Won't be worth eating, Sam said.

Parable of the Lost Chance

(JANUARY 1950)

THE THIRTEEN-YEAR-OLD boy, George, came in several times to ask questions about birds. Polly has always had a dozen birdbaths and birdhouses scattered about her lawn, just as inevitably as she has a sundial lettered in antique, "I number only the hours that are serene," though there could be no other kind of hours to number where Polly is. But she has never known anything about birds. They can't cast Citizens' Committee votes, there is no way of educating them to create a fairer world, it's hard to find in them any symbol that will hearten mankind on its way, and they have a distinctly biological aspect. Still, she answered George's questions not only with sunny patience but with what appeared to be alert and even vigilant interest as well. I observed suddenly that there were a lot of stuffed birds in the living room. They were as out of place among Polly's chairs and rugs and those arresting things she hangs on the walls as they would have been in a teller's cage at a bank.

But I have started this wrong. We have had a long, beautiful autumn in eastern Massachusetts, and there came an afternoon when I felt like getting out in it, away from the documents of seventeenth-century America I have lived among so long that deerskins and a cuirass would feel more natural than a dinner jacket. Polly and Pete live in a village out at the far edge of Middlesex County where I once lived too and it would make a pleasant drive. Besides I had lost touch with the right ideas, I didn't know what they were this season, and Polly always knows. Polly *is* the right ideas, in fact, and I hadn't seen her for months. So I telephoned. She said that Pete was spending the day in Worcester to do something or other about his new book but she would be home. (The society that has made war all but impossible wasn't doing anything today, then, nor the one that will federate the world before Easter, nor the Planned Parenthood League, nor the League of Women Voters, nor any of the study groups in sociology, foreign affairs, and the architecture of the future.) She said she would love to have me come to tea. Polly uses the word "tea" with exact botanical reference, but I love her and her mind, and she is most agreeable to look at, and maybe Pete who uses the word metaphorically would get home in time.

I saw George playing on the lawn and had that wearily familiar shock at time's acceleration, for I recognized him as Georgie. He was Polly's third pregnancy. In fact, he was planned Parenthood III, for Polly's mother had died and there was something about the passage of one soul into the universal and therefore the obligation, in our brief moment, to bring another soul into time. There were other urgent reasons too. Mattie was five years old and Little Pete was three and neither of them had ever before known about death, and now death had come right into the family. This was the first breach in childhood's perfect security, the first terrible intimation of mortality. It might create crippling fears, and unavoidably it would mystify the child mind and lay a burden on the child soul.

If it had been me, I would have left the problem to Pete, who in my opinion has written about death more profoundly than anyone else of my literary generation and ought to have been capable of handling his children's ideas. (A long speculation of mine has dealt with the relation of his books, which I admire just this side of idolatry, to Polly's mind and its wondrous workings in the institution of marriage.) But Polly has always known that there is a vein of insensibility, perhaps even coarseness, in Pete. Her mother — who I am sure wanted the children to call her Grandmother but whom they called Alice because Polly feels that discriminations based on age are unjust, and that though children are different from adults they are not in any way less — her mother had died in the spring. So strolling over one afternoon, I ran into a ceremony in Polly's garden. She had the two children there and they were planting heliotropes. This was for Alice. See, we put the seed in the ground, where we put Alice. The leaves that have died too, and the rain and the sunlight and the frost and the snow and the wind — all nature works in harmony and though the seed has been lost in the earth forever, when summer comes there will be flowers and their beautiful colors and their sweet perfume. Alice has merged with beauty — how could there be anything terrifying in a flower?

Polly, however, felt that the ceremony was not enough and, as I have said, it was because of Alice's death that there came to be the little heliotrope named George and called Georgie, though I do not crudely specify the symbolism of the seed. Simply, Alice must be reborn in petals of infant flesh. But now, you will understand, another mystery might confuse the child mind. There was that danger but parents can always avert danger if they are courageous and imaginative. And furthermore these rosy petals would be of life, not death, and therefore this was really an opportunity for the imaginative, courageous parent. As long as I have known Polly she has recognized opportunities far off and risen to them. One day when I dropped in I was surprised to find a cat in the living room — surprised because Polly's county and woodland emotions had always run to dogs, large, tweedy ones. But I learned that the cat was for the enlightenment of the child mind: Polly was going to convert danger into security. Soon now she was going to get . . . big. I am sure that Bryn Mawr gave her A in all her courses and they must have included zoology, and country living had also repeatedly exposed her to instruction. She knew therefore that presently the cat, a black and white scrub which the children had named Clara, would also be getting . . . big. So the child mind would develop none of those erroneous theories that Dr. Freud had, rather insistently, shown might do harm.

Mattie and Little Pete would see gravidity as not mysterious at all but as something widespread in nature and quite jolly. They could have no dark ideas about Polly's pregnancy because of Clara's, which would seem to them just a droll romp of a pet. While Clara was helping the heliotropes merge their grandmother's death in nature's loveliness, she would also be sanitarily shaping their minds to nature's ordinariness.

Polly has an infinite capacity to surprise me, never more so than with that cat. For I perceived that if Clara was to grow big it must be by overeating. I said so but Polly said, nonsense, I was wrong. She has always been saying that to me from the summit of an honors degree at Bryn Mawr and her intuitive understanding of life's beneficence, and so I repeated my assertion rather forcibly and with reference to the anatomical evidence. But Polly shook her head and for thirteen years I have treasured the sentence with which, smilingly superior in knowledge and understanding, she waved away, besides the evidence, the slight coarseness of mind which she has always felt is my bond with Pete. She pointed out that Clara was black and white and, she said, you must know, Benny, for everyone knows, that black and white cats are little girls.

She brings this same infrangibly sweet assurance to Congress, a united world, the poll-tax problem, but when I drove out last week I was not briefed on the current right ideas. We were off to a good start, I thought, when she said that at tea recently she had heard a variation of the old desert-island question that had made her do some extremely serious thinking. That old cliché, you remember, runs: "If you were forced to spend the rest of your life on a desert island with just one person, whom would you choose?" I reminded Polly that the inquiry had been closed forever a couple of years ago when a ship reporter asked the question of a movie actress just back from Europe. With an admirable good sense that made all the front pages, the girl said, "I'd choose a good obstetrician." I was clearly being coarse and Polly told me that the question was serious and so we had to ignore All That. The disturbing variant she had been asked was. "If you had to spend the rest of your life on a desert island with just one person, would you choose a man or a woman?" That, Polly said, brought it down to the deepest lessons you had learned from life. It required the most searching analysis and the most detached balancing of values. Basically, of course, this was a problem of social systems. Of a special social system, to be sure, but one in which the elements were so starkly isolated that you saw the psychological constituent of society.

I said that I wouldn't hesitate for a moment, I'd choose a woman. Polly, disregarding All That, nodded gravely and said, yes, that was the inescapable decision. In order to make the social system work you, whether you were male or female, would have to choose a woman. To survive on a desert island society would, most of all, need realistic thinking; otherwise the primitive environment would snuff you out. And only women thought realistically; the realist mind was woman's mind. Next to that, society would need adaptability, elasticity of personality and mind, for there would be just the two of you and society would perish of civil war unless you could adjust to each other. And that was woman's foredestined and eternal job, it was women who absorbed life's centrifugal forces and cushioned the shocks of society, it was women as stabilizers who kept society going. Women were the cohesive binder in the social group. . . . But here George came in for the fourth time with a question relating to birds and I asked, parenthetically I thought, what all this was about. I knew at once that it was serious when Polly spoke of Country Day. I had a child at Country Day for a while, till my wife and I took him out because it wasn't development toward a fairer world we wanted for him but some schooling, and so I knew that at Country Day everything, at every moment, is very serious indeed.

So it proved. Polly would have been alarmed, except that nothing justifies the A-plus and realistic mind in feeling alarm, and Country Day (where she has long been a Delegate in the Parents' Senate) had, as always, caught it in time. How long it had been repressed in the boy's unconscious Polly did not know, but it had become overt one afternoon when the closing bell rang.

George got his books together and went out of the room. As he went through the door he picked up a stuffed eagle, set it on his head, and walked out with it.

I felt an initial skepticism, for a stuffed eagle seemed improbable at Country Day. The eagle is a symbol of jingoistic national pride, which is one of the things the school is abolishing so that peace and brotherhood will be here in time for our children to avoid the fearful mistakes we have made. Eagles, I felt sure, must be a barrier across the way to the good society. They must be as abhorrent as the swastika or the dollar sign used to be or the sickle and hammer are now. (For though wives of Country Day are always forward, the husbands are Republican and the school has learned that Russian education is not the liberating force it seemed to be ten years ago.) But I understood when Polly said that old Mrs. Graves had given it to the school. That would be why it was not kept in the room where they teach civics: Country Day does not affirm the validity of political compromises.

With the eagle set splendidly on his head George walked past his teacher, past several other teachers on the path, past the secretary, and past Miss Perkins, the principal. At your school any of these would have rung down the curtain by saying, "Take that damned bird back," but your school does not recognize the significance of behavior. Significant behavior is Country Day's preoccupation till the going-down of the sun. So everyone understood that something dire and festering in George had reached the surface, and Miss Perkins called a special committee into being before he was off the grounds. They remembered to phone Polly, so she was able to prevent Pete from more deeply agitating that small, troubled psyche when it got home with the eagle. Country Day is a precision instrument for revealing neuroticism in children who have cunningly concealed it, though saddeningly often it fails with resistant, more primitive types. The committee broke up into subcommittees and for a week there were consultations with psychiatrists, child-guidance counselors, intelligence testers, and similar specialists till the faculty was sure of its ground and its duty.

Pete, who is enthusiastic about Country Day since it has kept him in copy for years, refused to accompany Polly on any of the consultations the school called for and in fact quite failed to see the significance of the case. But that was not wholly a loss, for the case needed the realistic mind — all the more so because the final diagnosis was that something must be wrong in the child's home life. (I once asked Miss Perkins if she had ever known an instance when a child was wrong and its parents right. She answered that Country Day's unintermitted problem was the parental ego which supposed such a thing possible.) This determination was intensely painful to Polly, who has built her home life on the right ideas and has always conducted it so that the child mind might be free, sweet-scented, and unwarped. But the realistic mind knows better than to demur when Country Day lays guilt on the line. It was not, Polly told me, that any of the right ideas had failed but only that we are fallible and that one or more of them must have got overlooked. Clearly George would not have taken the eagle if something deep in him had not forced him to, and her shame was that she had not observed the then tiny cause years ago and rooted it out before it could grow so big.

The school saw the rape of its eagle as antisocial behavior, and at Country Day that is equivalent to both treason and dementia praecox. The fear was that worse would follow, and Polly must amend her family life at once. She knew she must too, for it had been proved unhealthier than adultery, alcoholism, or divorce could have made it.

On being interrogated (oh, ever so considerately), George said that the reason he had taken the eagle was that he felt like taking it. This showed how severe the trauma was, the school pointed out, for his motive had been repressed and buried, had been glossed over as mere impulse. Clearly, it was so grave that only deep therapy could uncover it and that would take the school's united efforts for a long, long time. Meanwhile it could only watch and, as its primordial predecessors would have said, pray. It had, however, a temporary, stopgap prescription. The upper meaning of this theft was that George was symbolizing his conflicts as a strong need of stuffed birds, and he had had none and had therefore taken one. Polly must provide stuffed birds for him in plenty and so contain the neurosis till the school could uncover and resolve it and George could be socialized. So Polly had found a museum that had put away a couple of hundred stuffed birds in its storeroom because they were a little moth-eaten, and had bought them for George. There were stuffed birds all over the house now.

It was working, Polly told me, for George had shown no further antisocial behavior — here she colored faintly and added, at least at school. The revelation had shaken her, she said, and her great quest now was to find out wherein she had gone so dreadfully wrong. She gazed for a long time at the silver tea service inherited from Alice and then turned toward me those deep, candid eyes that could have been disturbing, on a desert island, if backed by a less realistic mind. She said, I can't hold you responsible, for I should have been realistic enough not to be put off by your cynicism. It was just like a cat killing a bird; Georgie was a big cat killing that big eagle. I'm quite sure it's a birth trauma, and it must come straight from the mystery Georgie's being born was to the other children. I should not have let you laugh me out of what I knew: I should have been strong enough to get another cat, a girl cat. Everything would have been different for Georgie.

It was on that grave note that we said goodby. I went out into the autumn twilight and Pete was getting out of his car. He led me back for a cocktail and he said, Has Polly told you her theory? — I'm sure it's wrong, the real mistake she made was in not having the kids plant Alice in the garden. George was coming in too, his arms full of birds and materials that I had no trouble identifying. He seemed to me happy and tranquil in his neurosis and I asked him how he was coming with his new hobby. He said, Just fine, sir — for another of his conflicts makes him a reactionary child with no acceptance of his elders as his equals. He said, I'm getting a lot of fun out of it; I think I'm going to be a taxidermist, and I'm thinking of stuffing Miss Perkins.

Almost Toujours Gai

(MARCH 1950)

I AM AFRAID that this piece is what one of the characters it will mention used to call eheu fugaces stuff. The New York *Sun* died early in January. In the stories that surviving newspapers ran about its passing I did not see any allusion to the obituary which the *Sun* itself printed about its greatest editor. It read merely, "Charles Anderson Dana, editor of the *Sun*, died yesterday afternoon." As unostentatious as a battleship firing by salvo, that obit appeared fifty-two years ago and has resounded in newspaper tradition ever since. When I was young there was always a newspaperman who had "worked with Dana on the *Sun*." The phrase was a negotiable gold certificate; title to it could pass from hand to hand for a few beers; it would get any old warhorse a job on any paper for at least two weeks. I suppose few or none of the species are left; they always seemed to be in their seventies thirty years ago and God knows how old the youngest of them would have to be now.

Last week, apparently some months late, I ran into a reprint of a book by a man who worked on the *Sun* for a long time, though not with Dana. Mr. E. B. White has written an introduction to the new edition. . . . In September of 1919, on my way east to finish my college course after two years in the Army, I had a couple of hours in Chicago between trains. (Some of the boys in the best clubs at the college I was returning to were walking police beats in a very tranquil Boston, carrying nightsticks and suppressing the Revolution by the example of the well born and well heeled. Governor Coolidge, who had been out of town at a canny moment, was off toward the Vice-Presidency in the cloud of dust that would obscure him from then on.) I went into a bookstore and asked for a copy of *Prefaces.* Chicago was about to be called the literary capital of the United States, so naturally the clerk asked me if I meant A *Book of Prefaces.* But my dues were paid and my standing among the well informed was fully as high as his and I said, certainly not, I had mailed home a copy of Mr. Mencken's book from an Army camp two years before. I wanted *Prefaces,* I repeated, and the clerk got his disdain well enough in hand to discover that Kroch's had it. (Eheu fugaces! The price still penciled in the corner was $1.50.) How long was the Chicago-Boston run in those days? Probably a couple of hours shorter than it is now, for the New York Central used to run its trains on time. Anyway, *Prefaces* made some hours of that road-bed smoother than I find it these days.

It is a collection of prefaces, none of them longer than one newspaper column, to unwritten books. The last page is a "Preface to a Book of Prefaces," which says that this book is not precisely what the author intended it to be and that as a matter of fact his books never are. The next one, he is determined, is going to be a Volume with a Moral Purpose, "but it may turn out to be a Volume with a Moral Porpoise. Things of that sort happen to us." . . . E.f.! when last week I bought at a moral bookstore the book Mr. White has written a preface for, the clerk spoke of the author as Don Markee. The next evening I had dinner with a young professor of literature at Harvard. He carries easily the heavy scholarship of his trade and he is mellowed in light learning besides, but when I began to talk about Don Marquis he did some fast footwork and got off on Finley Peter Dunne. Clearly he had grown up in a barren time, and the next night an even younger instructor, finding me at my devotions, asked, "Who in hell is this Marquis character anyway?" A tale so sad, so sad! Ah, welladay!

That is a quotation.

I don't know how to answer the young man's question, and Mr. White has the same trouble, remarking that when he edited an anthology of humor which had about a dozen classifications in it, Don seemed to fit them all. Mr. White ends by deciding that at bottom he was a poet. Yes, for you need a dozen classifications for his poetry, but again no, for you need a dozen more for his prose. One of the prefaces in the volume I have mentioned is to introduce a Book of Fishhooks. It tells a story the basis of which Don probably picked up at some cracker barrel in rural Illinois, whence, I do not doubt, its lineage could be traced all the way back to Noah and Jonah and Captain John Smith (strummin' golden harps, narreratin' myth). It is the story of a bullhead whom Don called Mr. Hoskins and who learned to live out of water so successfully that when he fell into a cistern, one tragic day, he drowned. Noah lifted it without credit from somebody but Don gave it twists of his own that have proved helpful to people with retentive memories and a taste for good storytelling. Six weeks after I got back to Harvard I spotted those twists in a story turned in to Dean Briggs by a young man who has since made quite a name for himself on the most austere plane of literature, and ever since then I have spotted them about once a year in fiction by very notable hands, some of them supposed to be stained the good brown color of our folksy American earth.

Here I was going to support my point by some quotations from *The Old Soak* but I find it has disappeared from my shelves. Don's books have a way of doing that, but I think I remember a thief who was reading this one with me reverently a few months ago and I will get it back. Well, remember Peter, the parrot, who when he tasted some home brew by a friend of the Old Soak's laid an egg. Remember the Old Soak on Christmas Day, locking himself in his room with his hooch and his memories. Remember his outrage, his feelings of intolerable blasphemy, when he found out that his wife had made a raisin pie — " 'Woman,' I says to her [it must run], 'don't you know that raisins today ain't something you eat?' " and, I think, he taken that pie and had it fermenting in the basement right now. . . . Well, we have got to make room somewhere for *The Old Soak* and, as Mr. White remembers, there is *The Almost Perfect State.*

It is the damnedest book, but which of Don's books isn't? You learn from it that the soul comes just down to the midriff. You run into superbly angry outcries against man's nature and man's fate, usually with topspin and usually in the vernacular he had forged and burnished from the current slang. At least fifteen different ways of establishing the Almost Perfect State are explored in detail, but there are going to be no reformers in it for it is better to behead a man than to reform him, and the inhabitants are going to be equally divided between radicals and conservatives who will never work at either trade. At one point the Home Must Go but later on it has to come back again; and the same with the legal system: the State must have a lot of laws, for "The progress of humanity consists in the violation of laws," but on the other hand there are going to be very few, but anyone who wants to violate any of them will be free to do so but must "withdraw to a distance from his fellow men, so that the violation will not interfere with them," but also at any time a law may seem desirable anyone is free to make one up to fit. If a question of statecraft proves refractory, it may get summary treatment: "Economic problems that cannot otherwise be solved should be abolished." Or, just as likely, an Outcry from the Back of the Hall will protest something and there will be a "Response from the Platform: We don't know any more about it than you do." But ultimately the best guidance will come from the insane, and "Unless you have levity and wings you shall not enter into the Almost Perfect State," and "There will be in the Almost Perfect State a chance for everyone to go to hell. This is a promise." Dialogues so exquisite and cockeyed that partial quotation would spoil them are scattered through the text, and so are bits of Don's verse, played on every instrument from a violin to a kazoo. At intervals the way is cleared for another instalment of his theory of history, that the decadence of peoples and the fall of nations can always be traced to baked beans. So the book carries an appendix which begins, "*If* you *will* eat beans, here is the way to prepare them.". . .

Almost Toujours Gai (March 1950)

I wonder what books they read at Harvard now.

A year or so ago I tossed an allusion to Hermione into a review of a silly book; at least one scarred veteran of her era was soothed by it, for he wrote and told me so. Mr. White, though I gather he doesn't think these days any less preposterous, says that that dewy age was "pleasantly preposterous." It was at that, but Hermione is with us still, and Fothergil Finch, and her whole Group. Their stuff is in a different key from the original one; but only the key ever changes, the melody is the same forever and one of Don's agents even turned it up in king tut ank amen s time. Hermione still thinks that the Bhagavad Gita is simply *wonderful* and she thinks Tagore is too, though he is using an alias now. It still comes back to her "again and again how Primitive I am in some ways"; and "What would modern thought be without Subtlety?" Not much, as you cannot escape seeing for yourself and as the Ineffable reminds you too often, and it remains true that Nobody but the Leaders of Thought can dream what Martyrdom is. Fothergil's poetry is less concerned with Virility than it was, but that has merely left more room for the Cosmic All. Nevertheless, Don gave Fothergil his due and let him write the legend of Citronella and Stegomyia. Page 100. Its equivalent, paraphrased as, say, Toynbee, might serve you in the precinct where Hermione never dies, "Thought's Underworld, the Brainstorm Slum." That phrase was rude of her creator but a kindlier Garbage Man reminded him, "Into the Ashes Can the whole world goes. . . . Eventual they dump 'em down the bay." The same bay, the same garbage scow that Mehitabel must come to sometime.

But Mr. White is right: it is the poet we come back to in the end. The world seems a little uneasy and may distress those who observed Mr. Eliot's difficulty in deciding just what Kipling wrote. (On page 191 of Mr. White's reprint you will find: the cockroach stood by the mickle wood in the flush of the astral dawn.) Well, all right, it's just wonderful stuff to read. Throughout the *Sun Dial*, throughout the books, you keep coming on verse that delights you and frequently holds you breathless while you watch a jagged and vertiginous imagination shoot through the air like a skyrocket, giving off odd-shaped and slightly drunken stars of gold. The line with "welladay!" in it I have quoted is from one of the Sonnets to a Red-Haired Lady. Most of them end with "welladay!" — the Gentleman with a Blue Beard who writes them has had sorrowful experiences with wives. They can begin, "Splendour Incarnate! Great Auroral Blaze!" or "My Torchlight Dame! My Frail Incomparable!" They can speak of the girl as "A Bonfire in the Autumn of my Life" or "Gulf Stream of my ocean deep," and of an injudicious admirer as "That rodent-minded, mutt-faced, wolf-eared Mose." But a clear, disturbing music comes through the oddest contexts; and maybe you had better look up those contexts, and some crystalline images, and the last four sonnets, before you decide what classification Don Marquis fits. I'd be willing to waive taxonomy, if some scholar would turn up fifty unpublished ones, or even two.

There are other sonnet sequences but this one is the best. Let's admit that some of Don's verse is tolerably bad; I could never like, for instance, the variations on brains, eyeballs, poached eggs, and pickled onions as interchangeable parts. But you can never be sure. The most innocent-appearing start may presently pull the rug out from under your feet as "The Country Barber Shop," or as "God and Magog" may bump you dizzily to the edge of mania. Or a trite line suddenly breaks in a curve and gives you a glimpse of something dreadful or insane or damned, or a glimpse of beauty from the murky fire-opal that was Don's mind.

But Archy and Mehitabel have everything. All of them that has survived newsprint is in the book Mr. White has introduced, *the lives and times of archy and mehitabel*, 477 pp., $2.50. I am not going to risk competing with Mr. White. I am glad that he explains the exigencies of time in relation to space in the newspaper business, and that he muses about a metropolitan press which does not manage to climb this high any more. There has never been anything like Archy and Mehitabel and there never will be. Don Marquis got all his rich and strange talent into a cockroach who had the literary urge because his soul was that of a *vers libre* poet, and a cat on her ninth life who had been

Cleopatra and many other adventurous, unlucky dames but who was always a lady in spite of hell. Only fantasy was wide or versatile enough to contain him; his mind kept escaping through cracks in the sane, commonplace world out into dimensions that were loops and whorls and mazes of the unpredictable. And he would not stay put.

The world of these creatures was mainly after dark. Even the scrubwomen had gone home, though not till they had scattered the roach powder through which Archy had to pick his way all the time, just as he had to keep a wary eye on spiders, just as he had to be forever ready to leap inside the typewriter, for a gleam might come into even Mehitabel's eye and she had a deadly paw. The world of deserted office buildings and back alleys in from the river, lighted by a grisly moon that was usually frozen. You can sum it up with Mehitabel dancing all night to keep her blood moving because she had no place to sleep but reminding herself to

pick your guts with your frosty feet
they're the strings of a violin.

(The fundamental purpose of the Almost Perfect State was to get rid of loneliness.) As a superior roach Archy felt no great respect for the intelligence and ethics of bugs but he sided with them in regard to men, whom he had known, from a pharaoh who spent four thousand years with sand in his esophagus, right up to the boss. He put it,

the trouble with you
human beings is you are just plain wicked.

When the uprising of the insects came he would try to save the boss because

you have so many
points that are far
from being human.

His thought is spun of contempt and holy anger, down some dizzy slant of the mind where only he could keep his feet—happily, he had six. But this same world erupts with ribald, belly-shaking laughter, and through innumerable abductions that end with her slicing an eye out of her gentleman friend Mehitabel is toujours gai, and the Martian scientist who got a look at our planet

laughed himself to death crying out
goofus goofus goofus all the time.

He said that from the way it looked to him it would not possibly have any other name. Archy agreed with him. But Don was caught between Archy's judgment that

it takes all sorts of
people to make an
underworld

and the sympathy the parrot expressed for Shakespeare, whom he had known at the Mermaid, on learning that his plays were now well esteemed:

poor mutt little he would
care what poor bill wanted
was to be a poet.

You have to be as alert with this stuff as Archy was about the roach powder, for at any moment a thousand volts may hit you. I suppose there isn't any grave name for it. As Mr. White says, Don Marquis "was never quite certified by intellectuals and serious critics of belles-lettres." Simply, it was wonderful to read in those "pleasantly preposterous" days and reads better now. I have difficulty in remembering the names and books of a good many writers of that time who got the right certificates with red wax seal and dangling ribbons, and my inability is pretty widespread. But no one who ever read Don Marquis has forgotten him and on the publisher's word as of the end of 1949, the sale of *archy and mehitabel* remained "really astounding." That is a criterion to which Archy, along with Hermione and Fothergil Finch, was superior but it is an omen of good fortune for the young who are coming up. Nobody is going to write that way for them.

Let us avoid offense by calling it literature, which is a uniform substance that reacts dependably to standard tests, whereas Don Marquis is always slipping through your fingers. But the shelf his books stand on is not crowded. There is a small bulk of writing, winnowed out from the massive and rewarding, that people insist on reading for its own sake, regardless. They have always held it more precious than rubies and if it isn't literature, then literature be damned. There is no chart of the bay toward which the garbarge scow is headed, but his fellow passengers will always find Don Marquis good to read. I'd say that his books may be in the pilothouse.

An It in the Corner

(AUGUST 1951)

TOWARD MIDNIGHT I decided that I had heard as much about the new novel Sam had just turned over to his publisher as I could honestly feel was significant for American letters. So I undertook to shift the conversation to my new book. I have found that novelists, and Sam wears an even smaller fig leaf than most, regard as a deplorable breach of taste any allusion to the existence of other books than their own. Your mother may be spending her last years in a sanitarium for dipsomaniacs but that is not something to be witty about at the dinner table, is it? They will therefore rapidly — if temporarily — turn to the state of the world or the newest scandal in literary circles. After sweetening Sam's highball, I said there was a great truth which the poets had not quite phrased. I was going to phrase it and I did: Something there is that does not want a book written.

Sam looked startled. For God's sake, he said, how did you know that? Why shouldn't I know it? I asked. He explained that it wasn't something one was likely to know except by experience. Not even, I said, not even considering the willingness of novelists to drag from the fascinating caves of personality the mysterious secrets of their experience and put them at the disposal of mankind? Novelists of course, he said, but I wouldn't think — well, the kind of books you write. . . .

I long ago had to accept it as given that books of non-fiction are written straight off, without labor or difficulty. You just look up some facts and write them down and publishers, with unfeeling obtuseness, pay you the same royalty rates they pay to novelists. For some years I have treasured a remark by another novelist, younger than Sam and nowhere near so good, one whose lostness would not rate more than two lines from the stern and monitory intelligence of John Aldridge. Fighting boredom at a cocktail party for some other writer, he observed to me that he'd heard I had finished a book and I must feel relieved. Since I had aged at least ten years in a four-year expenditure of energy that would have furnished forth a dozen such novels as he writes and by stubbornness and staying power had imposed on the book more discipline, form, and finish than he would ever understand were possible, I did feel at least convalescent. I wanted to reply that a man who has just had an infected gall bladder removed or a woman who has just been delivered of triplets probably feels relieved. But I protect the fineness of artists from contusion and simply said, Why? But of course! he said, now you can get back to creative work.

What I said now was, Sam, there's nobody here but me, and not only have I known what we will agree to call your mind for two full generations, I carry a card myself, I'm in good standing. You and I are pros, you needn't anatomize your agony and fortitude for me. I like your stuff, I even respect it. And at our age it's easy to explain the basis of respect: I know that you get up and along about nine o'clock you start writing, and by the end of the day you've done a day's work, and tomorrow at nine o'clock you sit down at the desk again. Let the semipros vibrate like jangled violin strings; you and I know that a writer is a writer who does a day's work. Relax, we will not go into the somewhat repulsive question of why people write at all. I merely remarked on the mysterious obstacles that get in the way of finishing a book, whereas nothing but lack of cash delays, say, a real estate deal. And how many inexplicable things go wrong while it is being written, whereas someone who repairs automobiles, say, simply goes on repairing automobiles.

An It in the Corner (August 1951)

Sam was uneasy. I don't think we ought to talk about it, he said — we're running a foolhardy chance, we might both get hexed. What says you can't finish it is a thing, an It. Sometimes I've thought I could see it, though I probably couldn't, but I've damn well heard It often enough. There It is just on the edge of the water, saying, You think you're going to get away with this one, Sam, but you aren't, I'll take care of that. Didn't the Indians you write about set out a nice meal for the bears before they tried to kill one, didn't they go through a lot of ritual and prayer? (I was not touched; I'm sure he has not read my stuff, it's an open question whether he knows how to read, whether any novelist knows how. He had heard me say this about the bears and had stored it up for some character of his to say.) I don't know how you propitiate It. I'd be willing to give some doves to the priest or send the virgins out to find the first mayflower.

Remember old Joe's hay fever? Sam went on. When you heard he was wheezing to death again, you always knew he'd started a new novel. Worst attack he ever had was in Maine in January; that couldn't have been pollen, that was an It. If a guy is on the alcoholic side, sure as hell halfway through a novel there'll be two interns and a psychiatrist working on him and the book goes over to next year. Or there's this thing, well, in the trade we call it love. Bill Whoosis publishes Martha's stuff, she's practically his meal ticket — though, Sam said conscientiously, God knows what people see in it. Well, she has never started a novel yet but heaven sent her a new man and true love at last with all its wonder. She has to go through five acts of a Christopher Fry 0-point-five-poetic tragedy before she can get on with the book — be money in the bank for Bill if he could get her committed to a convent for the duration. I can't believe that a dumpy and squint-eyed wench like Martha is a *grande amoureuse*. Simply, an It comes swimming in from the deep blue sea and says, this gal thinks she can write a book, well, let's go. What, he added, what is the normal course of any novel? Chapter Three, two weeks brawling with the school that wants to kick your daughter out for sliding down the rainspout to meet some Exeter Casanova.

Chapter Seven, a month lost because they carry your son home with a busted leg and he has to play the goddam radio all day long. (This was the artist's intuition. The numerous women who have divorced Sam have kept his children in protective custody at safe distances.) Chapter Twelve, your old ulcer kicks up again and another month is shot, Chapter Sixteen you have to referee a friend's adultery, and that's the way it goes. There's an It in there pitching all the time.

I said, What kind of ball does your It throw? How do I know It isn't here listening? he said, looking round the room. Well, I'm not a hypochondriac or an alcoholic and I never have had an ulcer or any woman-trouble. (From such fantasies do novels grow.) Besides, I've been in the league a long time. Oh, maybe I get to realizing along about Chapter Ten that if I'm ever to hear the music at Salzburg it's got to be now, for next year the Russians will have it or my publisher will be wondering whether he can collect that last advance from my estate. I battle that one for a month and can't write a word for reading new travel guides and gossiping with ticket agents. Or maybe a scene will go a little sour and I'll think it isn't much better than A——'s scenes [I censor here] or something will stare at me from the page that suggests a character is beginning to act like one of those Little Rollo jerks that B—— turns out. A notion like that would get anybody fed up with writing novels and maybe I have to take a little time off to get in some golf, take some Turkish baths, and get into a realistic frame of mind again. But I never have any serious It trouble, Sam said very loudly, see?—nothing worth talking about. You tell me, what holds up your books.

The haste with which he was getting out of the batter's box was revealing. I said, Skip it, I just look things up and write them down, I haven't got a bloodsweating artist's soul. Still, I would like to know what makes a man write down precisely the opposite of what he means to say. Or why I find I've mentioned Lloyd George when I meant Thomas Jefferson, or the Ohio River when I meant the Cascade Mountains. Normally my mind is capable of retaining an uncomplicated fact for as long as a week, but I may have to get up from my desk and cross the room to the map up to six times because on the way back to the desk I've forgotten where St. Louis is. I can tell you offhand when your birthday is but if I need to mention the date when the Declaration of Independence was proclaimed, I have to look it up, and then I write it down wrong. Why do I make rivers flow upstream, why do I have people delivering famous orations fifty years after their death, why do I find myself alluding to documents that I know quite well never existed, why do I call Aaron Burr the Archbishop of Quebec, or Abraham Lincoln a fiery advocate of secession and slavery?

That's an It getting sore because you've licked it, Sam said. You've outmaneuvered and outstayed It. You've taken all It can dish out, all the ulcers and radio-playing children and suicidal impulses. You've put this book over and with any decency It would wave you across the plate and say, Okay, pal, I didn't think you could do it, see you next time. Not at all. You knocked that one way out to the fence but maybe the book can still be made to look absurd — maybe you've beaten the throw in but you can still tear your pants sliding home and the stands will get a laugh. Nobody, Sam said, nobody ever tells a man these things and I guess it's just as well. When you're young and virginal, you know that writing is an artist's life and you'd only sneer at anyone who mentioned them. Your heart tells you that writing is ennobling, it brings out the best in a man's soul, only a hack could get thrown out at first.

Well, I said, I'm over the hump with this one, from here on in it's downhill all the way. Sam was out of his chair instantly, and he was appalled and genuinely alarmed. You mean you haven't finished it? he said. Practically, I said, I've come into the stretch, three or four months more will see me through. Sam actually groaned and it was an unselfish groan. And here you sit talking about it! he said. That did it, no point in telling the bears how much you admire them now. Look, have your meals sent in, don't ride in any airplanes — no, there's no use, but maybe you could get a big insurance policy, even at your age, and your family would be grateful. You unspeakable fool, you've wrapped everything up and handed it to your It. And what a moment when the executor picks up that first draft from your desk and starts reading. You know what a first draft is like. Tear your pants? — it reads as if you didn't have any pants. Even in your coffin you'll shudder.

I said that the superstitions of the fiction-writing trade did not scare me and I didn't believe, either, that you could turn the wind by spitting into it or pick the winner in the fifth by asking someone what he dreamed last night. I added that as a matter of fact the last part of a book, say the last quarter, was where you got your fun. By that time it had come together and you were solidly on top of it. If it's any good, if you're any good, from here on it will write itself; all you have to do is keep a hand on the wheel.

Sam sat down again. I was feeling sorry for you, he said, but I can't feel sorry for a fool. So now you're talking like Madam President of the local poetry society. Like an English instructor who has just landed a fearless review with some hand-sewn quarterly. Fun, is it? I bet you never feel truly yourself till you go into your study, shut the world away, and pick up the typewriter. Or maybe you're the uplift, maybe you write books to do good. Fun! — see here, amateur, this isn't tennis, it isn't square dancing. This is deadly stuff, it's for keeps, it's shooting the moon.

I had not supposed we would talk about my stuff very long. Do I understand, I said, that you write as a kind of penance or mortification of the flesh? You don't get any satisfaction out of it? I have been listening for more than twenty years, I said, to what I will concede is an absorbing if undeniably verbose account of your adventures in the wonderland of creative art. You now affirm that it has been a sad business all along?

Again Sam inspected the room for the possible presence of an It, then shrugged like an infantryman throwing a cigarette away and getting out of his foxhole. Sure I'm a pro, he said, I sit down at nine o'clock and pick it up where I left off yesterday. Sure, it's just a chore and you'd snicker if the chore boy proved to be too fastidious a spirit to go on mowing the lawn. Did you ever stand on the end of a dock in Maine during a northeaster, knowing you had to go into that water? That's nine o'clock. I'd thank God for a ruptured appendix that would justify putting it off. Madam President likes to write, the English instructor likes to write, but not anybody who has ever been there and felt that dankness start seeping into his soul. Then It warms up and look what I've been writing — a clotted, gelatinous mess. It isn't prose, it would disgrace the prenursery grade of a progressive school. I stare at the emetic stuff and It snickers a little and says, Stinks, don't it? — and is It right! So I'm supposed to enjoy turning out that strawberry junket, me, a grown man, not senile yet, all my parts and members intact, and with an IQ that got me through college more or less.

I said, You just have the animism of all primitive minds, Sam — you're personifying the critical faculty. That isn't an It, that's what saves you from appearing in the quarterlies. It is too an It and I'm a fool for talking about It, he said. Well, after a few pitches It gets Its arm in and begins to burn them across. One neat trick is, after you've boiled yourself in enough oil, the stuff stops stinking and you get interested. All of a sudden it isn't a halfwit's spastic attempt to say something, it's saying it and saying it right. I grant you that's a moment, it's like a shot of honest hooch on an empty stomach — you've got it *said*. When you've got it *said*, nothing can touch you. You're good, you're terrific. Out of the way, Proust, here I come.

Sam poured himself a shot of honest hooch, gulped it, and slumped mournfully in his chair. Yeah, and that one is Its best ball, he said. Don't quote me in print but Proust doesn't have to sit up nights worrying about me. You're not Madam President, you've been there, you carry a card — well, tell me how long your stuff looks good to you or even tolerable. Maybe this delusion It sets up in you lasts through the galleys, but one fine day you get half a dozen advance copies in the mail and they look pretty handsome, even if the picture of you on the jacket ought to be pinned up in the post office with an offer of $10,000 reward. But open the book anywhere and what hits you in the eye is an asininity that turns your bones liquid and so lousily written that A—— himself would be touched by a slight shame. I've never read ten pages of the printed book yet. And that's It over in the corner cackling and holding Its sides. But It has still got a Sunday pitch left. Five years later I pick the thing up and read a little and it goes pretty good, and I think, you know, five years ago I could write, what's happened to me since then?

No, Sam said, at our age we don't have to kid ourselves or each other. You don't write a book because it's a pleasing and rewarding experience—amateurs love it but any pro would choose pneumonia as more comfortable. You don't write it for the reading public, for nobody is going to read it, or if he does he won't understand it, or if he understands it he'll only patronize you as a boob—he could have done much better. You don't write it for the brethren—nobody ever walked out and offered your Indians his scalp. You write it because you enlisted in this war and as a man of honor and an enemy of Its, you'll damn well fight it out on this line if it takes a lifetime. That's a long, dark, chilly corridor that leads off to the left of your desk, and you've got to walk it alone, naked, and with a hex on you. But It has bet you'll never make it and by God you will—you'll get to the far end with a finished manuscript under your arm and heave it square at Its teeth. Quality of manuscript best not specified but you won the war.

I wondered what balm could close this wound. I tried to phrase a proverb, *post poema omne animal triste,* but that seemed unkind as well as indecorous. I said, well, this one has gone off to Bill, what's the next one about? Sam said, Getting kind of late, isn't it? He looked at his watch. Hell, two o'clock isn't late. I've got hold of something this time, something that will blast you right out of your socks. Listen. . . .

III

City Desk

Doctors Along the Boardwalk

(SEPTEMBER 1947)

BACK HOME — which might have been Iowa or West Virginia or Oklahoma — they probably called him Doc, and most likely Old Doc; for he would be close to seventy, his untidy Vandyke was white, his shoulders were stooped and there was a slight tremor in his fingers. Seersucker will not hold a crease and God knows how old his straw hat was. He liked to stand in a corner at one of the pharmaceutical exhibits in the Technical Exposition. Behind him were large charts showing the molecular structure of the firm's newest product, photographs three feet by four showing how it was synthesized, and equally large graphs with red and green lines curling round the black one to show its results in the treatment of anything you please — rheumatic fever, hypertension, duodenal ulcer.

Doc stood there and talked with the young man from the drug house, who had all the statistics by heart and because he had been trained in public relations never gave a sign of boredom but went on smiling and nodding. Doc described his cases back home and told how he handled rheumatic fever or hypertension, and said he had always got good results from potassium iodide, and ended by taking out a pad and writing down his favorite prescription for the young man's consideration.

It must have been a different Doc from hour to hour and from exhibit to exhibit but he always seemed the same. One observer remembers him as clearly as anything else at the Centennial (and ninety-seventh annual meeting) of the American Medical Association, at Atlantic City in the second week of June.

Everybody else was there too, at least by type and category. There were the elite: bigshots, famous researchers, occupants of celebrated chairs, heads of great clinics and great hospitals, representatives of the various government medical services, Distinguished Foreign Guests. There were the actual wielders of power and those assistants to them who have to be called the politicians: the Trustees, the House of Delegates which is at least theoretically a parliament, the presidents and secretaries of the state associations, many county association officers, editors, committeemen on legislation and public relations and hospitals and medical education, and the permanent bureaucracy. There was every variety of physician and surgeon: young men recently out of the services and bewildered, older men looking for an opening, men of all ages apprehensive about their prospects or about what is happening to "medical economics" or about what is happening to the world. But mostly they were your family physician, come from everywhere in the United States to Atlantic City, for the purpose of learning something about what has been going on, and for the further purpose of having a good time.

For this was a convention, the autochthonous folk festival of the Americans that is part professional forum and exchange, part vacation, and part debauch; and it had convened at Atlantic City, a specialized social organism that has evolved to take care of conventions. The town is a resort, atypical only in being oversized, with a range of accommodations from squalid summer flophouses for the impecunious to palatial-looking sucker-traps with Hollywood lobbies and battalions of servants in funny uniforms, where the rich and those who want to appear rich for a few days are robbed as arrogantly as anywhere in the world. Specialization achieves efficiency and the managers of this convention city, given in advance an estimate of the crowd they may expect, can calculate on a slide rule everything that will be needed, from the number of girls who must be kept on call to the number of coffins that will be required. The town is engineered to sustain a crowd on holiday. Municipally, it *is* a crowd, constantly changing in composition, forever the same in mood and behavior. So it has the anonymity of a crowd; unless you go there with a convention you will never see anyone you know.

The 15,667 doctors who convened there in June were by a good deal the largest assemblage of medical men in history. They did not wear comic hats or carry canes with pennants on them as a good many conventions do, from the BPOE to college classes on reunion, but they clowned just as much. If there was anything that distinguished them from any other crowd it was that they looked a little more unhealthy than most. There were rather more men than one might have expected to see who were overweight and putting strains on their hearts that a physician would have cautioned them against, rather more men who looked underweight and harried, whom a physician would have suspected of gastric ulcers. Too many of them had not been getting any exercise; too many worked too hard and lacked the relaxation of hobbies and extraprofessional interests; the incidence of hypertension was probably high.

Otherwise they were any Atlantic City crowd. They and their wives and daughters promenaded the boardwalk, that endearing climax of vulgarity, or were trundled along it in wheeled chairs. They dropped in on the auctions whose closing day has been tomorrow ever since the town was built and listened to the barker's grief over the pittances bid for this genuine or*mew*lu clock, and sometimes bought it. Natural selection assisted by engineering research has given the boardwalk every conceivable device for lifting money from those who in a holiday mood are not too reluctant to see it go. There were brokerage offices with boards and tickers for the Michigan Boulevard diagnostician who wanted to keep an eye on his investments, and next door a humbler colleague could get "5 photos while you wait for 25¢." Side by side shops offered mementoes for the doctor's wife, a ten-thousand-dollar diamond in the window of this one, a six-dollar diamond next door; mink coats here and dyed rabbit two doors farther on; the cottons that become linens newly arrived from Ireland on the way here from Paterson, and The Trousseau Shop, Lingerie of

Distinction. Salt water taffy could be mailed home from fifty places, and there were at least that many where at any hour you could see your GP playing skeeball or pokerino, popping at iron ducks in shooting galleries, rolling the balls of innumerable prize-games, or peering into the optimistically advertised peepshows of the arcades.

On the sundecks the more affluent and especially their women-folk sat disdainful of so much vulgarity, themselves surrounded by the town's vulgarest gimcracks. There were always swimmers on that amazing beach. Drifts of deep-sea fog blew in sometimes. From midmorning till late at night the boardwalk was murmurous with the sound of people having a good time. Inseparable from it was the rustling-straw whisper of surf and this grew louder after dark, the lights came on, the colored signs that are very beautiful when too far off to be read, the glare from concessions and amusement piers, and the shadows that are somehow darker because of the soft sea air.

They had a good time, somewhat pathetically, in the manner of people who are usually too rushed to have a good time and are therefore a little awkward and press too hard when the chance comes. Certain manufacturers set up bars and held open house. When the cocktail hour came there were many parties, proprietary, official, private, select, political. By night one heard the usual singing and roaring. Physicians have to be abstemious when working at their jobs and surgeons have almost to be teetotalers, and moreover in our town a man has got to watch his step if he wants to build up a practice. So the jubilation was in no light-minded mood. "My God," a woman remarked at one of the parties, "if somebody should keel over with a heart attack there isn't anyone here sober enough to take care of him."

II

A PART of the gigantic auditorium had been allotted to a display by the American Physicians Art Association. There was some magnificent photography, there was a scattering of sculpture, woodcarving, pottery, ironwork, inlay, but the medical man who takes up art appears most often to be a painter. The hundreds of canvases showed every degree of ability, from the Brooklyn primitive to the very good indeed, and one observed that a conspicuous prizewinner was a study of a graveyard. The medical eye is glad to turn to landscape when it can — the scarcity of nudes is understandable — and the medical landscapist is usually a romantic. Hillsides had evening mists on them, the prettiest vistas had the house by the side of the road to fill out the balance and were washed in sunset, or the woods showed shadows that were italicized mystery. The artists thought rhetorically of their profession too, and if a few had looked at surgical operations for the moment of intensity, far more had looked at them for "the doctor's consecration to his task" that produces verbal rhythms whenever doctors congregate. In fact one manufacturer had offered prizes for paintings that would show the heroism and nobility of medicine. Here and there one found a canvas that had been done in an expressionistic or some other advanced idiom, but most of them were academic to an extreme. Artistically, medicine does not lean toward the experimental.

Many acres of the exhibition floor were devoted to what the program called the Technical Exposition: in less scientific words, the advertising display. The program's estimate of "more than 282 firms" seemed conservative and the show was inexhaustibly interesting. It fascinated the profession; at any hour it was much more crowded than the other half of the floor, where the doctors themselves, in the Scientific Exhibit, displayed the results of their researches.

They had registered officially on arrival and they went on registering at the Technical Exposition, lining up in queues to make sure they got the house's literature. Their pockets gradually filled with comic devices like those you buy at a joke shop and with samples of proprietaries small enough to be taken away. Samples of poison ivy salves, vitamin tablets, liquids to be injected for bursitis, Old Doc's potassium iodide in a new and handier form — of the innumerable preparations that have just about relieved the modern physician from any need to study the United States Pharmacopoeia. Samples too of health breads, reducing wafers, dietary soups, a multitude of fruit and vegetable juices recommended for this or that condition, Pet and Carnation Milk, Heinz and Borden baby foods, Similac, Pablum. So much food was being given away that it must have reduced a good many expense accounts, and one saw demonstrators from the Scientific Exhibit slipping over to the advertising section for lunch.

Everything that touched the doctor's life or practice was there. He could begin by hiring a receptionist from one of the employment agencies that listed girls who were trained in the techniques of meeting patients and keeping their records straight. He could furnish his waiting and consulting rooms in complete sets or piece by piece. Every conceivable appliance for sterilizing instruments, assisting diagnosis or treatment, or facilitating the routine of medicine was on display—X-ray and fluoroscopic equipment, a "cathode oscillograph," an "infatometer," ampoule openers, a "rhythmic constrictor for the treatment of peripheral vascular conditions," "Tidal Irrigators."

One bystander sometimes left this multiplicity of machines to wander over to a display in the Scientific Exhibit and gaze at the booth that exhibited, with other devices, a set of Perkins' Tractors, which in 1796 would both diagnose and cure ailments of whatever kind. But he would come back again, remind himself how much capital it takes to practice medicine these days, and explore the exhibits some more. Operating tables, a thousand kinds of surgical instruments, sliced-ham machines for skin grafts, bronchoscopes with a display of the unbelievable objects they have fished from the human interior, the New Emerson Respirator Dome which maintains the patient's breathing while his limbs and torso are being separately manipulated and is equipped with a bookrest and a rear-vision mirror. There were competing makes and models of iron lungs and a variety of resuscitators, aspirators, and inhalators. Ansco had cameras to record operations, General Electric a pawnbroker's window of devices for therapy, Bausch and Lomb a whole catalogue of ophthalmological equipment. About here the exposition became too much for the reportorial mind, which began to whirl with "insert diapers" called Disposees and other diapers called Chix and Chux; cosmetics for allergic girls; artificial arms with an armless veteran demonstrating them; Sopranol for *tinea pedis* (athlete's foot in ads elsewhere), Globine Insulin, Gynergen, Cedilanid, Digilanid, Prostigmin Roche, Hygeia the Safe Nursing Bottle, Evenflo Nipples, Thyroid Armour — just register here, doctor, and we'll make sure you get literature and samples.

Doctors like something for nothing as much as the rest of us and lined up by the hundred to receive a twenty-cent pack of cigarettes from the Philip Morris Company. While the queue inched forward they could read the placard and graphs that composed "A Tale of Two Cigarettes." This monograph dealt with the rigorously scientific test which had established that the use of diethylin glycol instead of glycerine as a hydroscopic agent makes Philip Morris by a wide margin the healthiest of all cigarettes. It was disconcerting, fifty yards farther on, to see other hundreds in queues scrutinizing another display which established by a similarly rigorous accumulation of scientific data that most physicians smoked a cigarette which obviously had not proved so healthy in that test. But the Camel Company was not only giving away a twenty-cent pack of its product; it was putting that pack in a ten-cent plastic case with Old Doc's name stamped on it while he waited.

Sharp & Dohme had a series of six booths illustrating the manufacture of influenza vaccine, and assured the most careful scientific attention to the process by having each step of it performed by a singularly pretty girl. This method was more thoroughly developed elsewhere; a good many advertisers were striking the Minsky note. Thus the demonstrators of the Mennen Company's baby oil were fully adult and had been given costumes that left most of the torso bare. An untrained observer, however, would award the blue ribbon to the Richard Hudnut Company. One had not expected to encounter this firm at an AMA convention, but it runs what it calls the Du Barry Success School. A course there will improve the posture of any girl and will peel away superfluous pounds in the suggested areas. There were large X-ray photographs that showed the spine of a graduate before and after she had taken the course. But a more telling testimonial was supplied by a girl who had nothing whatever wrong with her spine or any other part of her. She had survived a selective process that would have flunked most movie stars and fashion models, and there had been applied to her, in small quantities, a fabric which stretched tighter than any other of which brassières and briefs have yet been made. The Hudnut display was always crowded. Across the aisle from it a manufacturer was exhibiting a new kind of splint that could be washed and ventilated. But the chairs he had provided were usually occupied by specialists in anatomy preparing clinical reports on the Success School.

III

If the Technical Exposition made the medical profession look like the crowd at a county fair, the Scientific Exhibit put it in the light that we and the doctors themselves most like to see it in. Here several hundred exhibits reported on the current progress of medicine, and (since this was the centennial year) a number of others on the progress of a century, and (since this was the AMA) still others on the activities of the bureaucracy. Into these displays had gone a labor and ingenuity that reflected the labor and ingenuity of the researches they were summarizing. Most of them were by hospitals, clinics, research foundations, or medical schools, though a few were by individuals and a few others by societies or institutions not directly connected with medicine. Many of them lacked the detail and complexity and doubtless some lacked the authority of similar exhibits at meetings of the medical specialties. But they signalized one of the most heartening realities of life, the steady advance of medical science.

The medical researcher and experimenter, while working at his trade, is just about the most admirable of human beings, and there is probably no other human activity that can show such steady and undeniable progress. The trouble is that, like a number of other sciences, medicine has advanced so far and in so many directions that the average practitioner cannot possibly keep up with it. In many aspects his practice necessarily lags behind what has been made known. The convention exhibits and the discussions in the general and section meetings are an admirable way (less valuable, naturally, than refresher courses) of keeping in touch with what the researchers have been finding out. They are the chief professional reason why doctors attend the AMA conventions: of the sixteen thousand at Atlantic City a majority may be assumed to have come from small towns or at any rate from places that are remote from a medical center.

There is little point in detailing the material displayed. The exhibits ranged over the whole field of medicine. They used every kind of aid — graphs, tables, drawings, specimens, especially photographs. (Medical photography is superb both technically and esthetically and several exhibits gave instruction in its use and suggested new extensions in hospital and private practice.) Most of them were staffed by men or women who had done the research and who were there to answer questions, explain methods, and consult with all inquirers about the problems involved. Most of them distributed mimeographed or printed reports or abstracts to be studied at leisure. The visiting doctor sought out the subjects of most interest to him and got a briefing on the latest developments.

Three theaters ran motion pictures, most of them in color and with sound, of surgical operations, new techniques in anesthesia, diagnostic procedures, and a miscellany of problems in public health, the treatment of convalescents, health education, and related subjects. Such movies have long been used in medical schools and shown at meetings of county medical societies; when it is feasible to make movies they have a quality that the static exhibits cannot achieve. One of them struck an ominous note; it was by the military and it was called "Operation Crossroads."

A couple of goats that had survived Bikini were exhibited elsewhere.

For two days the convention met as a whole, morning and afternoon, to hear papers and panel discussions on stop-press news from the research centers by exceedingly distinguished medical men. Thus Sir Howard Florey, one of those who developed penicillin, reported that the evidence did not support a spreading suspicion that micro-organisms could quickly develop immunity to it. Specialists from the Mayo Clinic reported on two substances (one of them taken from fermenting hay) which have sharply reduced the mortality from certain thrombo-embolic conditions — they operate to prevent the formation of bloodclots and to break them up when formed. There were reports on the present status of streptomycin, of drugs used to treat various heart ailments, of experiments in the use of radioactive substances — and so on. Then for three more days the convention broke up to meet in the seventeen "sections," fields or specialties of which one could be designated no more exactly than "Section on General Practice of Medicine" and another one "Section on Miscellaneous Topics." Here too there were papers and symposiums summarizing what the profession has come to know, and in a couple of sections what it has come to hope and fear. They were far too diverse to be touched on here but the roentgenologists, the allergists, the pediatricians, the otorhinolaryngologists and everyone else you please were reporting themselves for the benefit of your family physician.

A lay observer would venture only one observation — on the accelerating spread of the idea, which was derided by medicine as a whole less than a generation back, that the mind has an important relationship to bodily conditions. The psychiatrists have come in off the back porch and the psychosomatologists, who but yesterday were indulged as fanciful though probably harmless theorists, are practically drum majors now. A patient's ideas and emotions are now seen to be important to the way he feels physically. A few papers acknowledged that his social surroundings are important too; this idea is, for organized medicine, radical indeed, and there was evidence that such a frame of reference will have to fight harder than psychiatry did.

Here, one repeats, is where the medical profession looks best — looks better than most groups of men, looks almost as good as the messianic or megalomaniac rhetoric of its orators makes out. Here it shows the attributes that have enabled medicine as a science steadily to push the frontier of knowledge farther into the area once marked unknown, and have kept medicine as an art of human relations a constant solace to men in pain, fear, and sorrow. Patience, ingenuity, courage, skepticism, faith, the experimental spirit, the open mind, readiness to test innovation, laborious and exhaustive analysis of data, a constant quest for new data — such things as these have steadily carried medical knowledge onward to repeated victories, repeated subjugation of diseases that seemed impossible to subjugate, repeated solutions of problems that seemed insoluble. The mind of the medical researcher is the human intelligence at its most admirable, and the total personality of the good doctor dealing with a patient is human skill and wisdom fused inspiringly. Moreover, the profession as a whole shows an eagerness for greater knowledge and greater skill that no other art or profession quite equals.

Such realizations are forced on you when you see sixteen thousand medical men gathered in professional consultation. It is just as well, therefore, that different realizations are also forced on you when you see the austere scientific intelligence come out of the laboratory and consulting room, and either docilely or with belligerent enthusiasm accept the propaganda fed it by its own specialists in obscurantism, neglecting to apply to an undiagnosed syndrome any of the processes whatever that it has been insisting on applying to other syndromes.

IV

Monsignor sheen reminded the assembled physicians of the nature of their relation to their patients and gave them some excellent advice, then marred it somewhat by delivering one of those sideswipes at psychiatry which have lately marked his discourse and which, a layman thinks, he would do well to discuss with his confessor. A past-president of the National Association of Manufacturers made a skillful speech; there is hardly any need to tell you what he said: it is summarized when his former office is named. As you know, freedom, initiative, self-reliance, and risk capital have been dying in the United States ever since 1932. As you also know, class-consciousness that will prove (redundantly) fatal is being systematically encouraged by our collectivist government, and taxes are (fatally) not being reduced, and (fatally) the faith of our people is being insidiously undermined, and (fatally) a young man cannot acquire a competence, and a hell's brew of fatal hormones have been New Dealishly injected in the national bloodstream, and it is later than we think.

The past-president of manufacturers had a progressive mind, as he freely confessed, and so he realized that organized medicine must find some way of enabling people with small incomes to procure adequate medical care for themselves — to procure the kind of care for which the convention was repeatedly congratulating itself. He had applied hard thought to the problem, especially in relation to "politicians and reformers." And he had reached a conclusion: that we would be wise to adopt "the voluntary plans for hospital and health insurance" that the AMA recommends.

That was what he was brought to Atlantic City to say. And in the course of his inaugural address the new president of the American Medical Association found occasion to say it again. They were talking about a fearful bugaboo, a national health program, and they were voicing the party line of the present actual rulers of the AMA. In organized medicine there is a general realization that such a program is certain to come, a realization something like that of a town which learns by telephone that a dam up the valley has burst and a flood is on the way. The dam burst long ago and year by year the AMA has prepared to meet the flood by saying that it must not get here, that the flood waters are communistic, that we shall all be lost if they reach the city limits.

Systematically and tirelessly, with all the means available to one of the most powerful pressure groups and propaganda machines in the country, the AMA has opposed every measure in which it detected any connection whatever with what is surely coming. It has done so sometimes suavely, sometimes with amazing crudity, sometimes by individual pressure the most dishonorable, sometimes by flagrant mass appeals the most mendacious. Its performance has reached such a point that one of the most distinguished of American physicians, Dr. Edward A. Parks, formerly pediatrician-in-chief at the Johns Hopkins Hospital, by temperament and background surely no revolutionist, told the New York Academy of Medicine a few months ago that "the behavior of organized medicine is humiliating and its leadership has seemed incredibly stupid." Dr. Parks went on to say, "Its much-touted ten-point program is no program . . . but only a series of pious platitudes or highly qualified indorsements of policies or activities initiated in the first instance by isolated groups of liberal-minded, socially-conscious physicians or laymen working independently of it. Its primary concern throughout, as judged by its behavior, has seemed to be aimed consistently at the preservation at all costs of the medical care system as it exists today." That system, he said, had developed to fit the distribution of money, not the distribution of medical need; it does not meet medical need and never can.

Organized medicine — which means primarily the AMA and the hierarchy of state and county societies which support it and whose policies it in part controls — organized medicine has, as Dr. Parks said, exerted its great power to prevent any change whatever in the status quo. But events have changed the status of medical care, and the AMA has had to adjust not only to pressures from the social organism but also to discordant energies within itself. Step by step its original absolute rejection of all change has been modified — modified so slowly that the threat of public assumption of control has steadily increased, but modified nevertheless.

It is only a few years since the Wagner-Murray-Dingell bill was, in the editorials of the *Journal of the American Medical As-*

sociation, pure communism instigated by conspirators in the national government who were acting on orders direct from Stalin. That bill contained six main provisions; since Stalin phoned his orders to the New Deal the AMA has, by official resolution, indorsed five of them. In 1938 it met with all the ruthless force at its command the challenge to its policies made by the Washington Group Health Association. That fight ended, disastrously for the AMA, in the Supreme Court of the United States, and in 1947 there is no possibility that such methods can be used against such institutions ever again. Many smaller defeats mark the slow abandonment of the impossible position which the rulers of organized medicine at first tried to maintain. All the outposts and subsidiary defenses have been surrendered; the rulers are now defending what they regard as the citadel itself.

That ultimate and minimum is this: There must be no federally controlled health program; the program whose coming is seen to be inevitable must be based on states rights. There must be no national imposition of medical standards apart from those which organized medicine itself imposes. There must be no federal control over the practice of medicine and no government or public control of the bodies that will ultimately direct the program: all effective power must be reserved to organized medicine. There must be no form of *compulsory* health insurance — since this would make the previous provision impossible. There must be no "third-party intervention," by any nonmedical board or panel or supervisor, between doctor and patient. (Medical third-party intervention is all right, however, and nonmedical third-party intervention is accepted for the poor.) And nothing, at least nothing not a part of organized medicine, must interfere with "the free choice of the physician," a freedom which only a minute percentage of our population have now, which that percentage relinquish when they patronize any of the famous clinics, and which only a few of those who have it can exercise except ignorantly and as an act of faith. To sum up: organized medicine insists on complete, unsupervised control of any health program that may evolve; and it requires that plan to interfere with the fee-for-service system as little as possible, not at all wherever there is any way to maintain the system.

This stand, of course, is so unrealistic that it suggests the need of psychiatric scrutiny. Congress will not appropriate funds without providing for supervision of their disbursement, and if the AMA's propaganda were a thousand times as formidable as it is it could not kid the public into accepting a plan which the public did not itself control. The greatest desideratum of any health program, the practice of preventive rather than remedial medicine, is impossible for most of the population without some kind of compulsory insurance. And finally without compulsory insurance there is no way of providing complete medical service, except by the group practice which organized medicine disapproves, or by setting the prices of "voluntary" schemes so high that they will be out of the reach of most people.

At Atlantic City the realities had no force. Those who determine AMA policies certainly know that the Taft bill for a national health program is not meant to pass or even come to a vote, but they threw their support to it and an outsider can only decide that they did so to confuse the issues and to postpone as much action as possible as long as possible. The bill is a political measure only, an assist to Senator Taft's presidential campaign. It records him as favoring a national health program, which should get him a lot of lay votes, and it assures organized medicine that he wants that program left entirely to its control, which lines up one of the most powerful pressure groups in the United States in his support. It has the approval of the AMA's governors and so it will have the approval of the rank and file. The governors have guessed that we are going to be Republican for a while and so there need be no further retreat, in fact much of the ground lost to modernity can be regained. The public relations counsel whom the AMA hired last year and who advised it to get in touch with popular demand, was allowed — or forced — to resign, on the ground that nothing need be done after all. The governors and the bureaucracy (so far as these are not the same) were at their suavest and most practical in backstairs manipulation of downstage attitudes, in committee-of-the-whole disposition of dissents or proposals that might look awkward, at paralyzing with bureaucratic red tape the efforts of those who think otherwise than the governors think it best for them to think.

In a way some of the resulting spectacles are truly superb. The practice of medicine is furiously competitive, and much of the behind-the-scenes activity at Atlantic City resulted from the AMA's efforts to umpire and arbitrate competition — fee-splitting, rebates, contract practice, and the like; but there must be maintained a dignified outward pretense that doctors obey the code of ethics which forbids them to compete. Again, nothing is surer than that the evolution of health insurance and the like will provide not one health program but a good many — as many systems of medical practice, say, as there are systems of banking, from wholly private to wholly public — but the machine must continue to grind out the propaganda which the *Journal* has been purveying for nearly twenty years: that the reds are forcing on us a single all-or-nothing, either-or, black-or-white choice between freedom and slavery. Again, throughout medicine and even in the AMA there is much rejection of, and rebellion against, the official attitude toward what the propaganda insists on calling "state" or "socialized" medicine — but at all costs organized medicine must publicly appear to accept as inspired truth the party line of the Trustees, the House of Delegates, and the bureaucracy.

Of course, a large part of the profession does just that. Old Doc is the dauntless deathfighter the orations say he is, and the clinical researcher is — inside his lab — as inspiring a figure as he has been acknowledged to be herein. But they are busy men and they get little time to think about social matters; and Dr. Morris Fishbein, the veteran editor of the Journal, has been providing them with approved ideas for a long, long time. Typically, when you ask them what they think about the Taft bill or the Wagner-Murray-Dingell bill, or compulsory health insurance, or federal provision for the "medically indigent," you get back what Dr. Fishbein has been saying. When you press farther they tell you that they haven't read the bill, or haven't "looked into matters" very far; and when you ask why, you are told that the profession has delegated such problems to brilliant and specially qualified men and those men will find the right solution. If you still press them, a large part of the profession stops being practitioners and clinical investigators and begins to yell like any angry group of the unsanctified. Dr. Fishbein has told them they must not be pushed too far.

Scarcity of objective thought, ignorance of economic and social developments, neophobia, docile acceptance of the fuehrer principle, above all conditioned response in the automatic functioning of institutions which work as propaganda machines at the very moment when they are also working as guilds — these are the group characteristics one generalizes. They make the AMA, in regard to "medical economics" and the greatest single problem with which American medicine must deal, biased, obscurantist, and reactionary to an astonishing degree. But the AMA, like every other human institution, must yield to the pressure of events; and it is yielding now.

After all about 35 per cent of the doctors in the United States do not belong to the AMA; that is a sizable group and its attitudes and actions will necessarily influence the AMA's. Moreover, inside the AMA there are many groups whose attitudes toward the big problem are different from the official one, varying from passive dissent to active and sometimes violent opposition. The number and size of such groups are increasing; with whatever reluctance and however slowly, the AMA must maintain with them a working compromise that will constantly give ground, for it cannot afford rebellion and secession. In the county societies (which are in many ways far more important to the individual doctor than the AMA), the headlong social change of these times is constantly forcing more doctors to practice their profession in ways contrary to the official policies and therefore certain to alter those policies. A comparable influence is being exerted by medical schools and hospitals which have found that federal funds — so subversive and corrupt in the official view a few years ago — are increasingly necessary, and that the individual researcher who is supported by these funds is not a slave after all. From now on some of the ablest groups among the elite of the profession will have only formal reasons for supporting the party line. And there is the inescapable reality that the constant advance of medical knowledge constantly increases the cost of medical treatment and constantly reduces the number of people who can afford to pay for it under the present system.

In short, the AMA exhibits the paradoxes of any living institution and at this moment is more interesting than most in its all too human confusions. At Atlantic City there was always some orator telling you how noble medicine is, how selfless, how dedicated to the search for truth and the service of suffering humanity. He was right, when you listened to the papers or wandered through the Scientific Section — and when the convention delivered a report on what may be expected in an atomic and biological war, a report thoroughly cool-minded and objective, an admirable example of the human intelligence at work on a tremendous problem. And also he was pure ham, the voice of any group of self-congratulatory men kidding themselves, succumbing to the rhythms of speech, mistaking prejudice for public spirit, and glossing over unpleasant realities with personal illusions. The same mind that produced an objective report on atomic emergencies also produced a resolution to the effect that students at medical schools (who are indoctrinated with the official ideas all through their course anyway) must be instructed formally so that they will resist Dangerous Thoughts. And that same mind could be heard bellowing or bawling with an emotion something less than scientific whenever Old Doc went into his political or his sociological phase.

That seemed to be the moral of Atlantic City: the medical profession, so far as the AMA represents it, badly needs to bring a little of the laboratory method to the study of political behavior, and it needs some realistic instruction in the facts of modern life. Whether it will get them for itself or have them thrust upon it from outside made an interesting question to muse on as one watched the doctors strolling on the boardwalk in the fading afternoon. It seemed, as the former president of the NAM told them, later than they thought.

The Smokejumpers

(NOVEMBER 1951)

IN AUGUST 1946 a dry lightning storm, a thunderstorm without rain, started a fire in a remote part of the Boise National Forest in Idaho. Two fires which were burning at the time had strained the defenses of the forest but the fire control officials started toward the new one as many men as could be spared, rented bulldozers from the nearest contracting firms, and sent out an emergency call for firefighters.

You do not extinguish a forest fire. You make a fire line round it, clearing away brush, stumps, and the decayed organic matter that is called duff till you reach soil or rock, and hope to hold it within the line. Firefighters equipped with shovels, saws, and axes patrol the line, felling dead trees ("snags") on both sides of it, putting out small spot fires that have been started by sparks blown beyond it, rolling old logs out of the way, and starting back fires if they are called for. Violent winds made the new fire hard to control and by the end of the second day it had burned some three hundred acres of timber. By the fifth day 361 men were fighting it and sixty others were on their way toward it. Rain is almost unheard of in August in central Idaho but on the sixth morning there was a short fall and the fire was promptly brought under control. It had burned about seven hundred acres, destroyed about $2000 worth of timber, and cost $37,000 to fight. Both size and expense were trivial, considering the possibilities of a fire that had got so dangerous a start. In 1931 fire in the Boise Forest burned some 35,000 acres.

On the second day plans were made to construct a line well back from the one which the fire had leaped over. Part of it would run along a ridge separated from the base camp by a number of gulches where there were no trails and which men and equipment would therefore take a long time to cross. Ordering bulldozers to start making a trail toward it, the fire boss radioed a request for smokejumpers, the Forest Service's parachuting firefighters, to land on the ridge, construct the line there, and hold it till they could be reached in force. A small unit of smokejumpers was based at McCall, Idaho, fifty miles away in an air line, but all of them had been dispatched to three fires in the Payette National Forest. Missoula, Montana, 150 miles away by air and the headquarters of the Forest Service's system of aerial fire control, therefore answered the request with twenty smokejumpers in two Ford trimotor planes. Long obsolete for other kinds of flying, the old Tin Goose remains the only large plane that can do the kind of work necessary in these operations.

I first saw smokejumpers in action on this occasion. I was staying in the Boise Forest, getting extensive and for a man of sedentary tastes very strenuous instruction in various aspects of forestry. When I reached the ridge the smokejumpers had already landed there and were setting up a rough camp some distance down the reverse slope, but a Ford was circling the site dropping equipment and supplies. Twice during the afternoon it came back with additional supplies. To be under those drops was a spectacular and exhilarating experience.

I took shelter under a tall ponderosa pine, for these were pinpoint bombers and in 1946 the Service dropped more packs without parachutes than it does now. The bedrolls came down that way, hitting with a thump that sounded like a bomb explosion and bouncing high in the air. (I doubt if the Ford was ever less than two hundred feet off the ground, which was practically stratosphere flying compared to what I saw this year.) When a parachute carrying supplies lodged in a tree, a smokejumper put on a pair of climbing irons and went after it, if it looked as if it could be easily cleared. If it didn't, one or two chopped down the tree. Landing in a tree was desirable for it broke the force of the fall — the smokejumpers themselves like to land in timber unless it is very high — and the Service had worked out ingenious methods of packing to prevent breakage. Everything came down intact except when one chute stuck in a tree and dropped its load, which must have been imperfectly lashed. Part of the load was a crate of eggs, which hit the ground with a soul-satisfying splash. A single egg, however, rolled end over end downhill for an incredible distance and then came to rest unbroken.

Smokejumpers are simply firefighters who reach fires from the air. As soon as they had set up their camp, they got to work clearing the line along the ridge. A portable radio kept them in touch with the fire boss, the base camp, and a small plane that was reconnoitering the fire. They worked till dark but soon after they started again the next morning the bulldozers and a crew from the base camp reached the ridge and took over. The smokejumpers headed for the nearest road. They left all their equipment to be brought out by a packer and his mule string and forwarded to Missoula. They themselves would travel out of the forest by truck and return to Missoula by bus or train.

II

THIS WAS NOT a typical use of the smokejumper. Their great value to the Forest Service is that they can get to a fire much faster than any other firefighters. If he reaches it early enough one man can control a forest fire with a shovel or an axe or even by stamping on it. Many areas of the Western forests are a long way from a road or even a trail, in exceedingly rugged mountain wilderness. I have seen fires that were not reached until the third day and know of some that have required longer. At the end of such a period a fire may be so big that hundreds of men will be needed — and, traveling a large part of the way on foot, they may be exhausted when they get there. Whereas the smokejumpers can travel up to 160 miles an hour and so can reach nearly any fire in less than two hours — though Missoula will send them distances of up to four hours' flying time — and will be as fresh when they land as when they started. Commonly, therefore, they are dispatched in crews of from two to six.

Region One of the Forest Service — Montana, northern Idaho, and parts of Washington and South Dakota — has compiled some impressive figures about the saving that results. From 1905, when the Forest Service was organized, to 1930 the forests of this Region suffered an average annual loss from fire of 252,000 acres, worth at present-day prices $40,000,000 on the stump (there are four other Regions in the arid West), and the average rate of travel toward fires was two and a half miles an hour. In the next decade, because the building of roads and trails in the forests had made possible more extensive use of trucks, the average rate of travel was fifteen miles an hour and the annual loss dropped to 65,200 acres, worth $3,500,000. In the decade from 1940, the year when the small beginnings of smokejumping were made, to 1950 the average annual loss in Region One was 8888 acres, worth $350,000, and fires were reached at a speed that ranged between 80 and 160 miles an hour. In 1950 the entire cost of smokejumping operations in Region One was $171,624. Assuming the average annual loss of the preceding decade, this expenditure saved the public $3,150,000.

The figures, moreover, cover only the stumpage value of burned timber. In a big fire other losses may total far more: destruction of cattle, sheep, game animals, and other wild life and impairment of grazing ranges; alteration of soil chemistry with subsequent degradation of new growth; impairment of watersheds which may mean floods, damage to farmlands and to dams, irrigation systems, and city water systems; destruction of many kinds of public and private property, such as amusement and recreation areas, summer camps and cabins, resort hotels, ranch buildings, sawmills and stacked lumber, roadmaking equipment, railroad tracks and cars.

The Smokejumpers (November 1951)

The Forest Service began dropping supplies to remote fires as early as 1929. Though it has a few small planes of its own, which it uses for reconnaissance, survey, and search, practically all the flying connected with actual firefighting is done on contract by private firms. The principal one of these, the Johnson Flying Service of Missoula, owned and operated by the famous Western pilot Bob Johnson, has had an extremely important part in the development of aerial control. By 1936 Mr. Johnson and Forest Service experts had developed what is called the static line, a device which opens parachutes automatically and so relieves the jumper of responsibility for what had previously been the most uncertain and dangerous part of his jump. It made the Army's use of paratroopers possible. Two years later the same collaborators developed a quick-opening chute which could be steered and maneuvered more effectively than any before it.

The Service made its first experiments with parachute jumpers at the end of the fire season of 1939. The first jumps to actual forest fires were made in 1940. In that year too a board of Army officers studied the training system which the Service had worked out; as a result it became the basis of the training given to paratroops. The smokejumping program was expanded during the war years and later. In 1949 the Service had 252 smokejumpers, most of them based at Missoula but with two small sub-bases in Idaho, and one each in Washington, Oregon, California, and New Mexico. They made a total of 1335 individual jumps to 354 fires. Unusual weather conditions in the West made 1950 a comparatively easy year and the total number of jumps was less than half as large. The figures of 1951 are not in as I write but it has been a bad fire year.

Very few smokejumpers are permanent Forest Service employees, for the work is seasonal. All of them are young and many are college undergraduates. The pay is preposterously low but since they get overtime after eight hours they may make as much as $450 a month. The training course, which precedes the fire season, lasts three weeks and concentrates on precision jumping, though it also includes physical conditioning and instruction in firefighting. It is obviously effective. Although smokejumpers are used only in a country so difficult and dangerous that the Army would never use parachuters there at all except on rescue missions, none has ever been killed while making a jump. Severe injuries are astonishingly infrequent. During 1950, for instance, on the 188 jumps made to fifty fires in Region One there were three injuries serious enough to take the victims off the job. One man suffered a broken ankle, another a broken rib and some strained back muscles, and the third an ankle strain that incapacitated him for just one day. At Missoula this was considered a depressingly poor record for the year. Not only the training program accounts for such extraordinary success but the aerial techniques and the equipment which the Service and its civilian collaborators have developed.

The two-piece jumping suit — which on long flights is not put on till within a few minutes of the fire — in made of canvas and is padded with felt. Straps of webbing secure the legs under the jumper's boots and the jacket has a high stiff collar flaring back from the neck to protect him from tree branches. A pocket on the right leg holds streamers of bright-colored cloth for signaling to the plane and from 65 to 125 feet of rope. The rope is the jumper's means of reaching the ground when he has made his favorite landing in a tree. He hitches it to the lines of the chute, unbuckles the harness, and slides down.

Underneath the suit he wears a belt of heavy webbing with stiff leather braces front and back. He also wears an ordinary football helmet, a mask of heavy steel wire, gloves, and logger's boots, which are heavier than those worn by paratroopers. He has an emergency chest chute with easily detachable harness; a sheathed knife is attached to its under side. His main chute of course is on his back and is attached by the static line to a steel cable above the door of the plane.

So clad, the jumper simply steps sideward out the door of the Ford or from a metal step riveted below the door to the side of such single-engined planes as Travelairs. He straightens his legs and back so that he will hang erect and crosses his arms till he has cleared the plane and the chute has opened. He takes no equipment with him, everything being dropped to him when he has landed. All parachutes are made of nylon, which besides being more substantial and more easily packed than silk is unpalatable to grasshoppers. Personal chutes, which are used in rotation, no jumper being permitted a private one, are specially made for the Forest Service; cargo chutes are Army surplus.

III

In August of this year I spent ten days in Missoula, lecturing at the State University of Montana. It was, as I have said, a bad fire year. In my first seven days Region One had 215 fires, to 51 of which jumpers were dispatched, making 190 individual jumps. Resolved to see a smokejumping operation from the air if possible, I went to Hale Field, the private airport of the Johnson Flying Service, met Mr. Johnson, and got his permission to accompany a flight if smokejumpers should be called for at a time when I was not busy at the university.

Bob Johnson was one of the original group, and is one of the few survivors, of the adventurous men called bush-pilots who pioneered mountain flying. There is no more dangerous flying in the world and none that requires more skill. Treacherous and unpredictable winds, violent updrafts and downdrafts, and the liability of sudden storms are ever present hazards. In the summer the air above peaks and canyons is so turbulent during the daytime that except in emergencies even these treetop pilots are reluctant to fly between midmorning and late afternoon. (All forest fires are emergencies and most flights to them are made during the worst hours.) There are few landing strips and so emergency landings are all but impossible. Instrument flying is out of the question, and in any event there is no substitute for the skill and knowledge required by the special circumstances, one trouble being that a man may lose his life while acquiring them.

Conditions are even worse when fall and winter storms set in; a biography of Mr. Johnson would be a succession of hair-raising stories of bravery, risk-taking, danger, and escape. Since a book about him and his associates is now being written I will say here only that after flying and talking with him I was convinced, as hundreds before me had been, that he is one of the great pilots.

On my first Saturday, Forest Service officials showed me the training installation twenty-odd miles from Missoula and the parachute loft and equipment sheds at Hale Field. I also went through the Johnson Flying Service shops. It is engaged in a general flying business, of which its Forest Service contracts are only a part, and mountain flying demands the best possible maintenance. There can be no engine failures — so at Hale Field engines are torn down and rebuilt after only half as many hours as the standards of the CAA require. The Johnson Service owns three Ford trimotors which it uses (besides smaller planes) in its smokejumping contract. The great value of the Ford is that it is the only large plane which can be landed on short strips in the bottom of canyons and, though large, it can be flown slow enough to permit parachute jumps in mountain terrain but still has power enough to pull up fast. It long ago became impossible to obtain replacement parts and so they are all made at Hale Field. Since the youngest of these three planes was made in 1929 presumably no part of the original engines is left.

Twice while I was at the field on Saturday smokejumpers were despatched to fires but in single-engine planes which they and their equipment filled, leaving no room for me. Fords went out twice the next day but I was off in the backcountry of the Bitterroot Mountains, photographing sites on the trail of Lewis and Clark. On Monday afternoon, however, I was summoned to the field. A fire had been reported in the Lolo National Forest, in an area which I had crossed the day before, and smokejumpers were being sent to it in a Ford. Mr. Johnson himself was going to pilot the plane.

The fire — always called a "smoke" when reported — was fifty-five miles in an air line from Missoula, on the side of a canyon in the Bitterroots. It had probably been started by a lightning strike on Friday and had smoldered in a single dead stump or snag until today, when it reached the duff of the forest floor. It had been sighted at 1.52 P.M. by a Forest Service lookout in a fire tower on a peak some miles away. He had needed just eight minutes to locate it on his map, check his observations and calculations, and report it by Forest Service telephone to fire control headquarters in Missoula. Smokejumpers had been ordered to it because the nearest place from which any other firefighters could be sent was a ranger station in the same canyon but fifteen miles from the smoke, too great a distance to be covered that afternoon.

The lookout had reported it as "a large spot, burning on a gentle slope," which meant that it was still very small. Normally therefore only two smokejumpers would have been sent but the map showed that it was burning near what the Service calls heavy fuel, in this case an area studded with windfalls and snags. To make sure that it would be stopped short of such highly inflammable stuff, four smokejumpers were ordered to it.

Two of them were veterans of a year's experience, the other two were in their first season. Besides them there was the man in charge of the jump, known as the spotter, and since he had just been promoted to this crucial job, in fact would be in full control for the first time, a "check-spotter" of long experience went along to keep an eye on him. An observer from Region One headquarters, Mr. Johnson the pilot, and I completed the party. When I reached the field the last equipment was being stowed in the plane — forward from the door; the jumpers' chutes were aft of it. Fire control headquarters had provided maps for the pilot and the two spotters, ringing with colored pencil marks the quarter section — a square with half-mile sides — in which the smoke had been located. But none of them really needed maps; the whole enormous forest was as familiar to them as their own backyards.

We took off at 2.30, exactly thirty minutes after the lookout's report reached headquarters. Until we reached the long canyon in which the fire was burning we flew across successive ridges of the Bitterroots. Though I have known those mountains for a long time I had never acquired so vivid an appreciation of their wildness and ruggedness as a few minutes of flight gave me now. When we reached the canyon we gave up air-line flight in order to follow its innumerable twists and turns. The memorably clear Lochsa River, part of the headwaters of the Clearwater River, was a shining ribbon at the bottom of the canyon and turned Mr. Johnson's thoughts to trout fishing. I was sufficiently occupied with the flight itself; since he later described it to me as "mediocre," I will merely call it absorbing. I have indeed had rougher rides on passenger planes but hardly in circumstances so, well, stimulating. At one point Mr. Johnson pointed to the altimeter; an updraft had lifted us a thousand feet in less than a minute. This, however, was gentle stuff; pilots frequently have to manhandle the plane by main strength to keep it flying and are physically exhausted at the end of a flight. And the sky was cloudless and there were no storms within hundreds of miles.

Perhaps there was more motion back of the nose, where I was occupying the co-pilot's seat, but I suspect that a psychological element helped to make one of the veteran jumpers sick. These young men are entirely nonchalant and businesslike. They have complete and justified confidence in their skill, training, and equipment, and everyone in the Service assures me that from the first few days of training on fear is no problem. Yet there must always be some unconscious anxiety — considering the cliffs, the rocky slopes, and the treacherous air, how could there help being? It was interesting that when the spotter decided two jumpers would be enough one of those passed over, a first-year man, got sick.

Forty-five minutes after the take-off we sighted a thin column of smoke rising desultorily from a place about two-thirds the way down the canyon slope. Five minutes later we were over it. The fire was burning in a thick stand of ponderosa pine and Douglas fir, big, tall trees — too tall, in the spotter's judgment. It had not of course reached the crowns of the trees but was burning in the duff; the gray, burned-over spot looked about the size of a handkerchief. Mr. Johnson estimated it at a quarter of an acre, the size of a small building lot. We had demonstrated the entire function of the smokejumpers: an hour and twenty-eight minutes after the lookout first sighted the smoke we had reached it. Our first run over it showed the spotter that it was sufficiently small and sufficiently distant from the highly inflammable dead timber to be handled by two men. He selected the veterans.

I think that his silent critic, the check-spotter, may have picked a landing place for the jumpers on that first run. Our man, however, was making sure — when I later complimented him on his success he said adequately, "We don't get much room for mistakes." So we circled the fire three times while he examined the terrain. Knowing nothing about the requirements except that he thought the timber too high to be landed in, I saw several places that I thought feasible and silently chose a bare spot of slope which I thought not too steep, perhaps half a mile and somewhat uphill from the smoke. The spotter, however, had seen a small opening in the trees somewhat downhill from it and perhaps a quarter of a mile away. It was a clear space about as large as the fire, a quarter of an acre, and level except at one edge where it began to slope upward. As we completed the third circle he made his decision and directed Mr. Johnson to go down to about 1400 feet. This intensified a spectator's interest in the flight for it brought us below the ridges and one saw just how narrow and twisting the canyon was.

The spotter, wearing a chute and standing at the open door with one arm hooked over a short length of rail, was directing the pilot by hand signal, motioning right or left for small changes of direction. As we approached the fire on our next circle he released a brightly colored drift chute to determine the strength and direction of the air currents. Its angled, gliding descent was unintelligible to me but it told the spotter that he had been off the target when he dropped it and we circled again so that he could send down another one on a different approach. When it landed and collapsed he nodded; this one was right.

The two jumpers had been squatting at the other side of the door, the static lines of their chutes connected to the cable above it. The spotter had minutely inspected their dress and chutes and had pointed out the place selected for their landing every time we crossed it. Now they stood up, raised the masks over their faces, made sure again that the static lines were not fouled, and were ready.

Suddenly it was one of those moments charged with tension and a kind of beauty when the thinking, planning, and skill of many men come together for a single, irrevocable act. For that moment there are no individuals but a joint personality making a joint effort. Spotter, jumpers, pilot, training, equipment, experience — it was the instant of commitment. I was aware of everyone's poised intentness and then an indescribable excitement rose in me. The pilot was following the same course as on the last run, watching over his shoulder for the spotter's signals. He throttled down the engines. Then when the spotter's arm swept down in a violent chopping motion he cut them entirely. The spotter rapped the first jumper on the shoulder. He stepped out and down and was followed at once by the other one. I saw only that they ducked their heads as they went through the door.

I thrust my own head through the window beside me, having previously been warned by Mr. Johnson to take off my glasses, and saw the chutes opening as he gunned the engines. Before the tail cut off my view I snapped a picture of them, achieving as it turned out an excellent record of half the window frame and a patch of sky.

Their descent seemed to take forever and they seemed alternately to be motionless and to be traveling at express speed. I could not read the angles of their glide and as they neared the ground I several times thought they were in the treetops which it had been the spotter's design to avoid. I could see, however, that they were manipulating the slotted chutes and, with a final curving swoop, one after the other they came out between the trees to the minute clear space. One landed running, the other rolled and stood up. I could see them freeing themselves from the chute harness and even before they made the OK signal — waving their colored streamers — everyone in the plane knew that the jump was a success.

I had a firm hold on my camera. But, I found, my glasses, exposure meter, adapter-slide, notebook, and pencil were scattered about the nose. Someone in the co-pilot's seat had been a little flustered.

IV

FOLLOWING the jump the pilot takes charge and gives directions to the spotter, who is now officially designated "the dropper." We completed the circle we had been making in order to watch the jumpers' descent. (If either of them had been injured the other would have so signaled with a streamer, presumably the other two jumpers would have been sent down, and a radio message would have been sent to Missoula ordering out the Johnson helicopter, which can land on a dime or hover over one.) We began another circle for the first cargo drop. On that first run we dropped two fire packs, each of which contained a sleeping bag, a personal kit, three days' rations, a mess kit, compass, maps, shoulder-pack frame, shovel, and pulaski. (The last is a special fire-fighting tool, a combination axe and sharp-edged grub hoe, named for its inventor.) If a radio had been dropped it would have been lashed between these two packs for greater protection. On the next run we dropped a five-gallon can of drinking water. These all went down by chute but the big crosscut saw lashed to a plank which we dropped on the third run had only a long cloth streamer to slow its fall. One of the cargo chutes had lodged in a tree and the jumpers signaled for climbing irons by arranging four of their colored streamers on the ground in the form of a square. (The manual calls it an O.) So we circled again and dropped a pair, also bound to a plank and attached to a streamer.

The spotter made these drops on Mr. Johnson's shouted command but I did not watch their descent, my interest in flying having been poignantly intensified. Cargo drops are made at the lowest altitude that will permit the opening of the chutes, which like the personal chutes have static lines. That altitude turned out to be remarkably slight and the plane liked to drift still lower after the drop. Mr. Johnson approached his chosen release point at what seemed to me a steep angle and I had never before been so intimate with treetops. He cut the engines and yelled, "Let her go!"

Crouching at the door, the spotter shoved the stuff out, the plane sank noticeably, and the engines roared as we pulled out. Now not only were we neighboring with the trees but the wall of the canyon seemed to be less than spitting distance ahead of us. I suppose that from some angles daylight would have been visible between the plane and the mountainside as we slid up it, but until the wing rose for the turn not much daylight. It must have been the creative imagination that made me smell friction. I asked Mr. Johnson how far above the trees we had been when he gunned the engines. He said, fifteen to twenty feet. I said that by careful, detached calculation I made it somewhat less. "Well," he said, "call it eight or ten feet."

It was 3.55 when we dropped the climbing irons on our fourth cargo run. We made one more circle to be sure that nothing was needed below. If anything had been needed the jumpers would have signaled for it with their streamers. If the spotter had had any directions for them, a message attached to a streamer would have been dropped from the plane. And if this had been a bigger fire he would have radioed an estimate of its size, of its probable extension, and of the force needed to fight it, and the fire control headquarters at Missoula would have been drawing up a plan of action and designating men and equipment before we got back to the field. Since everything was in order, however, we turned homeward after the last precautionary circle. There being no need to follow the canyon now, we climbed out of it and flew across lots. We landed at Hale Field at about 4.30, two hours after the fire had been reported.

I have specified the times because they tell the story and carry its moral. Because of the speed with which they reached the fire, the smokejumpers had it under control before dark. (They would clear a line around it, fell any nearby snags and any small stuff within the line that was not too hot to handle, and shovel dirt on the burning duff wherever they could. The shovel is the principal tool in firefighting.) They stayed on it the next day till sure that it was out. (Meanwhile a patrol from the ranger station reached them and the job would be inspected and checked again by the packer who came in for their equipment.) Only negligible damage had been done and the fire had been suppressed at minimum expense.

The jump would not have been made if the ground wind had exceeded thirty miles an hour. Several days earlier a flight found such conditions at a fire in the Mission Range north of Missoula and returned to the field, then went back again in late afternoon when the wind had fallen. Similarly, jumps are not made if the terrain is found to be too difficult. In 1946 I saw a plane on two successive days repeatedly circle a fire that was burning high on one of the peaks of the Sawtooth Mountains and turn back without dropping smokejumpers because no safe landing place could be seen among the cliffs and boulders that surrounded it.

Aerial control is the most effective technique for fighting forest fires ever developed and the smokejumpers are its cornerstone. They have become indispensable to firefighting throughout the West and in its most arid and difficult areas, as in Region One, they are the principal means of attack, the spearhead, the basis on which all other methods rest. They are one of the most remarkable achievements of the Forest Service, which has had many remarkable achievements. I have sufficiently indicated the saving they have made possible in the protection of a precious national resource. (Well, one more instance. While I was in Missoula twenty smokejumpers and fifteen other firefighters suppressed a fire in the Bitterroot National Forest that had got a much better start than the one I have described, at a total expense of $2000. In 1945 a fire in the same forest to which smokejumpers were not sent, burning in similar timber and under almost identical conditions, destroyed a thousand acres and cost $70,000.)

They have spectacular incidental use in the rescue of injured people, sportsmen for the most part, and in the search for people who have got lost or planes that have crashed in the mountains. And their importance for defense must not be ignored. During the war the Forest Service trained Army, Navy, and Canadian personnel for search and rescue work in the wilderness; it has been training Canadians and Australians this year.

It operates under the considerable handicap of a congressional tendency to choose queer places to economize. The parachute loft and equipment sheds at Missoula are old CCC shacks which can barely be kept rainproof. They are firetraps and if the stables of the fair grounds across the road from them were to catch fire in a moderate breeze all smokejumping operations would be automatically suspended for a year while equipment was being replaced. (Thus insuring in Region One alone a loss of three and a half million dollars, nearly four times what it would cost to modernize the installation.) Furthermore, various parts of the plant are scattered about Missoula at inconvenient distances, the barracks for the smokejumpers in one place, the radio tower in another, and fire control headquarters in a third. And housing developments are reaching out from town to surround Hale Field.

Plans have been drawn for a new plant, ample, modern, and efficient throughout and concentrating everything at a new field on the edge of the municipal airport at Missoula. Land, building, and equipment would cost just under a million dollars, a third of the annual saving in Region One. A bill appropriating the necessary money met determined opposition last year and could not get by a Congress which appropriated more than half a billion dollars for dams in the West — some of them of very questionable utility and none of them destined to return the investment. This year a similar bill has at last been reported out of committee. The most elementary bookkeeping shows that to pass it would save a lot of money which, if no other use should be found for it, could be put into dams.

Motel Town

(SEPTEMBER 1953)

MOTEL TOWN is always a suburb. It may be the suburb of a village; when it is, it may itself be a village but it may also be a metropolis. It may be, that is, a couple of motels a hundred yards down the state road from the J. C. Penney store, about where the sign says "Speed Zone Ends." But if at such a distance from the Penney store and Marty's Filling Station two trunk highways intersect, it may be a longitudinal development a quarter of a mile long and more populous than the village. It will always be such a metropolis when it is the suburb of a metropolis, as at Indianapolis, but it will also be one if the intersecting highways are important and the distance to the next town is considerable, as at Cheyenne. On freeways it is an aggregate located where an exit road straightens out at the end of its cloverleaf and has no relation to any other factor, social, economic, or geographical.

The quality of the motorist's lodgings does not necessarily depend on the size of the suburb he finds at hand when he decides to call it a day. Since the quality of everything else usually does, however, he will be wise to keep on till he finds a motel metropolis, though he may have to turn off his route or drive another fifty miles. Otherwise he runs the risk of finding himself benighted in the nadir of roadside accommodations, a small town where the lunchroom and the drugstore close at 6 P.M. and no one, no one at least in public, has ever known the taste of coffee.

Village, town, city or metropolis, the roadside community proves that the vigor and staying power of the Americans remain undiminished. They will not in remunerative numbers drive as much as a thousand feet off the highway in order to find lodging. Between the highway and the No Vacancy sign there may be only the width of a sidewalk; very seldom is the space as wide as a third baseman's throw to home plate. One might as well spread a sleeping bag beside the pavement. Everywhere the legal speed limit is lower at night than during daylight but this is by statute only; when the stars come out the customary 65 or 70 steps up to 75 and beyond. The whirr, hum, and flick of passenger cars continue all night, modified just enough so that the ear cannot make a rhythm of them as it does by day. They are a powerful assault on the ear, bolstered by the screech of tires under suddenly applied brakes. But they are only a murmur compared to night town's quadrupled frenzy of trucks.

There is usually a slope at one or the other end of Motel Town, and there is always a stretch of frost-heaves or a band of patched pavement at the bottom of it. Diesel-engined truck-and-trailer combines roar down the slope, hurdling the bump, or ascend it through a series of laborious and atonal shifts, crescendo and full pedal. They too travel at 65 or more, a discord of baritones and basses; the wayfarer spends much time trying to decide whether the engines are worse than the crunch and grind of the twenty-ton load doing its best to reduce the inequalities of the highway. Neither, however, is so bad as the sudden acceleration on straightaways, which is scored for two instruments, a machine gun and a riveter's hammer. Yet even this is a lullaby compared to the tone poem of a truck achieving full momentum after a dead stop, with solo passages for each gear united by the percussion effects of backfires. It is endlessly repeated through the night as truckers, having refreshed and comforted themselves at Jody's Drive-In, take off again past the sleeper's open window.

The highway is one edge of our suburb, then, and a mysterious law of nature, doubtless geographical, has made the other edge a railroad, or two railroads, sometimes of two or four tracks each.

Motel Town (September 1953)

The tracks are no farther away than second base, and two hundred yards below Motel Town the highway makes a right-angle turn and crosses them. Freight trains average 125 cars. They slow down for the crossing; couplings clank and jolt; airbrakes exhale; the diesel locomotive hoots greetings beforehand and farewell afterward, obeying a statute of 1880 that stands unrepealed in the electronic age. Worse still if they stop, for the multiple engines of a diesel locomotive are vocal and versatile beyond the aspiration of trucks; and worse when the freight is a red-ball express at 70 miles an hour or when a streamliner passes at its advertised 90; but worst of all whenever the horn blows. Remarkable ingenuity, arising in our nostalgia, has been expended in an effort to make the diesel's hooter resemble the whistle of a steam locomotive, whose proud and melancholy tones we remember as always at a tranquil distance. The results differ from road to road but have succeeded nowhere; at trackside all the hooter's tones are shattering, all terrifying, all a torture. Throughout the night they salute the crossing and carry the conversation of engineer and brakemen, for if the radio telephone we read about has been installed it has always blown a tube.

There are occasional augmentations. If a charted flightway follows the railroad through the valley, an overcast may bring airliners down to a neighborly distance. Or in rural areas the space between tracks and highway may be occupied by a field whose owner has a tractor and gets to work with it at dawn.

Nor does the wayfarer demand to sleep in darkness. Neon tubes stripe the front of his motel, outline its eaves and gables, and frequently frame the windows as well. Columns of neon, six to twenty-four inches through, three to six feet high, stand before the suburb's proudest establishments. Some are floodlighted in addition and none is too humble to possess a flashing sign in blue, orange, crimson, and green. The tourist closes the venetian blinds, turns out the lights in his room, and may still read the Gideon Bible without eyestrain. If he wakes at 2 A.M. he will for a moment believe that he has overslept and that morning is well advanced.

Before we scrutinize the other establishments, what of the motel, this contemporary stage-stop on the National Road, this lineal descendant of the tavern whose potsherds an archaeological dig would turn up at the same site? "Motel" is an awkward word, a coinage from the folksiness that named the suburb's Kan-di-Korner. But it designates a functional, and admirable, response to the needs of the highway. A motel may be dingy or uncomfortable but at its worst it is always better than the highway's slum structures, the corn cribs and chicken coops called, offensively to our pioneer tradition, "Cabins." It is the highway's hotel. In cities of a hundred thousand or less it is almost always better than the local hotels and everywhere it comes increasingly to compete with all but the very best. For the motorist it has conveniences that make it superior to a hotel, conveniences so important that they outweigh the drawbacks, which may sometimes be serious. He need wait on no one's time, a clerk's, a bellboy's, or an elevator's. His car is always at hand if he needs to run an errand; his supplementary baggage and his professional or technical equipment are in it; he need take into his lodgings only what he will need for the night. Rooms are more spacious than he is likely to find in a hotel. He pays in advance and may depart at any hour, in a tenth of the time it would take him to check out at a hotel and with much less fuss. Procedures are swift and there are no rituals.

The average motel is clean and nearly all proprietors have by now learned a lesson long withholden from them, that beds must be comfortable. In the plains, mountains, and deserts, many motels are air-conditioned; some are to a welcome degree soundproofed. Those which may be called first-class have an adequate amount of comfortable furniture, walls and curtains and carpeting in good taste, adequate service, and usually room telephones. Beyond this (and not only in the vicinity of resorts) there is a class which are truly luxurious, which are equipped and furnished with genuine distinction, and which provide some of the services of a luxury hotel. They are likely to be large, to have a restaurant and a bar, and to be surrounded by landscaped gardens. They may run to beach umbrellas, their own stationery, and a swimming pool.

There is a class hierarchy and motels of the second class or below it may have annoying inadequacies. Some are architectural: the rooms are too small or in awkward relationship to one another, or cross ventilation may be impossible, or the angle of the sun or the prevailing winds has not been taken into account. More often they result from parsimony or insufficient financing. The bathroom lacks towel racks and has a cheapjack shower; towels are small and in short supply. There is no closet and only a few clothes hooks, or none at all, have been provided. Paper cups have been substituted for drinking glasses; there are no reading lamps or upholstered chairs. A common and annoying deficiency is the lack of anything that can be used as a desk or writing table; indeed, this is a diagnostic sign to the many travelers who must keep in touch with the home office or file reports or write up field notes. (Equally reliable indications are the size of rugs and the presence of a list of Dont's for Our Patrons.) The proprietor of the place has failed to understand that he is in the hotel business. Or he may be an elderly man or a semi-invalid who hoped to retire to an easier but income-producing business, could not get a sufficient mortgage, and did not realize that he needs adequate equipment and professional skill.

Among a motorist's basic requirements is a prompt breakfast near at hand; there is no worse inconvenience than having to drive a considerable distance from his motel for his morning egg and coffee. To find himself in the village suburb of a village is therefore his hardest luck. There is no lunch counter at his motel, there is no all-night restaurant for miles, and the town's establishments do not open till 8 A.M. or even later. He may have to drive up to twenty miles for breakfast and then go back to his motel to pack his outfit and get ready for the road. It is for this reason above all others that he seeks out a metropolitan Motel Town; if he does not, his only recourse will be that other economic specialization of the highway, the drive-in.

The drive-in is Motel Town in embryo. It originated as a small restaurant, with a counter and a few tables, what the vernacular calls a diner. As the tourist's luck runs, it may be a good or indifferent restaurant but is more apt to be bad. (To fry an egg requires skill and though to boil one badly may require talent it seems to be a common talent; toast needs more attention than it usually gets, and 98 per cent of the highway's coffee is vile. Pray that you may find a place operated by elderly women, preferably women who have hired a male cook.) But by now the restaurant is merely the core. The humblest drive-in sells cigarettes, cigars, pipe tobacco, three or four headache remedies, and a couple of proprietary caffeine pills with some such trade name as No Doz. Above this minimum, there seems to be no limit to the merchandise sidelines. Buddy's Drive-In may carry sunglasses, handkerchiefs, gloves, key rings, ballpoint pens, jackknives, flashlights, cigarette lighters, razor blades, soaps and lipsticks, sunburn lotions, laxatives, wallets and handbags, an assortment of joke-shop novelties, and the fearful, inexplicable junk called souvenirs. It may have punchboards and pinball machines and, in states where they are legal or tolerated, slot machines. It is certain to have gas pumps but do not patronize them: go to a filling station.

The drive-in, this is to say, undertakes to supply the wayfarer's casual needs. The longitudinal metropolis, Motel Town, undertakes to provide all the goods and all the services he may require. Glance at it. It has grown up round a series of neon-lighted and imaginatively christened motels — half a dozen, a dozen, perhaps more, some consisting of a few units, some up to a hundred. There are a couple of restaurants in glass and chromium, half a dozen drive-ins, a Bar-B-Q, and Kan-di-Korner's cousins which purvey malts, shakes, cones, and the poisonously colored water ices that have been frozen round a stick. There are up to four garages with wrecking service and adequate repair departments and filthy toilets (comfort stations in the vernacular), and six or eight filling stations with scrupulously clean ones. We are in Texaco land, Socony land, among the satrapies of Tydol, Gulf, Conoco, Amoco, and Shell; rival principalities have such pleasant names as Marathon, Skylark, Kanotex, Zephyr, and Bronz. At a gasoteria you can save a couple of cents a gallon by filling your own tank from coin-operated pumps. A mototeria is a Rube Goldberg assembly of sprays which will wash your car in five minutes, but a carena is an open-air movie theater and attracts what the vulgar call the horizontal trade. There are a couple of secondhand-car lots, in case your heap has broken down beyond repair or you have lost an argument with a truck. A few doors down the row you can get the purchase financed and buy accident insurance.

This is only the beginning. There is a Laundromat, a laundry, a dry-cleaning establishment — one day service if desired. Some are prefixed by the adjective "drive-in," which is here used in the original sense, meaning that you need not get out of your car. Besides the drive-in theater there will be a drive-in drugstore and a drive-in church, which advertises redemption for miles down the highway and brings heavenly grace into competition with Burma Shave. There may be a dress shop; there is certain to be a Kiddie Shop and a Men's Toggery which features rayon slacks, cowboy boots, and the crazy-quilt sport shirts that represent Florida and California joining hands across the continent. There are a bar, a café, and a cocktail lounge, indistinguishable from one another and, unhappily, absent in the states that have screwball liquor laws. Maw and Paw will sell you fishing tackle, mineral specimens, *objets d'art;* Jody's Place is bottled goods, Nan's embroidery and table linens, Buddy's handworked leather goods and belts with silver buckles, Edith's (and this is inexplicable) shrubs and seedlings. Do you want underwear, smelling salts, sculptures in native woods, decals (from the vernacular: decalcomania stickers for the windshields), water bags, a haircut, a trailer, a veterinary for the poodle, Chanel No. 5, agates or crystals or jadeite, shotgun shells, bottled spring water, or invisible reweaving? In the desert or in the high country back of beyond, Motel Town will supply it at a specialty shop or a super department store. And there are always the souvenirs, the pennants, the fox tails, the myrtle wood, the birch bark, and the balsam pillows.

This is a province of neon, Places, poetry, and no last names. Here are Melba and Joe's Place, the 2 J's Place, Sonny's Place, Your Pal's Place, Stevie's Place, Cliff's Place, Juanita's Place, Honey's Place, Sweetheart's Place. In a row are Mel's Steak-ette, the Hasty-Tasty Drive-In, Dewey's Diner, the Poor Boy Café, the

Meal-a-Minute Eatery, Flock Inn. Here is Seat-Cover Charlie's: "I want to give them away but my wife won't let me." He must be doing well for Seat-Cover Dave has set up a few doors farther on. Bob's specialty is turkeyburgers, Lulu's is fries, which means chicken, not potatoes, and all too often means some paralyzing conception of "Southern fried" that may run to glued-on apple fritters or nearly anything else. Pete (or Petey) offers chicken in the rough (or ruff) or chicken in a basket; next door Franny and Freddy's Place has all these and chickenburgers, samburgers (*sic*), foot-long hot dogs, and shrimps in a basket. Indeed the frozen shrimp is the endlessly repeated culinary triumph of the American road and has infiltrated everything from canned soup to cheeseburgers.

Art's Place, however, is a nite club. It has a name band and a singer of what are intended to be smutty songs. God help the Republic if these ballads are a dependable aphrodisiac; God help it if the gals who sing them are held to be personable. Beyond Art's, Milli-Kin-Clean-It and beyond Millikin, or Milly, Chief Glad-to-Mi-Chi operates a souvenir stand with artifacts from the Bulgarian, the Alaskan, the basketmaker culture, and South Paterson. Next to the Chief is The La Fiesta Bowlaway and beyond it is Ole's Big Game Bar. Ole's specialities are frosted on the mirror. He has Storz, the Orchid of Beers, and two other beers which call themselves champagnes. His masterpiece, the mirror says, is a cocktail called The Atomic. No report is offered on it here. No report is offered on any roadside cocktail: the reporter is a bold and reckless man but he is not that bold and he sticks to whisky.

Enter freely and enjoy. Every alcove of it is rewarding and there is no dull Motel Town. But do not expect drinkable coffee. You will find it exactly once per thousand miles. Note, moreover, as a final poem of the road, that a competitor of Storz is the Beer from the Land of the Sky-Blue Water.

On a Note of Triumph

(JULY 1945)

I HAD BETTER offer this as personal opinion without trying to call it literary criticism. For my colleagues who have reported so far disagree with me unanimously, and this is one that cannot be talked out at Joe's. If they are right, then I am not only wrong but irretrievably wrong — fundamentally, from the first step on. But if I am right not only my colleagues are wrong but also some of the methods — and basic admirations — of what we have begun to call the art of radio.

Mr. Norman Corwin's "On a Note of Triumph" had been under way for a few minutes when I chanced to tune it in on May 8, but there was no mistaking who had written it or what radio was trying to do by means of it. It had Mr. Corwin's signature and it was backed up by the full resources of CBS. Moreover, it was trying to do something that we wanted done, the millions of us who had spent most of the day at our radios and who spent most of the night there, too, after Mr. Corwin's broadcast was over. Our emotions of that day were inexpressible but we welcomed attempts to express them. We could take in only a little of the day and we knew how to understand only part of what we took in, but we were trying to give it order and recognition. We wanted instruction, realization, imaginative confirmation. Nothing could fully have satisfied our desire or fully have lived up to the theme — but we were favorably disposed, and would have regarded any dignified and moving failure as an overwhelming success.

After the broadcast ended the air was full of proclamations that "On a Note of Triumph" was just that, an overwhelming success. By Sunday the book reviewers were agreeing that something momentous had occurred; radio art had achieved a memorable triumph. And when the program was broadcast again on Sunday evening, the production had an aura of self-confident and generally admitted greatness. I listened to it again that evening, this time not as a civilian seeking emotional fulfillment on the day of victory but as a journalist and critic checking second thoughts against my original opinions and those of my colleagues.

I must report that my second impression was the same as my first. I listened with a distaste that only occasionally yielded to satisfaction but frequently intensified to distress. "On a Note of Triumph" fell far short of what was reasonably to be expected of the art of radio on May 8. It not only failed to live up to the greatness of its opportunity, it contrived to trivialize that opportunity and to touch with vulgarity the most tremendous events and the deepest emotions of our time. The factual broadcasts of CBS that preceded it on May 8 — by John Daly, Bob Trout, Bill Henry, Major Eliot, and many others — had a professional cleanness and clarity that gave them an esthetic quality as well. Their reports roused and satisfied the very emotions that "On a Note of Triumph" tried but failed to satisfy. They fertilized the listener's imagination as Mr. Corwin did not. The reportorial and editorial aspects of radio were superb. But when an acknowledged master of the art of radio got to work on the same stuff, he was dull, windy, opaque, pretentious, and in the end false.

For some of this effect the conventions of radio may be to blame; the industry may be paying a fine for some of its practices. Take the interlocutor, the narrator, the voice, the emcee — whatever is the proper designation. He was called on to convey to the audience awe, portentousness, triumph, bitterness, irony, commiseration, and a wide range of other emotions and states of mind by purely vocal means. That is not an easy job, though it is one all competent actors are trained to do. But this actor had to achieve his effects by means of conventions peculiar to radio, conventions which radio has developed for itself. It derived them originally from an obsolete and overblown oratory and then went on to associate them with the advertising business. Repeatedly when the voice of "On a Note of Triumph" was supposed to be attuning us to extremities of hope or tragic realization, it had to work with the exaggerated, unctuous, and richly phony elocution of any commercial announcer. However real the emotion of the part he was reading, the tradition of his medium required him to represent it as unreal. A convention was bringing in two echoes along with Mr. Corwin's program. One was an echo as of some cheap orator tearing a faked emotion to tatters. The other was an echo as of a thirty-second break in a dance program when some drug company commands us to move our bowels.

And not the voice of the narrator only. Radio has thought it necessary to develop specific Voices, character Voices, typed so that they will be instantly identified at the first syllable. It has chosen to compose many of them of pure glucose. There is the Candid Feminine Voice, the Voice of a Mother with All That Motherhood Implies, the Sweet Voice of a Girl, the Voice of a Tough Guy with a Heart of Gold. Sugary earnestness is their hallmark, they probe you for tears over the heroine's agony, and then they pump the same sugar into a candid, motherly, sweet, and golden message that you will save both your money and your stockings if you will only use our earnest soap. They are certainly no fault of Mr. Corwin's, but there they were. There they were vulgarizing and travestying what the radio intended to be great. The mother of a dead aviator had to speak with the syrup of a morning shopper fishing for the change in a housewife's pocketbook, for radio holds that women must speak in that way. The awful symbols of the dead themselves, here to be given a voice, could be given no voice by radio except the phony one of Gangbusters and the cereal ads. Radio was impelled by its entire development to commemorate victory with the same saccharine, the same preference for the unreal, that it thinks effective in commercials.

Such things as these, and such further things as the shuffling steps of doom that fail to signify doom because they also signify Captain Midnight and the like, were, however, only the smaller part of what I found distasteful in "On a Note of Triumph." One might accept the conventions, in fact, as a kind of mechanical condition and presently disregard them. The failure of the program was the failure of an attempt, and perhaps also it was the failure of a conception of art, but it was not the failure of a medium. What was wrong with it was inferior imagination and bad writing.

An excellent contrivance had a hillbilly song reappearing throughout the program at opportune moments. I do not know whether it was a Tin Pan Alley hillybilly song or a real one, one of the spontaneous translations of real emotion into simple songs that ballad singers sometimes achieve by themselves. Whichever it was, it was an artistic success. It did what Mr. Corwin did not do; it was genuine, realized, achieved. Whenever that song, "Round and Round Hitler's Grave," came into the program there was a moment of emotion, comment, and effective highlighting. It invariably made Mr. Corwin's book sound tinny. The introduction of the Te Deum and the Psalms had exactly the same effect. So that at both a humble and an exalted level, genuine art showed up the counterfeit. The book could not meet the competition of either the Te Deum or the hillbilly song — you heard its pump working too clearly.

In form "On a Note of Triumph" was a rhapsody. Radio reserves that form for its most solemn efforts and Mr. Corwin has worked in it before. Perhaps Mr. Pare Lorentz did not invent it when he composed "The River" for a different medium but it still shows his impress. It was not a particularly good model, for Mr. Lorentz's rhetoric was shoddy and his devices were not substantial, were in fact cheap. "Black spruce and Norway pine, Douglas fir and red cedar, scarlet oak and shagbark hickory" — well, yes, mildly, but at your risk when you use it more than once and Mr. Lorentz used it a dozen times. He did not bother to provide a reason inside his idea or his emotion why it should be black spruce rather than witch hazel, or scarlet oak instead of mountain laurel, or why we should stop at any given breathing place before some other tree got into the catalogue. It did not develop from within, it was something brushed on from outside; it tinkled pleasantly for a moment, perhaps, but it got irritating pretty soon. "Down the Mississippi, New Orleans to Baton Rouge, Baton Rouge to Natchez, Natchez to Vicksburg, Vicksburg to Memphis. . . ." The sequence has no significance and no necessity; there was no reason why we might not just as well travel the other side of the river and make it "Rosedale to Friar Point, Friar Point to Helena, Helena to Osceola," or for that matter, "Change here for Winchester, Ashuelot, Nashua, Keene, and stations on the *Fitch*burg line." Mr. Lorentz was not deeply engrossed with his words and failed to engross us. He played a slight tune, easily, with an easy rhythm, and left the rest to the waters flowing on his movie screen. No particular imagination went into the effort and no distinction came out of it.

Nevertheless radio took his hint and has since acted on it whenever it set out to be rapt, ecstatic, awful, or compelling. Mr. Lorentz kept coming through clearly in "On a Note of Triumph," and at the same time you heard a parody of Mr. MacLeish. Now Mr. MacLeish's ventures in the art of radio were frankly experimental. I don't think that his experiments altogether succeeded but he is a fine poet and the distinction of his language gave the instruments he was trying out a strength they have not got in other hands. To Mr. Lorentz's attack Mr. Corwin tried to add Mr. MacLeish's idiom. "Kentuckians are padding through the junglelands of Burma: Sailors from Ohio navigating coral seas: Texas rangers bombing in pagoda country." That was the catalogue, all right, but why this particular series, why not Minnesota and Somaliland, why not any names from the Postal Guide and a directory of gainful occupations? And he missed out on the idiom. "And the tourists bought postcards in Estes Park, the Rocky Mountains taking the whole thing casually; and Kate Smith was in her usual good voice; and the Loyalists kept on in Spain." That falls a good deal short of Mr. MacLeish. It does not convince you that all can play the tune now since all have got the key. Played thus, the tune is cheap, not Mr. MacLeish's tune at all. But he was writing poetry, whereas in a preface, with an accuracy seldom repeated in the pages that follow, Mr. Corwin finds a word for what he was writing. He calls it a non-poem and that, I think, is right.

The truth is, "On a Note of Triumph" is bad writing. "Every leaf and every frond knows all about it, and the humus in the ground is hep (grass has an active international)." The parenthesis is intended to be knowing and the "hep" is meant to have impact but both are merely glib. Mr. Corwin is making a show of doing something that competent novelists and poets do on every page without any show at all, but he fails at it. Or "Hey nonny-nonny, achtung, and well-a-day," or "Next week, umbrella dance at Munich — Salomé bearing the head of John, the Czech." This is meant to be exceedingly hard but it is soft; it is meant to be caustic and embittered but instead it has a bargain-counter jauntiness. It doesn't look like poetry, or even non-poetry, even momentarily; you spot the costume as rented. "And in June, sumer is icumen in with the sound of another broken treaty," "And the thoughts of the mother are tall, straight thoughts," "You must not forget to take along your homework in the barracks bag." Not sardonic; something too easily done, an essentially cheap effect. "And the wave of the future swept all before it, and the Century of the Uncommon Aryan opened up ahead," "However, in the matter of the kid who used to deliver folded newspapers to your doorstep, flipping them sideways from his bicycle," "For nature in all its wisdom and notwithstanding its proven generosity, made no allowance for blast" — no, definitely no. It pretends to have an elevation it simply has not got. It is a semi-clever talkativeness. It is bad writing.

Good writing, whether poetry or prose, would have worked this same material into symbols deeply felt and so capable of evoking a deep response. But these associations are commonplace and this imagination is vulgar. It is a flip rhetoric, a rhetoric so flip that it degrades the emotions presumed to have created it. It is radio beginning by being pretentious and so once more ending by being cheap. It is a mistake from the first line. Didn't Bernard Shaw once explain that he was in a hurry and so had to write a play in non-poetry because it took too much effort to write sound prose?

Radio has shown a marked liking for this bastard form of speech, which has neither the discipline of verse nor the structural strength of prose. It has shown so marked a preference for it that some of my colleagues have impressively decided that this is "the language of radio." I do not think it necessarily is the language of radio. I do not think that radio has to force everything it can into the form of a drama and then, when it can dramatize no further, trick out everything else in spurious rhetoric. If the simple newspaperman's language of John Daly, hardly an hour earlier, could evoke the sorrow and exaltation which Mr. Corwin tried hard but failed to evoke with his non-poetry, surely the art of radio can find instruction in that plain fact. Mr. Corwin even supplies an example of his own. His script quotes an actual news broadcast by William Shirer, a description of Hitler at Compiègne. Its simplicity and directness get home: no hearer could fail to feel what he is meant to feel. And then in his own person, Mr. Corwin immediately adds, "The gloating hour is to be remembered. File it away in a bomb-proof corner, if such there be, against a better time, if such can possibly arrive." Mr. Shirer's is good writing; Mr. Corwin will not deny himself the intellectual cliché, nor the jiggly rhythm, nor the pretentious phrase. "Elsewise, why the young mother in Baranovichi . . ." I think that does it in one word. Mr. Corwin brought a manner to the occasion, but what the occasion needed was a style. It needed a mind working on the situation and with words, a discriminating mind, a mind that could not possibly have written "elsewise."

I do not know whether the art of radio has fixed limits, whether this represents the best it can do with its present techniques. We are freely told that Mr. Corwin has mastered his medium, but it would be interesting to see whether a better writer might not be able to use the same techniques, limitations and all, to better effect. On the showing of "On a Note of Triumph," either poetry or prose would be much better than non-poetry. On the other hand, pretentiousness will fail in any medium, with any technique, and certainly pretentiousness, the radio's occupational disease, was a lethal mistake to have committed on May 8. Literature will need many years before it can achieve any adequate expression of that day, and the sternest, severest efforts conceivable were bound to fail. But we could have been spared the pretentious failure of "On a Note of Triumph." In the presence of those realities, those profundities, those significances, literature should have resolved to be what all arts most wisely are when they are compelled to deal with tremendous things — simple and direct and humble. The art of radio had been at work on its climactic program ever since "late in 1944." There was time, I think, to have worked through its conventions and its rhetoric to a decent understanding of its opportunity.

Twenty-Hour Vigil

(MARCH 1953)

THE IDEA was to see how a prolonged exposure to television would affect my impressions of the medium. They were pretty casual impressions, except for news and political broadcasts, the World Series, an occasional football game which I seldom understand, Ed Murrow and Dave Garroway, and such features as friends occasionally direct me to, sometimes to my regret. I have learned to avoid comedians whom I admired on the stage and to fish around for factual programs which assume a moderately high IQ. Of what I was familiar with, the highest achievement, the most moving program, was "Victory at Sea."

Boston is a two-channel town, a phrase which I am told is equivalent to "whistle stop"; while on duty I shifted from one channel to the other with nothing to guide me except, sometimes, discomfort. I spent one evening at it, from eight o'clock to sign-off. The next day I became the ideal audience and watched the screen from 7 A.M. to twenty-two minutes after midnight, except for an hour when G-men were getting shot at for our children. Consultants tell me that the day I chanced to pick, Thursday, was my tough luck. On any other day, they insist, I would have encountered stuff of better quality. That may well be true.

We can forget about the dramas I saw. In normal circumstances I might have seen two of them through to the end but I would have switched all the others off. Occasionally the narrative method becomes interesting and this is like the movies, which year by year steadily improve their techniques but keep the content forever the same. The content of television drama is negligible and may be summarized as, Life has a heart of gold, especially in the slums. There were no situations that common sense would not have resolved in thirty seconds. There were no characters who resembled people or acted from recognizable motives, and practically no genuine emotions. It came to a bleak rejoicing if for a moment a character was feeling anything at all, or if there was a bit of skillful acting or a flash of experience that seemed true. I have read somewhere that these dramas are written on the assumption that the audience is tired out, but behind many of them must be a suspicion that it is asleep.

The two that stuck out above the others claimed to be based on actual happenings — one dealt with a metropolitan police force, the other with the Treasury's Alcohol Division — and therefore needed only a little logic of structure and less of emotion. I suppose they are to be classified as crime programs and others that I saw certainly are. I had been told that they were packed full of unmotivated violence, and they certainly were — flogging, beating, slashing, torture, murder. Little of it was exciting and none of it horrified or appalled me. I doubt if this universal mayhem is the ominous gratification some editorials say it is, and I doubt if it is going to damage our culture as other editorials predict. I see numerous possibilities of cultural corruption in television but this isn't one of them. It may be sadistic in form but it isn't in effect. Just as you are about to shudder because the gangster is grinding out lighted cigarettes on the victim's naked chest, everything stops and the announcer reads a plug for motor oil. Nothing can kill horror or pervert bliss so fast as an ad.

This seems to me one of the basic handicaps under which television drama must operate; another is the limitation of time. Both kill the illusion. A movie runs about ninety minutes and a stage play at least two hours, but the norm for television is half an hour. One reason for the absence of personality, characterization, motivation, and emotion may be that the structure and development necessary to achieve them cannot be managed in the time at hand. And in any kind of drama, the beholder must succumb to the illusion. He has got to believe, if only for a moment, that he is seeing a real event happening to real people who feel genuine emotion because of it. Grant the dramatist the greatest talent possible — and still, just as the beholder is beginning to suffer with and on behalf of the heroine, an alien (and hoked-up) voice breaks in with the information that this is Station WBZ-TV, or that Mrs. Filbert makes the best oleomargarine you ever tasted and of her own impulsive generosity adds forty thousand extra units of vitamins to it. Gasoline is necessary to modern life and high-test may indeed work better than standard, but the illusion of young love will dissolve in either of them, and grief for a dying child terminates when we hear how a liver pill cures constipation by stimulating bile.

Most of what I saw in some twenty hours was intended to be entertainment, and most of this was, for me at least, a dismal failure. Scattered through the rest of the time was interesting, valuable, and even fascinating stuff and several very moving moments. I would never have seen most of it if I had not imposed the vigil on myself, for most of it came at hours when normally I am at work, when nearly everyone is at work. (This point might be raised when the networks tell us how devoted they are to the service of the public.) There was, for instance, a half-hour by the Massachusetts Extension Service, which dealt mostly with beef cattle, the cuts of beef, and a review of retail food prices. Its straightforward approach was admirable and I wanted to see more of it, though I am not one to wonder how much broccoli costs this morning. Some of the news broadcasts and some of the commentaries on them were excellent. The movie shots that accompanied some of them were surprising and good, the still photographs pretty awful, the animated cartoons (if "cartoons" is the word) ingenious and pleasing. Some weather forecasts made amusing use of these animations too, and this is probably the place to remark that the musical commercial which uses animations is sometimes enjoyable and always incomparably easier to take than an announcer reading a plug. Especially when the announcer interrupts his role as the hero of a tragedy in order to tell us about cigarettes.

There was also "Ask Washington," with some members of NBC's news staff answering questions, pointed and sometimes risky questions, and answering them well. The whole panel promptly trampled on a question (conceivably planted) that made a crack about the millions Winston Churchill was going to rob us of, and they discussed hydrogen bombs and the President's message to Congress. Then there was Charles E. Wilson talking about the Crusade for Freedom and showing a movie of it, illuminating and valuable but at 10:30 A.M. how many people were watching? Newsreel shots appeared on a number of programs that had nothing else to do with news and whenever they touched on the war in Korea they overshadowed everything else. Finally there is the program, of whatever kind, that presents someone who has the easy mastery of his trade for which we have no adjective but "professional." Anyone in or out of the industry who can do his stuff well seems to be good television material — for instance, a sculptor who appeared as a guest on a household program the rest of which was repulsively homey and phony. And among the pros I was particularly grateful, considering how many sodden and saccharine singers wandered through half a dozen variety shows, to Kate Smith and Dinah Shore.

But there are some questions to be asked about Miss Smith's show. She has a good and well-trained voice and she uses it expertly. She is not, thank God, beautiful (though I'm also glad that a girl on her program is) and she has individuality and personal warmth. It is good to watch her work and if she can sell millions of dollars' worth of her sponsors' products, that's all right with me — up to a limit which has got to be defined. At one point she wandered off into interpretation of the news and began to plug a cause which I happen to favor — but just how qualified is she? What gives her authority? Suppose Miss Smith does not know what she is talking about, or suppose she chooses to talk on the bias — what is to protect the large audience she influences or what is to protect us against the audience? And though the most moving thing I saw in twenty hours of television showed up on her program, its being there was dreadfully wrong.

We were, for some reason I missed, suddenly seeing news shots from Korea. It developed that they were not made by a newsreel company or by the military authorities but by, or at least for, Miss Smith's show. Somebody was interviewing some wounded Marines at a field hospital. It was a profoundly moving experience; somehow it concentrated and sharply focused the tragic necessities of this war. In a parenthetical remark one of them noted that he would have a choice of trades when he got home, for before enlisting he had spent his evenings learning to be an undertaker. Another one, told by the interviewer to end with some words to his family, addressed them in Armenian. The hold these poignant actualities took on your heart was almost intolerable. Then the shot ended and Miss Smith began to describe, with her personal and expert warmth, the merits of canned orange juice.

So two things. Why is the Marine Corps permitted to commercialize the bravery and suffering of Marines by putting them at the disposal of an advertising agency? And why are the makers of the goods which Miss Smith advertises permitted to profit from that bravery and suffering? This is not only wrong, it is tawdry and degrading, it is an unspeakable affront to everyone, and all the worse because it is so blithe. I alluded above to cultural corruption. Here it is.

Other programs get there by different avenues. I saw one, for instance, which undertakes to discover good, good neighbors who do good, good deeds, and to reward them. This lingo is the native tongue of many advertising people, who believe that we are encapsulated in glucose and who pump syrup at us all day long; and only a huckster could have thought up the program. The good, good deeds turn out to have been courageous, even heroic acts. Having brought the neighbors to the studio, the program transforms itself into a combination of quiz show and giveaway show. The spin of a wheel entitles the person who benefited from the courageous deed to reward his benefactor, provided he can answer some questions. "Pearl Harbor Day is December 7; what was the year of the attack on Pearl Harbor?" This was one of three questions asked a man who had been caught by the cave-in of a pit he was working in. By answering correctly he won $400 for the two companions who had rescued him after some hours of constant danger to their own lives. The program thereupon gave him a watch and showered on his rescuers the miscellaneous largess at the disposal of anyone who will name a product when he gives it away. Presumably the sponsor, so long as the rating remained satisfactory, did not care that courage and self-sacrifice had been vulgarized, that his ad-writers had besmirched human decency. But the sponsor — and the network — might take account of the revulsion which the spectacle arouses, the feeling that we have all been corrupted, the rescuers, the rescued, and those who have watched a private sanctity publicized to sell goods.

The man was an unskilled laborer; he spoke broken English and he had a massive, far from handsome face. Face and voice made him inherently more interesting than the smooth, practiced showmen who were using him. Television has rescued the human face from the nonentity Hollywood has bred it up to, and the industry is conforming to this fact. Though some announcers and narrators look like chorus men and some move as if corseted with whalebone, most of them are far from handsome; irregular features and even homeliness are at a premium and facial expressiveness at a higher one. A related fact, that naturalness shows up phoniness, has not made as much headway as one hopes it will. The laborer's halting English made ridiculous the stage-Irish and stage-Yiddish accents I had just heard in a drama of the golden slums. Mr. Wilson speaking effectively but in an entirely untrained way while his interviewer talked like "The March of Time," the sculptor intent only on the meaning of what he was saying while the woman who ran the household hour spattered him with verbal goo — such people make a point that has been intelligently acted on, here and there. Much of Dave Garroway's effectiveness comes from his avoidance of the elocutionary style and his indifference to slips of speech. Some announcers have clearly been cultivating hesitations, repetitions, and mismatched grammar; there is the threat that they may go on and rehearse spontaneity as if they were running for Vice-President.

But this trend has by no means gone far enough as yet. In a medium where actuality and naturalness are obviously the most effective instruments, there is a vast deal of manufactured falsity. Part of this is a holdover from radio's basic drive toward phoniness, especially vocal phoniness; part of it is the huckster mind, which like a diseased pancreas converts everything to sugar. Apart from some wan sniggers by comedians, the only awareness of sex I encountered during my vigil was in a commercial. While the screen showed a pair of hands, the announcer made love to Ivory Soap Flakes — so soft, so wonderful, how delicate they are, the secret of mildness is in them. He could say "delicacy" with a lewdness and lubricity that would have got him jailed if he had spoken the word from a Boston stage. Amorousness about soap is combined with stereotypes about nearly everything, and most of them afloat on a sea of molasses. Thugs have hard voices, private eyes have menacing voices, old ladies have old, old ladies' voices, and everyone has a golden voice. The woman who operates a cooking school makes salad and stew and biscuits but her manner is all cream puff and her voice marshmallow. The one who is angling for the pre-school child says "ooh" and "yes" and "fun" with grace notes and cadenzas encrusted with sugar (and a simper); her guest, the director of a zoo, is probably casual about his job when offstage but she talks baby talk to him so horribly that he catches the infection and talks baby talk to a monkey he has brought with him. The pre-school child is a resistant organism and probably tough enough to take this unharmed, but the rest of us aren't. For us it is corruption by caramel.

Or maybe we will be saved by the same principle that makes a healthy stomach reject poisonous food. The natural guest does show up the synthetics of his interlocutor. The emotion manifested in and evoked by such documentaries as the news shots of Korea, and by other bits of reality, mocks the falsity of the dramas. Even the blight of programs devoted to amateurs may show an instinctive awareness of this fact, for they sometimes give us vitality before it can be wrapped in a jellyroll. And if the actuality it can show is television's best instrument, realism has such offspring as parody, which makes the animated-cartoon commercial pleasant, and satire, which must sometimes be the impulse that turns the camera on the audience. These phenomena will not be permitted to work their leavening on television unless they impress the advertising agencies. Well, the way may be opened for such impression by another phenomenon, the revulsion, the feeling of shock and outrage, when a soup or a soap invades private decencies in search of sales, or when Kate Smith turns from wounded Marines to peddle orange juice. That revulsion can cost money.

I was surprised by the lack of variety in twenty hours. I had expected a greater diversity, a wider experimentation. This too must be the Madison Avenue mentality and again it is standing in its own way. The entire ethic and practice of modern advertising developed from a misconception, failure to understand that when the intelligence-testers classified the normal mind in the age group of twelve years, they did not mean that adults are children.

The public is brighter than advertising has ever believed. It is less dependent on sweets, and it is less timid. It is a damned sight less timid than the agencies or the networks. They fired George Kaufman because five hundred people wrote letters protesting Mr. Kaufman's protest of the commercial vulgarization of a Christmas carol. Many millions of the public certainly approved his protest, and some of those millions certainly heard it and omitted to write in — but five hundred letters did the job. That's timidity for you — the timidity of the same business that during my twenty-hour ordeal kept repeating, in a voice half choked by sugar, "Our kind of freedom knows no bounds."

Victory at Sea

(JUNE 1954)

THE WORD "liberation" has lost the force it had ten years ago but gets it back when you look at "Victory at Sea," which has completed its second run on television, this time with sponsors. Repeatedly you see the tears and ecstasy of people greeting their deliverers: the French in North Africa and Marseilles and Paris, the Filipinos, the Italians. They line streets of shattered buildings, they swarm over tanks and the fields are still burning behind them, against many backgrounds they are ravished by the fulfillment of hope. On half a dozen islands they come slowly down some path from the hills, starved, fever-ridden, carrying their sick and old. On Guam they stagger out from a concentration camp; at Dachau they have to be carried. At Tokyo they are American prisoners. Each of the twenty-six programs in the great war serial evokes the most powerful and most profound emotions, but the sight of deliverance moves the beholder more deeply than anything else. We forget too easily; everyone should see the whole series every year. It will be all right with me if Congress sees it twice a year.

For twenty-six Sundays last year neither the telephone nor the doorbell was answered at my house between 3 and 3:30 P.M. When the series was finished I pressured NBC and the Navy into showing me about half of it again. And recently I spent six evenings watching all twenty-six once more. The idea, apart from repeating a memorable experience, was to see if I could determine some of the principles of the medium which the drama employs. For it is a drama, a work of the imagination, art of a high order. And it is new under the sun. Since this is true, it would appear to have set one of the directions and broken one of the trails that the development of television will follow.

One thinks first of isolated moments and such special effects as climaxes. A falling plane skips on the surface of the water like a stone, or a burning plane sinks and the gas goes on burning. A Marine uses his helmet to shield the face of a wounded comrade from the rain. At Malta nuns shepherd school children into a bomb shelter. A baby shakes with terror at Okinawa. At Peleliu the surf rolls the body of a soldier in full combat pack up on the beach. Arabs dance to the pipers of a Scotch brigade on a dock at Oran. Someone is reading a letter which has kisses printed on it in lipstick. Firecrackers snap as the first convoy of trucks reaches the end of the Ledo Road. An old man weeps as President Roosevelt's coffin comes down Pennsylvania Avenue. The face of a captured German is pure hate.

Some moments restore in full emotions we resolved never to forget: Hitler's turkey strut at Compiègne, the tinny bravado that makes every picture of Mussolini corrupt, the anger and shame of Pearl Harbor. Or moments of excitement so intense that one could not stand much of them: the Anzio landing, a Kamikaze almost missing a ship, a convoy under torpedo attack, the flaming death of a carrier. "Roman Renaissance," the fourteenth episode, ends with the crowds hushed by the appearance of the Pope on his balcony. At the end of "The Conquest of Micronesia" crippled planes land on a flight deck and burst into flame and the film closes with a solemnity intensified by the fact that not only the body of a pilot but his plane too is committed to the deep.

The documentary instrument is used here and "Victory at Sea" must be the longest documentary film ever produced, as Mr. Richard Rodgers' score for it is said to be the longest symphony ever written. But that term, documentary, will not do. What we have is a factual instrument used to break the hold of fact for the purposes of imaginative creation.

Victory at Sea (June 1954)

A good many times we see men killed; the camera records an actual death. There is horror of a kind which the dramatic representation of death cannot produce; it is no more intense than the horror which fine acting in a fine play can create but its awful immediacy is unique. By itself it would be merely an assault on the nerves. But it is not by itself, and it is neither in artistic terms melodrama nor in reportorial terms mere shock. It is actuality used structurally in a work of art whose effect is on the imagination. Similarly with the faces of men, women, and children, combatants or civilians. These are not the faces of actors. The exhaustion, anguish, agony, sullenness, apathy, despair, or exaltation which the screen shows are not histrionic, they are actual. But the faces blend and generalize and build up, they create a realization of men in war, indeed a realization of war, and this is a function not of fact but of art. Probably the commonest camera subject in the twenty-six programs is something burning. What we see is some actual thing actually afire, but the result is a realization of war as fire that has abandoned fact, advancing so far beyond it that the substance is imaginative.

One must have the campaigns and chronology of the war pretty clearly in mind, as I took care to get them before seeing the series this last time, in order to perceive with what freedom time has been treated. On the stage and in the movies it is usually only in fantasies that more than rudimentary rearrangements of chronology are risked, and even in fantasies they tend to be pretty simple. "Victory at Sea" is as free as a firstrate novelist in its discontinuities and mixtures of time. The montage of time is as elaborate as the montage of scene. Just as a single half-hour will build up scenes that cover a whole ocean or two oceans, a number of battles, various approaches and headquarters, and a variety of shots of industry and agriculture and logistics — so the same program will arrange them in time relations that may have no regard to their historical sequence. This is structure for the final effect of one program. But there is an equally complex mixture of time among the programs, building the whole series structurally toward a final effect kept constantly in mind. Any given half-hour may go back in time before the preceding one or much farther back, it may disregard or recapitulate its predecessors, and it may leap ahead beyond one or more of the half-hours still to come.

That is, complex as the structure of a single program may be, the complete work has a structure far more complex than any of its parts; it has what must be one of the most elaborate forms ever worked out in any art. It is in twenty-six acts, it plays for thirteen hours — and its form is organic and precise, a unity wrought from a vast diversity. I know of nothing in the movies and can remember nothing in the drama that is at once so extensive, so diverse, and so single. Since the material is war, Hardy's *Dynasts* comes to mind but there is no likeness and one thinks again of the novel. The structure of *War and Peace* has a comparable multiplicity and occasionally the techniques are similar. But if there are similarities, it is clear that they provide no basis for comparison. "Victory at Sea" created its own form. It used potentialities that exist only in its medium. It is imaginative drama, it is art, but it is television.

Such moments and isolated effects as I have mentioned are, I suppose, primarily the province of the editor, Mr. Isaac Kleinerman. Structure, in both the individual programs and the series as a whole, would appear to be primarily the province of the producer, Mr. Henry Salomon, formerly a lieutenant-commander and for a considerable time an assistant of Samuel Eliot Morison in the great naval history of the war. It was he who conceived "Victory at Sea" and clearly he is, in critical terminology, the dramatist. As a dramatist he had the outline of his form set for him by the war itself, which had its own lines of development, conflicts, climaxes, and resolutions. But that is true of all artists who use historical fact, of all historical novelists and dramatists, and there is the corresponding handicap that such an artist may not alter his facts. He may create but he cannot invent.

Additional considerations must be mentioned. There was no single artist. The idea was Mr. Salomon's and he was the directing and unifying intelligence throughout the long development of the artistic conception. But in television artistic creation is not one talent at work; necessarily it is many. This cannot be called, even, a composite or collaborative art; it is a fusion. Mr. Rodgers' score could no more be separated from the film or the narrative than Stravinsky could be separated from Diaghilev in *The Fire Bird.* Mention of Mr. Rodgers brings in Mr. Robert Russell Bennett, who not only orchestrated the score but conducted the orchestra which played it. Again, there was a scenario to write, as for a movie, and a script as well. I assume that basically this was the work of Mr. Salomon. He must not only make such decisions as the one to spare no nerves in "Two If by Sea" and then build the structure by which they are not spared, but must also write the narrative. But part of the narrative — which has no clichés, is always understressed, and calls on many styles, including the grand style — some part of the narrative was written by Mr. Richard Hanser. (It is worth noting that the narrator, Mr. Leonard Graves, disdains the tricks so fearfully and permanently bestowed on radio by the overripe bass of "The March of Time.")

With each collaborator and each additional special skill, the odds against unity of effect, which is so memorably achieved in "Victory at Sea," increase geometrically. But I have by no means listed all the skills and talents necessary to produce "Victory at Sea." To name only one more, there is Captain Walter Karig, vaguely described as "official Government technical adviser." We must remember too that the production required a two-year search all over the world for combat films and related matter, in many bureaus of many nations, armies, and navy departments. Diplomatic negotiations were required to get some of it; much had to be declassified. Some required costly technical processing and this is only one category of the technological procedures that make television expensive. Finally, there was the job of reducing some sixty million feet of film assembled for scanning to the sixty thousand feet eventually used. These skills cost money.

We arrive at another condition of the medium and another basic requirement for such an effort: someone with sufficient power in television and sufficient belief in the experiment to commit a corporation to the expense involved. "Victory at Sea" cost NBC half a million dollars to prepare; I do not know how much twenty-six Sunday half-hours are worth if sold commercially but, to guess, call it between one and two million dollars. Granted that much of this could be written off as tax money, much capitalized in the books as public service and prestige, and much repaid by subsequent sales to sponsors — still half a million is a formidable deterrent. The necessary ingredient was Mr. Robert Sarnoff, the Executive Vice-President of NBC who saw the possibilities, had his imagination fired, put the resources of his company behind the enterprise, and surely was as responsible as anyone else for the triumph.

It has been necessary to list these necessary conditions and inescapable collaborations. For assuredly "Victory at Sea" created a new art form and assuredly the essence of its triumph is that it utilized the inherent means put at the service of art by the new medium, television. What we have is an imaginative drama of the war, artistic realization of a kind which is possible in no other medium. As I began by saying, it pioneered in one direction which television seems likely to develop. It is well ahead of the field, perhaps as much as ten years. Ten years from now its innovations and techniques may have become customary and even routine instruments. Certainly it foreshadows something, but not clearly enough to make prediction easy.

"Victory at Sea" was an experiment but it is not "experimental television" as that phrase appears to be used specifically in the industry. In that specific sense experimental television works in other directions and with other instruments. A large part of it is fantasy, disregarding the actual. It frequently uses puppets, ballet, pantomime, a great variety of technical expedients such as multiple projection, and other instruments of visual illusion adapted from the stage and the movies. I am told that some of its most interesting ventures have been made by small local stations which have to experiment because they lack money to produce the ordinary and usual.

But perhaps we can disregard cost as an item which, in this strange medium, is not relative to what we are familiar with in other mediums, even the movies. A movie may cost several million dollars but is played many times a day in hundreds of theaters for two years or more, whereas the usual television program is performed only once. The budget of one unsponsored experimental program on one network I happen to know about is $13,000 a week. Few other programs on that network have so low a budget, but on one hand $13,000 is not peanuts and on the other it actually is not much less than the prorated cost of one episode of "Victory at Sea." But it *is* peanuts when compared with the cost of, say, such mere vaudeville shows as last summer's Ford anniversary program or this year's General Foods program. Apparently somebody can always be found who will pay fantastic sums.

Well, you need the combination of many talents but the question is in what ratio to one another. The equivalent of Mr. Sarnoff is a prerequisite, to support an expensive venture which breaks with the familiar and sure-fire, and more especially to believe in experimentation, in the future, and in taking a chance. I am not sure that you need the equivalent of Mr. Rodgers and Mr. Bennett. Their contribution here was beyond price but their availability was a stroke of great good fortune: it is possible to believe that considerably smaller talents might create a score which would perform its full function, given a sufficiently fine conception and narrative to work with.

What is unmistakable is that you need the equivalent of Mr. Salomon, though the equivalent may turn out to be two people. You need, that is, an artist who can imagine the work of art which can be wrought from the material of art and an artist whose technological skill is of the same excellence as his imagination. Conceivably this could be a writer and a director working together, though I think it is more likely to be one man.

Plenty of combat movies existed, so many that "Victory at Sea" had to scan twelve hundred miles of film; all newsreel companies, all governments, all armies and navies had them and there were many in private hands. Out of material so copious that it could be called commonplace a major work of art was made. Documentary material was transformed into a drama on exalted themes. Out of horror, suffering, despair, endurance, and courage — out of these rather than the spectacle and excitement with which they were clothed — artistic imagination wrought the purging and purification of the emotions which is drama in the strictest sense, reaching beyond compassion to a reconciliation and exaltation which say as much as anyone has yet managed to say in art about the war.

But, one may think, there aren't any comparable subjects lying around. The destiny of mankind, the overthrow of despotism, the preservation of freedom, the justification of sacrifice — themes so tremendous are not easily come by. But is that pertinent, is it even true? When asked by another enthusiast what such a talent as Mr. Salomon's might engage itself with next, I said that certain sequences in "Victory at Sea" had suggested to me that industry, to mention only one subject, might perhaps be treated as illuminatingly as war had been.

My friend disagreed. You can document industry, he said. No doubt you can document it visually far better than anyone has yet done, and the result may well be spectacular, splendid, or whatever similar adjective you please. But it will nevertheless remain inert, untransformed — it will remain documentary. You cannot make documented industry live as art.

But this seems to me to miss the significance of "Victory at Sea." The significance, I mean, of what it has demonstrated, quite apart from its achievement. My friend's argument, in fact, seems a fair statement about the potentialities of television before "Victory at Sea." The material that art works with is human experience, be it human experience in war, in industry, or in anything else; it is in the experience and not in the accident of its setting that great themes are to be sought and found. Hitherto it seemed likely that fixed limitations inherent in television as a medium, precisely the limitations which my friend applied to industry as a subject, would always limit what the artist could accomplish. "Victory at Sea" has shown that they do not; so far as I know, it is the only demonstration yet made but we need only one. It has shown that television is a medium in which an artist can work freely, at the top of his bent, in a major key.

We know now, as we did not know before, that given an artist of proper size, television is one of the arts.

The War of the Rebellion

(FEBRUARY 1946)

THIS IS an appropriate time to talk about the Civil War, since Lincoln's birthday comes this month and since there is a new biography of him, Professor J. G. Randall's *Lincoln the President*. I wish somebody else would do this job, for it is going to be ungracious. I admire Mr. Randall's book, anyone who reads it must admire it, in earlier books he has supplied me with many of my own historical ideas, and all of us will be appropriating parts of his new one without quotation marks from now on. But I want to discuss some ideas that are part of the book's frame of reference, ideas which have been proliferating among historians for a generation. They seem to me a regression, a deterioration, which has reduced the validity of general ideas in American history.

Historians are mortal men. Also some historians tend to be timid about expressing judgments lest their colleagues deride them or prove them wrong, and some others hold themselves aloof from, or as they believe superior to, expressing judgments; these last feel that they are scientists working toward the establishment of fact, dealing passionlessly with inert data, without attitude toward them, working outside the area where judgments, especially moral ones, can apply. Nevertheless, even the cagiest and the most detached acquire a body of historical judgment involuntarily. They absorb it from more forthright colleagues who believe that the essence of historiography is judgment. The intellectual climate of their time affects them. Fashions in thesis and dogma sift under their study doors. Historians who are now mature, the generation to which Mr. Randall belongs, happened to be young and impressionable at a time when an intellectual fashion was developing the (erroneous) thesis that the United States could and should have stayed out of the First World War and the (false) theorem that we were betrayed into it by propaganda. Furthermore, of that generation many who took up the study of the Civil War happened to be Southerners; that is, men who from their earliest childhood had been nourished on the most active of American social myths. Few if any of them have managed to work all the mythology out of their history.

This generation of historians has built up a body of judgment about the Civil War. Some of it is certainly sound, some certainly unsound. Some parts of it are not reconcilable with other parts; some parts cannot be reconciled with common sense or with experience. Some of its end-products in general ideas have been proved untenable by the experience at large of our generation. No historian, I suppose, accepts all of it, but every historian has incorporated a large or a small part of it into his thinking and assumes some of it as judgment on the way to forming further judgments. Let me call the body of judgment about the Civil War as a whole "revisionism." Well, revisionism, this historical generation's conclusions about the Civil War, contains much solid truth but it also contains a number of fallacies, some of which suggest an apt and accurate designation out of history, "doughface." My point is that, as a result of those fallacies, general ideas about the Civil War are less trustworthy today than they were a generation ago. There has been a regression in history.

I can state here only a few theorems from this body of judgment. The basic one holds that the Civil War was avoidable: that the moral, economic, social, political, and constitutional crisis could have been resolved short of war and within the framework of our institutions. Corollaries follow: that it should have been resolved and that therefore someone was to blame for the failure to resolve it. Who were the villains? A fundamental thesis of revisionism is that they were extremists, radicals, hotheads, agitators, manufacturers of inflammatory propaganda. It turns out that the decisive ones, so to speak the operative ones, were Northerners: abolitionists, free-soilers, the Republican Party, more radical reformers — in short, everyone who thought that the slavery issue was in some degree a moral issue. One of the most influential statements of this thesis is Professor Avery Craven's book, *The Coming of the Civil War*. I have been told that its title in manuscript was "The North's Blunder" and that puts the idea into three words. An accessory theorem makes Stephen A. Douglas the tragic hero of the revisionists. His ideas ought to have prevailed: that they did not, which is the heart of our national tragedy, was due to the Republican or abolitionist agitation, which led the American people down a fatal path in pursuit of an unreal, a falsely represented, issue. In sequence, another theorem holds that, after Douglas had been repudiated, further Northern mistakes (procured by the radical Republican conspiracy) prevented a compromise which would have brought about a peaceful solution. A posteriori, it was the duty of the constitutionally elected (Republican) government of 1861 to abandon the constitutional structure and extemporize a new one which would contain the crisis — incidentally containing secession.

This is by no means all the revisionist body of judgment and, as I have said, probably no historian accepts all these theses, even as a system. But they have warped a lot of thinking, including some of Mr. Randall's. Now the Civil War is the crux of our history. You cannot set out to understand any part of our past, from the convening of the Constitutional Convention down to this morning, without eventually arriving at the Civil War. A few of the innumerable matters it involved were these: the successful functioning of constitutional government, the basic paradox and conflict in our social system, the basic conflict in our economy, the basic conflict and evasion in our political system. Whether or not the war was inevitable, the crisis was: these conflicts and paradoxes created problems which had to be solved. That they were not solved short of war is our greatest national tragedy. Our failure to solve them short of war is our greatest failure. The inescapable duty of historians is to explain that failure. But revisionist dogmas are carrying them farther from an explanation year by year.

Already those dogmas have made all but impossible the necessary first step, an accurate definition of the crisis. Take one which Mr. Randall accepts. The political conflict between the slave states and the free states entered a critical phase as soon as the invasion of Mexico made it clear that the United States was going to acquire an enormous new area by conquest. This area, which would be a national possession, would have to be organized as territories on the way to statehood. The prospect of so organizing it posed the question whether slavery should be legalized in it. This in turn forced consideration of a question which had been compromised, or settled, or evaded (depending on the point of view): whether slavery should be legalized in certain territories which were about to be organized in an area that was not part of the conquest. From that point on our central political, social, economic, and constitutional conflicts, all of which pivoted on slavery, were fought out on the question so posed, the status of slavery in the territories. So far as slavery was a cause of the Civil War or an issue of the conflict that ended in the war, it was nationally faced during the fifteen years before the war not primarily as slavery but as the question of slavery in the territories.

And that is a tragic fact. For it is clear to us today, and may have been half as clear to Americans North and South then as the revisionists say it was, that the economy of slavery could not possibly be adapted to or survive in the lands conquered from Mexico. And it is almost certain that slavery could not have been maintained in the territory of Nebraska and only a little less than certain that it could not have been maintained in the territory of Kansas, and these territories came to be the very vortex of strife. Therefore, according to revisionist dogma, the question of the legality of slavery in the territories was tangential, unreal, abstract, hypothetical, and almost immaterial. The pivotal strife in the fifteen tragic years that led to war resulted from the forcing of an unreal issue. Since the issue was forced by those who insisted on making the territories free soil (though why more by them than by those who insisted on making them slave is one of the more opaque portions of the revisionist gospel), the responsibility, after several lateral passes, must be charged to the Republican Party. Here, adopting the pure doughface doctrine, Mr. Randall looks on the men who stood by the central Republican demand, that slavery be forbidden in the territories, with a wild impatience. They were agitators; the best of them were bigoted or blind or misled, the worst of them corruptionists and disunionists. The principle on which they stood refusing to be moved was unreal, it had no existence. It was mere wind. They sowed it and the United States reaped the whirlwind.

But this is to miss the very essence of the national tragedy, and when history leads us off on this tangent it monstrously fails to explain our past. It is true that the question of slavery in the territories was a peripheral issue. But for historians and for those of us who try to learn from them *that is the point which must be explained.* It cannot be impatiently shrugged away or dismissed with a denunciation of some agitators whose blindness or wilfulness or bigotry is supposed to have dropped it in the path of men of good will and so swept them into the maelstrom.

Hold it to the light at a different angle. Slavery was at the very heart of our disequilibrium. It was the core of the social, the economic, the political, and the constitutional conflicts. But in the fifteen years left to the United States in which to face and solve the problem of slavery, the final decade and a half which ended in civil war, it did not face that problem but faced only a peripheral and even unreal issue that was ancillary to it. The federal powers and the state rights in regard to slavery, the future of slavery, the limitations of and on slavery, the constitutional questions of slavery, the relation of all these to the structure and functioning of our society — were fought out not in regard to themselves, the only way in which there was a possibility that they might be solved peacefully, but in regard to the status of slavery in the territories, where slavery could not exist. There, if you will, is a fact of illimitable importance. There is a fact which, if we are to understand ourselves, historians must explain.

To pass this off as an irresponsible mischief of politicians on the make is to go so far astray that history is forced entirely out of orientation and nothing less than a new beginning is required. What was there in the nature of the American people, in their institutions, in their development and way of life, or in the sum of all these and more, that prevented them from facing their inescapable problem squarely, in the nakedest light, with the soberest realism? What was there in the sum of American life that forbade us to go to fundamentals and forced us to escape through subterfuges into war? That is the question which historians must answer — the more necessarily, I submit, because in an answer to it there may be light or forecast, some judgment whether we are capable of squarely meeting the fundamentals of inescapable questions hereafter, perhaps even some wisdom that would help us to prepare to do so. But, because of the evolution of historical ideas which I have called revisionism, historians are farther from answering that question than their predecessors were a generation ago.

I do not venture to say why this regression has occurred. A friend of mine, whose hobby is the history of history, believes that in democracies historians have a tendency to romanticize defeated aristocracies. He points out that the English people, at the behest of their historians, especially the historians of this generation, are in a fair way to forget that they had a democratic revolution in the seventeenth century, that it settled basic problems for good and settled them in line with the development of the modern world, and that just because it did settle them Great Britain was able to maintain the domestic peace and exercise the world leadership that were hers during the two and a half centuries following it. It is certainly true that in English historiography today the picture of the Roundheads who gave representative government to the English people has a striking likeness to that of the Republican malcontents and opportunists which our revisionists have been sketching. "In song and story," Mr. Randall remarks, "it is the South that has won the decision at Appomattox." Check. And one wonders if the South may not be winning the historiographic decision too — by evasion.

For the process of revisionism has developed a habit of understanding certain things and passing quickly over others. That habit signalizes something to the inquiring mind; it looks like a repetition in the minds of historians of the evasion described above as a tragic failing of the American people, a repetition of fighting out the subterfuge instead of facing the fundamental reality. Thus the inquiring mind notes the agility with which revisionism dodges the question of minority dictation. A generation ago history clearly recognized that first the maintenance and then the loss of control of the national government by the slaveholding states, a minority, were important in the oncoming of the war. These facts have now been retired to the shadowy fringe. But there is a more central slurring-over which repeats the tragic evasion itself. In its concern to show that the Civil War was a product of hotheads, radical agitators, and their propaganda, an almost incidental result which could have been avoided if some extremists could have been induced to hold their tongues, history is in imminent danger of forgetting that slavery had anything whatever to do with the war. The revisionist gospel finds little time, and seems to have little inclination, to discuss whether in trying to understand the war we should take account of slavery as a social anachronism in the nineteenth century and as an obsolescent or even obsolete economy. It evades raising the question whether the Civil War had any of the quality that made the Glorious Revolution a struggle between the past and the future, whether it involved issues that were part of the movement of world society. As for considering even theoretically that the problem of slavery may have involved moral questions, God forbid. History will not put itself in the position of saying that any thesis may have been wrong, any cause evil, or any group of men heretical. A thesis may have been insufficient and a cause may have been defeated but, even at the end of the Second World War, history will not deal with moral values, though of course the Republican radicals were, well, culpable.

So, standing on this bulk of judgment, revisionism and Mr. Randall's book with it come to a crux of disorientation, a distorted perspective on what precipitated the war, secession. But if history cannot get secession into perspective, then it fails its job with the Civil War.

We have lately seen some younger historians whose specialty is the American Revolution come back forthrightly to the little red schoolhouse with a finding that, after all, the Revolution did have something to do with representative government, taxation without representation, and some of the things which the Declaration of Independence calls abuses of power. It is time to take a singularly radical, or reactionary, step and find some relation between slavery and secession on the one hand and the Civil War on the other. Next month I will recall certain currently slighted theses about both.

The Confederate Anachronism

(MARCH 1946)

AT THE END of the second volume of *Lincoln the President* Mr. J. G. Randall, now halfway through the Civil War, writes a chapter on the Gettysburg Address and its bearing on the problems of government. It is an excellent chapter. But it looks exceedingly odd at the end of two volumes which have been developing the revisionist interpretation of the Civil War. Most of the argument in his two volumes has been trying to show that the Republican position was wrong; that Lincoln was ineffective or in error except as he approached the position of the Douglas wing of the Democratic Party (to whose remnants, Mr. Randall says in three contexts, he was really nearer than he was to the Republicans); and that the "radical Republicans," who were diabolists and conspirators, were primarily responsible for the origin, continuation, and eventual tragic culmination of our national catastrophe.

Last month I discussed the tendency of modern historians to evade the central problems which the Civil War imposes on their science. This month we may state some theses about the war. They must be seen in relation to the two central facts which revisionism evades, secession and slavery, and in relation to the revisionist state of mind. That is a state of mind which, for example, impels Mr. Randall to explain Preston Brooks's assault on Charles Sumner in the Senate Chamber as a duty imposed on him by the integrity of his class and discharged impersonally, "with all the self-control he could muster," though with a natural distaste since Sumner was underbred and *parvenu.* It is a state of mind which reactivates the Democratic presidential campaign of 1864 and reanimates that moth-eaten tragic hero, General George B. McClellan. In retrospect, Southern generals used to admire McClellan because the greater general he could be believed to be, the greater their achievement in intimidating and defeating him; but the revisionists love him because the radicals did not. I lack space for military analysis, but the revisionist theorems leave out of account all we have learned about the conduct of war since 1865 — and all that U. S. Grant had learned by the spring of 1862. McClellan is Balder the Beautiful to revisionism precisely because he felt no urgency in the problem of slavery and because he supplies the *as-if's* which are absolutely indispensable to the revisionist view.

Thus Mr. Randall has only five pages for the War Democrats, who did at least as much as the radicals to defeat the Administration programs, but spends half a volume on McClellan and devotes long passages to speculating on what might have happened *if.* If, assuming that he could have taken Richmond in 1862, McClellan had been allowed to (*sic*). Revisionism supposes that the capture of Richmond would have ended the war and that (here is the payoff) the end of the war in 1862 would have meant the restoration of "the Union as it was." That quoted slogan meant many things in history but to the revisionists it means what it meant to the doughfaces: the Union restored with slavery undisturbed, the slave power unbroken and the South in a position to control the government again.

What this notion leaves out of account is that in 1862 the fall of Richmond (greatly desired by radicals and by Lincoln as well as by McClellan) would have meant little more than the fall of Richmond. The North would have had the capital of the Confederacy and the territory between there and the Potomac. Perhaps ten per cent of the Confederate war potential (which was much less centered there in 1862 than it was in 1864) would have been destroyed. Confederate armies in bulk far more powerful than the Army of Northern Virginia would have remained intact. The sources of their supply would have been untouched, the sources of their recruitment undisturbed. The Confederacy as a war-making power would have been little more impaired than the North was by Second Bull Run. No one can say certainly what would have happened to the Confederate will to resist — to crush which was the object of all Northern military operations — but one who supposes that it would have been seriously weakened underrates the Southern people. It was hardly weakened from First Bull Run to the siege of Petersburg and the loss of the capital could hardly have extinguished it in 1862. Wars are not won by the capture of cities.

Even with its *ifs* assumed, revisionism has to perform some astonishing operations on McClellan. Mr. Randall lightly waves away the general's megalomania and does not even print the most significant expressions of his dictatorship fantasy, explaining that after all most of these things were said in private letters and so are no concern of history, which deals with important evidence. Nor does he bother to make clear just what the radical opposition to McClellan rested on. Other revisionists are more helpful: the theorem is that the radicals wanted the war prolonged so that Northern bitterness would harden and allow them to enforce a vengeful peace. But McClellan was finally removed from command on the explicit and empirical ground that his conduct of the war was prolonging it. Mr. Randall fails to apply to *McClellan's Own Story*, an ex post facto polemic, the rigorous analysis to which he subjects Republican documents. He accepts it as a judicious statement of historical fact, which is a mistake. A lethal mistake.

In the last chapter of his second volume Mr. Randall focuses on the Gettysburg Address some remarks in Lincoln's message to the Congress he had summoned in special session in 1861. He quotes several passages, from which I repeat two sentences. Lincoln says that the war presents to mankind at large "the question whether discontented individuals . . . can . . . break up their government and thus practically put an end to free government upon the earth." And he says that war will teach "men that what they cannot take by an election, neither can they take it by a war." This goes to the heart of things, as the revisionist analysis does not. The Republican Administration had been elected by constitutional means, in strict accord with the established and accepted forms, and in complete conformity to the American tradition. It had no constitutional power, nor has anyone shown that any member of it intended any attempt, to interfere with any "Southern right" except the arrogated right of a minority to control the government. Revisionism has steadily refused to weigh that fact in the open where we can watch the scales. That refusal is bad history; it is history by ellipsis. Revisionism then fills the hiatus by offering a nonsensical speculation: the notion that the duty of the Administration was to recognize secession, which had occurred by the time it took over the government, and to call a convention of the states, for which there was neither precedent nor logic nor good sense. That is, the duty of the elected governors of the American people was to appease a revolutionary and anarchic faction by surrendering to its claims. Mr. Randall speaks of "solutions [impossible in 1863] that had been *easy* in 1860." My italics. What were easy solutions, what were any solutions whatever except the ones adopted, that did not recognize secession in law and in constitutional and political theory?

Moral criteria which history cannot ultimately disown could be brought to bear right here — but they need not be. For one need only do what revisionism has consistently neglected to do, what Mr. Randall's books fails to do. One need only scrutinize the government which was established as a result of secession, the Confederate States of America. Mr. Randall, as a biographer of Lincoln, could have found analytical scrutiny of it, theoretical and factual, in Lincoln's speeches, letters, and state papers. He could have studied the pivotal point in the Annual Message to Congress, December 1, 1862. It is a point so fundamental that the failure of Mr. Randall and revisionism in general to deal with it must be adjudged a gross error.

The Confederate Anachronism (March 1946)

The Confederate government was based on contradictions which it failed to resolve, which could not be resolved. Almost as important as military defeat in the collapse of the Confederacy was its inability to reconcile the states-rights theorems, which it had to accept, with the necessities of national existence in regard to which, so far as they concerned the United States, it had tried to turn the clock of history back. It also tried to turn the clock back in other ways and this attempt was even more important than the sum of its inherent contradictions. The fact that financial power was centralized in Northern cities had been economically disadvantageous to the South, but when secession made those cities foreign, putting New York on the same basis as Paris, the Southern economy committed suicide. The South had been paying an unjust operational tax to the Northern industrial system, but the Confederacy made itself a fief of the British imperial system. When it abrogated the Monroe Doctrine it abandoned one of the basic sources of the American power that had gone to produce it. For a continental nation it substituted a system of two small powers (which must have become three, if not more) and invited Europe in, an invitation which France accepted in June 1862. When it armed slaves and went on to promise, and in part effect, emancipation, it demonstrated that its fundamental assumptions were ultimately untenable and it turned its panic nightmare into realities. In sum, the Confederacy was established in disregard of everything that had happened to the American people from the time they crossed the Alleghenies on. In disregard also of the Americans who lived west of the Mississippi. In disregard, finally and disastrously, of the continentalism of the American nation. As a political system the Confederacy was anachronistic, absurd in logic, and unworkable in fact. It was a monstrosity which could be born but could not live.

This was what Lincoln had been saying, what many others from Jefferson on had said, and what defeated the Confederacy. Behind the idea of union were instincts of the deepest mystical power, sentiments which in defiance of Southern expectation bound Wisconsin to Pennsylvania and Iowa to Vermont, but we may leave them out of account too. For Wisconsin and Pennsylvania and South Carolina, Iowa and Vermont and Mississippi, were united by primary bonds which, if there was any meaning at all in the American experience, were as Lincoln said, indissoluble. The mountain ranges, the rivers, the valleys, the routes of trade and communication had to be enclosed within a single political system — or the United States had always been a paradox as monstrous as the Confederacy was. In terms of American life the Mississippi could not be a Danube and the Potomac could not be a Rhine. Let some Americans withdraw from the American system, make a foreign city of New Orleans, set up at Richmond a regional, rival sovereignty proposing at best a customs union, and war must follow inescapably. The American system must fight out that war to victory or extinction. Which is what happened.

History is supposed to learn from the experience it studies and from those movements which it calls historical processes. Forty-six years into the twentieth century it is supposed to understand the relationship of events in the nineteenth century. Finally, it is supposed to understand that in the nineteenth century some Americans were mistaken, some ideas fallacious, and some actions in error and certain to fail. Perhaps the Confederacy could have survived in the cis-Allegheny, hand-labor, mercantilist, eighteenth-century America from which all its ideas were derived. It was, however, inconceivable, an impossibility, in an America which extended across the Mississippi Valley to the Pacific, the nineteenth-century America which the industrial revolution, the centripetal forces of developing commerce and communication, and the free movement of population had welded into a single nation occupying a unified geographical system — fifteen years before secession. Asa Whitney, Eli Whitney, Morse, the steamboats, the post roads, the public domain, California gold, and the Oregon emigration had made Calhoun an antique.

This is the overwhelming historical reality that revisionism ignores. If I could devote a third Easy Chair to the inquiry I could show, step by step, that it does so by evading the problem of slavery as the American people did in the middle of the nineteenth century. Mr. Randall's position is typical: he perceives no economic obsolescence, no democratic frustration, and no moral urgency in the existence of slavery, and so he is exasperated not only by abolitionists but by everyone who wanted any kind of limitation put on slavery or who opposed minority control by slaveholders. So, since a cardinal fact is the gradual development among a majority of the American people of a determination to take control of the government out of the hands of the slaveholding minority and to fix a limit to the extension and power of slavery, he never even comes close to making the explanation which a historian of the Civil War must make. Revisionism in general has no position but only a vague sentiment: that if the South had been left quite alone, somehow the slaves would eventually have been freed, an equitable system established, and the evils of war and reconstruction prevented. In view of the South's treatment of its free Negroes and in view of a generation of increasingly intransigent threats by slaveholders to make war in uncompromising defense of slavery, threats eventually made good, this is untenable, even if it could be understood. But the point is twofold: revisionism will not explain why the opponents of slavery felt that something had to be done to limit it, and it refuses to face the economic fact that slavery was obsolete as a labor system or the moral fact that it was an evil.

Poets of the neo-Calhoun fantasy assure us that slavery was not abhorrent to the nineteenth-century conscience but was an estate ordained by God for the mutual happiness of whites and Negroes, and that if it had been preserved the world economy would not have collapsed in the twentieth century. But that is mythology, not history.

Here too a century is supposed to have taught us something. History is supposed to understand the difference between a decaying economy and an expanding one, between solvency and bankruptcy, between a dying social idea and one coming to world acceptance. It is supposed to differentiate between historical forces that are regressive, of the past, and those that are dynamic, of the developing future. It is even supposed to understand implications of the difference between a man who is legally a slave and one who is legally free. Revisionism will not make such differentiations, which is why Mr. Randall's book is querulous, usually indignant, unsatisfactory, and in the end unrealistic. That is why it fails to explain the mid-nineteenth century to people who are living halfway through the twentieth century.

As I said last month, the most important duty of American historians is to explain the Civil War. It may be that the Civil War was inevitable: people who are not historians have lived to learn that some wars are. But if it was inevitable, history has got to show us why. And if it was not, history has got to show us how, why, wherein, and wherefore the American people precipitated their greatest tragedy. As a result of a generation of revisionist concentration on "the North's blunder" we are farther from explanation than we were in 1920.

But the state of the world is such that we have got to focus this crucial part of our past on our present problems — fast. There appears to be no recourse for historians except to go back to the beginning and start over. Underlying the revisionist errors were our generation's fallacies about the origin of the First World War. They have now been corrected at high cost. Historians may begin by accepting those corrections, by acknowledging that we made mistakes, and by premising that some of our ancestors who were not abolitionists may also have been in error.

IV

Editorial Column

Due Notice to the FBI

(OCTOBER 1949)

THE QUIETLY dressed man at your door shows you credentials that identify him as Mr. Charles Craig of the Bureau of Internal Revenue. He says he would like to ask you a few questions about one of your neighbors. The Harry S. Deweys are friends of yours, aren't they? Yes, you tell him. How long have you known them? Ever since they moved to Garden Acres eight or nine years ago — or was it seven? no, thirteen. Mr. Craig says the Deweys moved into their house June 1, 1935, which makes it fourteen years. By the way, have they got a mortgage on it? Sure, you say, we all have. Harry didn't buy till about eight years ago. He is paying it off on a monthly basis; must be down to a couple of thousand by now.

Mr. Dewey's older son graduated from Yale this spring? Mr. Craig asks. Yes, you say. The daughter — she's at Vassar? Yes, she's a sophomore. And the other boy? — Exeter? Yes, first form. Mr. Dewey bought a new car last year, a Buick? Yes, he'd driven that Chevrolet for nine years. Who is his tailor? Gummidge? Pretty high-priced firm. Does Mrs. Dewey spend a lot on clothes? The trash barrels were on the curb when Mr. Craig came by and he noticed several empty Black and White bottles — do the Deweys drink a lot? Didn't they have Zimmerman, the caterer, for that big party last April? — Zimmerman comes high. Have you noticed their garbage — pretty rich stuff? What labels have you seen? Bellows & Co., maybe, or Charles & Co., Inc? Do you happen to know what Mr. Dewey's income is?

By this time you are, I hope, plenty mad. You say, for God's sake, it's none of my business. Mr. Craig explains. Investigation by the Bureau of Internal Revenue does not necessarily mean that the person being investigated is under suspicion. These checks are routine in certain kinds of cases. Orders to make them come from above; the local echelons do not initiate inquiries, they simply find out what they can. Then back in Washington the information thus gathered is evaluated. No improper use is made of anything and of course the evaluators know that most of the stuff sent in is mixed, idle, or untrue — they simply go through the vast chaff in order to find an occasional grain of wheat. The Bureau, Mr. Craig points out, is part of the United States government. It conducts its inquiries with entire legality and under rigid safeguards. The duty of a citizen is to assist his government when he is asked to.

So you say, look, Harry is district manager of the Interstate Gas Furnace Corporation and everybody knows that IGF pays district managers fifteen thousand a year. Yes, Mr. Craig says, IGF pays him fifteen thousand but one wonders whether he hasn't got other sources of income. How can he send three children to prep school and college, buy a house and a new Buick, and patronize Gummidge and Zimmerman on fifteen thousand? And he belongs to the City Club and the Garden Acres Country Club. He took Mrs. Dewey to Bermuda last winter. He has heavy insurance premiums to pay. He had a new roof put on the house last fall and this spring Mrs. Dewey had the whole second floor repainted and repapered. How come? Does it make sense? Where's he getting it from?

Does Harry S. Dewey belong to the Wine and Food Society? The Friends of Escoffier? Has he ever attended a meeting of either group? Does he associate with members of either? Has he even been present at a meeting of any kind, or at a party, at which a member of either was also present? Has he ever read Brillat-Savarin's *The Physiology of Taste?* Does he associate with people who have read it? Has he ever been present at a meeting or a party at which anyone who has read it was also present? Does he subscribe to or read the *Daily Racing Form?* Has he ever made a bet on a horse race? A dog race? A football game? Does he play poker or shoot craps? Has he ever been present at a meeting or a party at which anyone who makes bets or plays poker was also present? Does he play the market? Do you know whether Harry puts any cash into diamonds? Does he associate with people who own diamonds? Does he know any millionaires, or people who own cabin cruisers, or people who have accounts in more than one bank? Has he ever attended meetings of such persons? Has he ever been present at a meeting or a party at which such persons were also present? Does he read the *Wall Street Journal?* Has he ever been present at a cocktail party at which anyone who does read it was present? Is it true that Harry gave his secretary half a dozen pairs of nylon stockings for Christmas? Could she be fronting or dummying for business deals that are really his? What kind of girl is she? Does she always leave the office at five o'clock? Whom does she associate with?

Where does Harry stand on the Bureau of Internal Revenue and the income tax laws? Have you ever heard him say that the income tax laws ought to be changed or the Bureau reorganized or abolished? Have you ever heard him damn the income tax? Does he associate with people who damn it? Has he ever been present at a meeting or a party where people who want to abolish the Bureau or revise the tax laws were also present?

Let us assume that you remember nothing which indicates that Harry S. Dewey is a tax dodger or a crook. But Mr. Craig goes a few doors down the street and interviews Frances Perkins Green, who is a prohibitionist and has suffered from nervous indigestion for many years. She has seen truffles and artichokes and caviar in the Dewey garbage. The Deweys' maid has told Mrs. Green that they have porterhouses much oftener than frankforts, that they always have cocktails and frequently have wine, that sometimes cherries and peaches come all the way from Oregon by mail. Mrs. Green has seen many suspicious-looking characters come to the

Dewey house. She doesn't know who they are but it's striking that mostly they don't come till after dark, seven o'clock or later. Some of them, she says, are staggering when they leave at midnight. So Mr. Craig tries the next house and finds Henry Cabot White at home. Cabot is doing all right now but he had tough going for a couple of years after Harry Dewey fired him. Everyone in Garden Acres is familiar with the neighborhood feud and would tend to discount Cabot's revelation to Mr. Craig that Harry's secretary used to work as a cashier at a race track. He confirms the nylons but says there were a dozen pairs. Sure Harry is sleeping with her — Cabot has seen them lunching together several times. Matter of fact Harry only took Mrs. Dewey to Bermuda because she blew up about the girl. Yes, and do you know who was on that boat? Gooks McGonigle — you remember, he runs the numbers racket and they almost got him for wire-tapping. Cabot wouldn't like to say anything either way, but Harry took the same boat and Harry manages to lay his hands on money when he needs it.

I have hung this fantasy on the Bureau of Internal Revenue precisely because it does NOT operate in this way. When it suspects that someone is making false tax returns its investigators go to the suspect's books, his bank, the regular channels of his business, and similar focal points where factual evidence can be uncovered and made good. If Harry S. Dewey reads Brillat-Savarin or serves Stilton with the cocktails, the Bureau is not interested. It does not ask his friends or enemies to report on his wife's visits to the hairdresser as a patriotic duty.

But if it did, would you be surprised? In fact, would you be surprised if any government bureau sent round its Mr. Craig to ask you if Harry Dewey reads the *New Republic* or has ever gone swimming in the nude at Bay View? I think you wouldn't be surprised. What is worse, I think that for a moment Mr. Craig and his questions would seem quite natural to you. And this feeling that the interrogation of private citizens about other citizens is natural and justified is something new to American life. As little as ten years ago we would have considered it about on a par with prohibition snooping, night-riding, and blackmail. A single decade has come close to making us a nation of common informers.

It began with the war. Candidates for commission in the services or for jobs in non-military agencies had to be investigated. If enormous asininities resulted, if enormous injustice was done, they were inevitable, part of the cost of war. They are not inevitable now. But several branches of the government are acting as if they were. Several branches of the government and far too many of us private citizens are acting as if they didn't matter.

True, we have occasional qualms. The Committee on Un-American Activities blasts several score reputations by releasing a new batch of gossip. Or a senator emits some hearsay and officially unaccused persons lose their jobs without recourse. Or another senator blackens the name of a dead man and then rejoices in his good deed, though the people he claimed to be quoting announce that they didn't say what he said they did. Or some atrocious indignity inflicted on a government employee by a loyalty board comes to light. Or we find out that the FBI has put at the disposal of this or that body a hash of gossip, rumor, slander, backbiting, malice, and drunken invention which, when it makes the headlines, shatters the reputations of innocent and harmless people and of people who our laws say are innocent until someone proves them guilty in court. We are shocked. Sometimes we are scared. Sometimes we are sickened. We know that the thing stinks to heaven, that it is an avalanching danger to our society. But we don't do anything about it.

Do you think the questions I have put in Mr. Craig's mouth are absurd? They are exactly like the questions that are asked of every government employee about whom a casual derogatory remark has been unearthed, even if that remark was made twenty years ago, even if a fool or an aspirant to the employee's job made it. They are exactly like the questions asked of anyone who is presumed to know anything about him, whether casual acquaintance, grudgeholder, or habitual enemy. They are exactly like the questions asked about anyone outside the government of whom anyone else has reported that he has radical sympathies. Have you (has he) ever studied Karl Marx? Have you (has he) ever been present at a meeting or a party where anyone sympathetic to Communism was also present? Did you (did he) belong to the Liberal Club in college? Did you (did he) escort to a dance a girl who has read Lenin or is interested in abstract painting? Have you (has he) recommended the *Progressive* to a friend? Those questions and scores like them, or worse, have been asked of and about millions of American citizens.

The FBI — to name only one agency that asks such questions — tells us that everything is properly safeguarded. The investigators gather up what they can and send it in, but trained specialists evaluate it, and whatever is idle, untrue, false, malicious, or vicious is winnowed out. So the FBI says. But we are never told who does the evaluating and we have seen little evidence that anyone does it. Along comes the Coplon case, for instance, and we find out that a sack has simply been emptied on the table. The contents are obviously in great part idle and false, in great part gossip and rumor, in great part unverifiable — and unverified. Investigator K-7 reports that Witness S-17 (for we have to cover up for our agents and our spies) said that Harry S. Dewey is a member of the Party, or wants to make the revolution, or knows some fellow travelers, or once advised someone to read Marx, or spent a weekend at a summer resort where there were members of an organization on the Attorney-General's list. If K-7 is only two degrees better than half-witted, if S-17 is a psychopath or a pathological liar or Harry's divorced wife, no matter. And also, no one can be held accountable. If the same sack has previously been emptied for the loyalty board of any government department nobody can be held responsible for that act, either, and Harry Dewey has no recourse. He will never know and neither will you and I. We will never learn who K-7 or S-17 is, in what circumstance the information was given, whether or not it is true or deliberate falsehood, how far it has been spread or by whom.

In the Coplon trial the government did its utmost to keep from the public view certain information which it was using and which had been gathered by the FBI. That was a sagacious effort. For when the judge ruled that it must be made public some of it turned out to be as irresponsible as the chatter of somewhat retarded children: it would have been farcical if it had not been vicious. For instance, some S-17 had given some K-7 a list of people whom he considered communists or communist sympathizers. One of them was the president of a large university. In all candor, he is not continentally celebrated for intelligence but his economical and political ideas are a hundred miles to the right of Chester A. Arthur. He is a man of unquestionable patriotism, loyalty, integrity, and probity, incapable of any kind of behavior with which the FBI is authorized to concern itself. But it was the privilege of someone — perhaps a fool, a personal enemy, a boy who had flunked out, a maniac — to lodge in the FBI's files a declaration that he is a red.

Well, the university president will not suffer in public esteem. But his university may be damaged in many ways, now, next week, ten years hence. And Senator Mundt or Congressman Dondero or any public official with the gleam of a headline in his eyes can denounce the university, its students, and all who have acquired their guilt by contagion — on the basis of a remark which may have been made by an imbecile and for which no one can be held to account. And that remark remains permanently indexed in the FBI files. And what about humbler names on that list? How many people have been fired? How many are having their reading, their recreation, and their personal associations secretly investigated? Against how many of them are neighbors with grudges or senile dementia testifying to some Mr. Craig, hereafter and alias K-7? What redress have they got? What redress has anyone got whom anyone at all has named to the FBI or any other corps of investigators as a communist, a communist sympathizer, a fellow traveler, a bemused dupe, or just a person who happened to be in the bar at the New Willard when a subscriber to the *Nation* was buying a drink?

I say it has gone too far. We are dividing into the hunted and the hunters. There is loose in the United States today the same evil that once split Salem Village between the bewitched and the accused and stole men's reason quite away. We are informers to the secret police. Honest men are spying on their neighbors for patriotism's sake. We may be sure that for every honest man two dishonest ones are spying for personal advancement today and ten will be spying for pay next year.

None of us can know how much of this inquiry into the private lives of American citizens and government employees is necessary. Some of it is necessary — but we have no way of knowing which, when, or where. We have seen enough to know for sure that a great deal of it is altogether irresponsible. Well, there is a way of making it all responsible, of fixing responsibility. As one citizen of the United States, I intend to take that way, myself, from now on.

Representatives of the FBI and of other official investigating bodies have questioned me, in the past, about a number of people and I have answered their questions. That's over. From now on any representative of the government, properly identified, can count on a drink and perhaps informed talk about the Red (but non-communist) Sox at my house. But if he wants information from me about anyone whomsoever, no soap. If it is my duty as a citizen to tell what I know about someone, I will perform that duty under subpoena, in open court, before that person and his attorney. This notice is posted in the courthouse square: I will not discuss anyone in private with any government investigator.

I like a country where it's nobody's damned business what magazines anyone reads, what he thinks, whom he has cocktails with. I like a country where we do not have to stuff the chimney against listening ears and where what we say does not go into the FBI files along with a note from S-17 that I may have another wife in California. I like a country where no college-trained flat-feet collect memoranda about us and ask judicial protection for them, a country where when someone makes statements about us to officials he can be held to account. We had that kind of country only a little while ago and I'm for getting it back. It was a lot less scared than the one we've got now. It slept sound no matter how many people joined communist reading circles and it put common scolds to the ducking stool. Let's rip off the gingerbread and restore the original paneling.

The Ex-Communists

(FEBRUARY 1951)

A STANZA by a currently unfashionable poet ends, "The way is all so very plain That we may lose the way." Several stanzas farther along the phrasing changes a little, "So very simple is the road That we may stray from it." The poem happens to have a religious theme but what it says holds true for some crucial acts of the intelligence.

A number of intellectuals who were communists have lately been explaining why they no longer are: discussing the reasons that led to their conversion and those that have produced their apostasy. The theological terms apply, for it is apparent, and indeed was apparent all along, that the phenomena are primarily religious. The typical ex-communist American intellectual in fact has experienced two conversions; whereas evangelical doctrine holds that to be saved you must be born a second time, salvation has required him to be born a third time. Such an experience puts the greatest possible strain on the personality. There can be only compassion for the agony he has felt, the double disillusionment, the necessity of twice rebuilding his shattered personal world. And his careful analysis of his experience can be valuable and useful.

Embracing communism, like religious conversion, is an act of the total personality. It is packed with private and even unconscious as well as rational and objective reasons, with emotion as well as intelligence. What the apostates have been saying shows that frequently intelligence played only a small part in it. Yet it played some part and they are eager to show that it was decisive in their apostasy, their repudiation of communism. I propose to discuss only their intelligence. We will agree that the American intellectual who became a Communist was, typically, a generous, warmhearted man, an idealist deeply disturbed by the catastrophe of the modern world and deeply concerned for the betterment of mankind. But how good was his thinking?

The question is given more point in that frequently an odd claim accompanies the ex-communist's confession of error. In a book which I will return to presently Richard Crossman puts it forthrightly. Ignazio Silone, he remarks, "was joking when he said to Togliatti that the final battle would be between the Communists and the ex-Communists," but we must understand that there is a great deal of truth in the joke, in fact it is no joke at all. Only one who has wrestled with communism as a philosophy — unhappily Mr. Crossman's prose turns opaque here — but, he implies, only one who has come close to accepting it as a philosophy —"can really understand the values of Western democracy." And, climactically, "The Devil once lived in Heaven and those who have not met him are unlikely to recognize an angel when they see one."

Mr. Crossman was never a communist but he here voices in good faith the mingled snobbery, arrogance, and unreality that make communist thinking so hard to deal with as idea. The road to an understanding of democracy crosses the communist east forty. Before you can add a column of figures correctly you must first add them wrong. He who would use his mind must first lose it. Various ex-communist intellectuals are offering themselves on just that basis as authorities about what has happened and guides to what must be done. Understand, I am right now *because* I was wrong then. *Only* the ex-communist can understand communism. Trust me to lead you aright now *because* I tried earlier to lead you astray. My intelligence has been vindicated *in that* it made an all-out commitment to error.

The thesis thus abuilding gets indirect support from others. Diana Trilling isolates for examination one group of American intellectuals, those who during the trials of Alger Hiss hoped that he would be proved not guilty. She makes bold to say that this hope expressed an unconscious *absit omen!* They had come so close to accepting communism that they could see part of themselves in Hiss; they felt that only the luck of the draw had kept them from the prisoner's box; there but for the grace of God went they. And Alistair Cooke sees the Hiss trials as symbolic: an entire generation of American intellectuals was on trial, for an entire generation had been at least in part disposed to take the same fork at the crossroads. In the historical context, that is, in the United States during the nineteen-thirties, the acts charged against Hiss were, though not innocent, at least logical for intellectuals who were doing their utmost to understand and repair the world. Way back in the upcountry where the height of land separates the watersheds, there is only a narrow space between the rivers that reach the sea so far apart.

There is only a narrow space too — and a good many have crossed it — between this and the conclusion that whether or not to embrace communism was the master problem of the American intelligence in our time. As a corollary, everyone who was truly intelligent and tried to grapple with the modern world must have been powerfully impelled to accept the communist explanation and to support its measures. Conversely, anyone who never felt the powerful attraction of communism must have been insensitive or unintelligent or both, and at any rate was not deeply engaged with the problems of the time. Here is the kind of distorted simplification that did turn some minds to communism. A historian cannot let these ideas go unchallenged, for though they are wrong they might get lodged among the accepted ones that are brought to bear on the past.

What, in sum, is the recusant communist now saying? That he has come to understand that communism is an abhorrent dictatorship, a corrupt power which destroys freedom, robs human life of dignity, and obliterates the institutions of Western civilization which embody its morality and justify its hope. Step by step, conclusion by conclusion, affirmation by affirmation, he draws up an indictment of communism that corresponds in every particular . . . to what? To what the non-communist American intellectual has said about it from the beginning. Just how is this wisdom when voiced by a man who spent years convinced that it was nonsense? The ex-communist pleads error; he was deceived. There should be some presumption in favor of the intelligence that was not deceived.

We need not distinguish between those who became members of the party and those who, remaining outside it, accepted communism, followed the party line, and put their minds at its service. The number of American intellectuals who did either was very small, though high-church Republican politics finds a useful technique in representing it to have been enormous. The communist intellectual was a tiny subspecies; the generality of American intellectuals were never tempted to accept communism but instead recognized it for what it was, understood it, and opposed it. The unfolding of events vindicated their judgment — proved the accuracy of their analysis and the justness of their conclusions. The ex-communist has now added an independent if belated justification. With ideas, empirical demonstration is the payoff, and serves as at least a rough gauge of intelligence. If the side of a cube is twelve inches square the man who measures it and says that it is twelve inches square is right. A man who for some time maintains that it is a half gallon in the key of C-sharp and blue at that is not displaying conspicuously penetrating intelligence when he finally picks up a ruler.

The conversions were a phenomenon of the nineteen-thirties; we may safely disregard the rare intellectual who turned communist before the economic collapse. In the bewilderment and panic of the time the bases of conviction were brought into question. As some economic and political systems crumpled and those of the United States were grievously strained, as misery and want and despair spread more widely here than ever before, as the Nazi totalitarianism joined Italian fascism (and Russian communism) in a reversion to tyrannies supposed to have disappeared permanently from the civilized world, as another and greater war seemed to threaten, as belief and courage weakened — as the world of the nineteen-thirties revealed itself, a man whose trade was to use ideas had to determine which ideas could deal with it. The one who embraced communism did so in a belief that (Russian) communism was the wave of the future: that it promised a better economic order, that it offered the best possibility of social justice, that it was a force for peace.

The generality of American intellectuals held that this man was wrong. They said the same thing of converts to creeds which only a historian now remembers. Minute groups of true believers found a light in such aberrant gospels as Social Credit, Technocracy, Distributism, "Christian Collectivism," Monarchy (oh, yes, it is on the record and very winsome it is too), and a number of fantasies which declared that mankind was going to be saved by the abandonment of machine production, the restoration of handicrafts and the subsistence farm, and perhaps the reinstitution of Negro slavery. They appeared to have no commensurable quality, and yet if you followed them far enough you found them all converging. Eventually each of them substituted for law the will of whichever group was to hold power, abandoned representative government, impaired or destroyed individual freedom, and either repudiated the immunities of citizenship or undermined their safeguards. The typical intellectual said of them that they were not workable but he said something else which got to the heart of the matter in the first instance: that they began by giving up what alone could give value to anything they might salvage. The experience of the United States, of Western man, he said, was that nothing worth having could be bought at the price of freedom, citizenship, and government by law. And, he said, that goes for communism.

The evidence, the ideas, the experience on which he based his judgment were equally available to all minds. The communist must be granted some allowance for the anesthetizing power of any gospel and for the fact that his gospel was a mechanical formula. It explained everything; the mind that accepted it was not *required* to inquire critically into realities, it need only apply the formula. And his gospel was authoritarian as well as infallible: criticism of any kind was deviationism. Nothing else in the history of thought has so completely stifled critical inquiry, which non-communists take to be the essence of the intellectual process.

Communism made its American converts not as a system of thought but as an eschatology, a millennial faith. And here the evidence available to everyone included, by the nineteen-thirties, more than a decade of the U.S.S.R. It also included the content of American history.

The communist needed no knowledge of history and no understanding of experience, since his formula would reveal the meaning of either wherever he might apply it. This turned out to be a handicap; it blinded him to a defect in the millennial apocalypse. The non-communist intellectual understood that neither a proletarian revolution (such as the convert was predicting) nor one corresponding to that of the Bolsheviks would occur in the United States. Neither was of our nature or in our kind. If a revolution were going to occur here it would have to be in a pattern established by our inheritance. Our revolutionary radicalism would not suffice; their model was the I.W.W. (syndicalist and therefore anathema to communism) and no imagination could conceive of its seizing decisive power.

A native revolution must be by political fission followed by political coalescence, the model of the Civil War. And in the thirties for this single possibility one or the other of two developments was a prerequisite. There must first be either an overwhelming defeat in war or an absolute collapse of the economic and social system. Clearly, no nation was going to inflict the former. The communist assumed that the latter was inevitable; his formula explained that it was a part of the process of history, the decay of capitalism. But the non-communist dismissed this as fantasy; he knew what it left out of account. This was crucial knowledge and the judgment was a crucial test of intelligence.

That is: he knew the richness of American natural resources and the power of the productive plant. He knew the flexibility and responsiveness of the political system which had been developing for a century and a half. He knew that the political system was capable of resisting and containing great strains, whether social or economic, while readjustments were worked out. He knew that it had held while fundamental readjustments were being worked out in the past. He concluded that such a revolution as might be in store for the United States would consist only of a redirection of political control. He knew our history held a series of such revolutions, Jeffersonian, Jacksonian, Lincolnian, the unlabeled one that implemented the Grangerite-Populist revolt, Wilsonian. In all of these the social and political freedoms had been preserved and redirection of political control enabled the enormous natural wealth to resolve the conflict and work out the required amelioration. In all except the Lincolnian the social fabric had been kept intact. He judged that the possible revolution, and the one to work for, was the characteristic American revolution by "reform." The communist formula said that reform was impossible: the non-communist pronounced the formula defective.

What followed was the most fundamental, the most widespread, and the most thoroughgoing reform in American history. To call it the New Deal obscures the fact that it was a sweeping revolution which had already begun to gather momentum when Roosevelt took office and some fundamental parts of which were unrelated to the movement he headed. All that need be said of it here is that it worked. It demonstrated that the generality of our intellectuals had correctly analyzed the situation, and the generality of them had some part of it. (Historically, as against popular cliché, though the influence of the American intellectual on politics has fluctuated, there has never been a time when it was not considerable.) The revolution expressed the non-communist intellectual as a type. The communist intellectual had only two concerns in regard to it: to explain it as evidence of the progressive degeneration of democracy and to convert it if he could to the service of Russian foreign policy.

There was, however, an even more basic act of the intelligence.

The way is all so very plain
That we may lose the way.

The enemy was not fascism. It was absolutism. The non-communist intellectual clearly understood that what the communist intellectual was glorifying in Russia and working for here was dictatorship. And dictatorship always means abrogation of law, government by force, destruction of private and civil liberties, slavery (alias forced labor), forced starvation, mass murder. The master question of our time was never: Is communism the way out? It was simpler: Does freedom count?

No matter how inscrutable the future, the axiom at the basis of American experience is that freedom counts most of all. That the defense of freedom comes before anything else. Right there the non-communist intellectual took his stand. Whatever threatens freedom must be fought totally, first, wherever, in the immediate instance, from then on. The communist intellectual decided that the concept of freedom was a bourgeois sentimentality, that communism had established the necessity of destroying it, and that his job was to make use of American belief in freedom as an instrument for the destruction of freedom.

The choice offered the intelligence was as clear and simple as the quoted poem says.

The sequence of events that led the ex-communist to his break with communism may provide a scale of comparative intelligence, though on the other hand it may be an index to his capacity for self-deception. The recusants usually name three turning points or dramatic revelations of the truth: the great state trials (though they had been going on for some years before they caused any apostasies here), the treaty of nonaggression with the Nazis, and the attack on Finland. The non-communist grants their power of disenchantment but finds them no more revelatory than the massacre of the kulaks, forced collectivization of agriculture, planned famine as an instrument of government, police terrorism, transportation, forced migration, labor camps, execution for dissent, any other kind of liquidation, the treatment of the Spanish anarchists, or any other tyranny in the functional dictatorship. In this judgment, though he derided it throughout, the recusant communist now heartily concurs. But the non-communist thought of him, the communist convert, as having repudiated intelligence, and thinks of him now as having lived in a delirium which he took to be a vision of a better world.

A non-communist finds the serial apologia of the recusants astonishing. Here for instance is a gentle, unworldly literary man, one of the first who "jumped off the Moscow express." (The phrase is Mr. Cowley's but I am not referring to him.) His activity as a communist was not important. It consisted of slanting book reviews, helping to capture for the Party control of entirely insignificant organizations, writing resolutions which various "fronts" adopted and everyone disregarded, proclaiming his faith, and maintaining his doctrinal orthodoxy through the innumerable zigzags of the Party line. The long agony that preceded his break with communism and the despair that accompanied it were a profoundly moving tragedy. But, in his new enlightenment, what has he found out? Why, that freedom must not be given up, that treason is evil, that murder and terrorism must not be condoned, that communism is not democratic, that democracy is precious. That is his harvest from two dark nights of the soul, from a second birth and a third one. See it as pitiful waste or see it as the innocence of a saint, but what is it as intelligence? Where, for God's sake, where was he when they were distributing minds?

Or take the anthology of apologias from which I have already quoted Mr. Crossman, *The God That Failed*. There has been little discussion of its one truly shocking revelation. The talented authors, like all recusants who preceded them in print, describe in detail the process that led them to renounce communism, the slow, painful achievement of the stand which the non-communists had originally taken. But in doing so they also detail the reasons that had induced them to accept it. And they reveal a shocking simple-mindedness, a shocking surrender of intelligence, a shocking inability to grasp reality.

Richard Wright's admission of what his mind would accept as true, for instance, is almost benumbing. One searches fruitlessly for comparisons — Santa Claus, the stork brings the baby, pie in the sky by and by? Or Ignazio Silone's consternation when a communist assembly laughed at a delegate who protested, "But that would be a lie!" He discloses a credulity for which there is no word but infantile, a credulity that blocks off not only the critical faculty but the perception of reality. He had studied communism for years. He knew its doctrines and techniques and was acquainted with its activities everywhere in Europe. He had not only known Lenin and read his texts on revolution by conspiratorial elites but had had firsthand reports from his lieutenants on what was actually being done. Yet he was capable of believing that this was not a shooting war but boys playing with cap pistols. Somehow dictators, like children making their first communion, would be good and would use power only cleanly and justly. Communism would purify itself. It would restore "the possibility of doubting, the possibility of making a mistake, the possibility of searching and experimenting, the possibility of saying 'no' to any authority." Living in the presence of an absolutism never exceeded in history, of a ruthlessness greater than the civilized world had seen for centuries, of millions already killed or enslaved, he hung up his stocking to be filled with sweetness and kindliness. Even after experiencing communism at first hand, he believed that machine guns would turn into cap pistols if you only affirmed they must — and had to be told that he was a counter-revolutionist. Benignancy, magnanimity, altruism, greatness of hope — yes, all these are there. But intelligence?

The sinister part of the book is the introduction by Mr. Crossman, an editor, a member of Parliament, never a communist, and never a mature mind, either — sinister because though it analyzes and rejects the communist intellectual's fallacies, it retains unmodified most of the assumptions from which they originally issued. But the absolute disclosure is Louis Fischer's chapter; there has been no document of equal naïveté since Marjorie Fleming. The summary of his career as a correspondent distorting and withholding facts is unremarkable, for when a mind is put to the service of an absolutism, that is what becomes of intellectual integrity. (A commonplace cry at the mourners' bench: oh, yes, brethren, I lied but I had faith.) The point is that year by year this mind made out what the facts were and insisted on believing that what they were instead was what they could not possibly be. I must understand them as something else; it really is a cap pistol to the eyes of faith, the earth is flat for I can see its edge, and I must purge myself of doubt. When the job is finished at last all will be justified. Believe altogether that this is not so and on the Day of Jubilo it will prove not to have been so.

This may represent some vibration in the central nervous system but it is not intelligence. And what realization does he reach when at last a sign is given him? "No dictatorship is a democracy and none contains the seeds of liberty," and "There is no freedom in a dictatorship because there are no unalienable rights." Yes. Where had he been?

We are asked to respect these men not as believers but as minds. So to Arthur Koestler. Since he apostatized he has written a brilliant novel and several others not quite so good. An admirable artist, he evokes reservations as a thinker — as a reporter on Israel, as the compounder of a psychometaphysics. But he illustrates the usefulness of the ex-communist intellectual. He describes convincingly what communists have done, what they feel, what they think and believe, what their methods are, how they behave. And yet is "convincingly" the exact word? Whatever any ex-communist can tell us truly about communism will be useful. But it will always be at least a little suspect too. His recantation says explicitly that he was once easily deceived and thought badly. However brilliant, he had a conspicuous gift for illusion, for spinning beautiful fantasies out of abhorrent facts. In what he now tells us about communism, how can we be sure that he understood his experience or is able to report it reliably?

That, however, is up to us; it is an ordinary problem for the critical intelligence. But one possibility of danger latent in the ex-communist intellectual cannot be ignored. . . . In the sum, probably, our American ones were not very important, did not do much harm, were nowhere near so great a danger as a widespread fearfulness now assumes. Conceivably, it may prove in the end that only those who were engaged in espionage did any harm at all. . . . But they were communists and it was only because their ideas were not accepted that they did no harm. Their ideas were dangerous and will remain so even though they may be wrapped in tissue of a different color.

Let James Burnham show how. As an expounder of communism he offered us the poison that kills freedom, representative institutions, democratic life, the integrity of individual men on which the existence of free society depends. His recantation describes communism as exactly that. But he has devoted himself to offering us the same stuff out of a differently labeled sac. If you drop the word diamondback and substitute for it *Crotalus adamanteus* you have changed only the words, not the effect. What the sac holds is still poison to freedom, free institutions, democratic society.

The convertites confess that once upon a time they were not very bright. What we must remember is that once upon a time they were authoritarians.

"The flight from freedom." They have given that old phrase a new currency to explain what happened to them. To explain what, in another renewal of a familiar phrase, they call *la trahison des clercs.* Freedom lays on anyone a heavy burden of obligation, it is the heaviest of all burdens, and perhaps we should feel compassion for a man who could not bear up under it. But the point about the ex-communist is that he did not bear up under it, a little while ago. He fled from freedom to the absolutism that relieves a man of responsibility and his mind of obligation to do the mind's work. His but to accept and obey; the authority, the gospel, the Party would take over. By this act he repudiated everything for which the free intelligence, democratic society, and the dignity of the individual stood. His confession says in humility and grief that now he has learned better.

But the original problem is still there. It has not changed since the nineteen-thirties. It has not changed since Jefferson wrote, "I have sworn upon the altar of God eternal hostility against every form of tyranny over the mind of man." It has not changed since mankind began to work out the conception of free men in a free society. The enemy is still the same: absolutism, authoritarianism, dictatorship, tyranny, whatever threatens freedom. And the burden that freedom lays on the human mind and soul has not decreased; it has grown heavier. The strength of every honest man is needed in its support. There is no impugning the honesty of a man who says, "One thing I know, whereas I was blind, now I see." There can be only rejoicing that he has found his sight. But what about his strength? The essence of his plight, and of ours who must appraise him, is that neither was there any impugning his honesty when he was blind. Freedom was once so intolerable a burden that he fled from it; will it again prove too much for him? Not as a penalty for error or as a punishment for sin but as a precaution against a known and self-confessed weakness, he must be put to a double scrutiny in whatever he tells us or proposes. His courage failed once; in what he now offers us has he succeeded in deceiving himself into some other acceptance of the gospel of despair?

But Sometimes They Vote Right Too

(NOVEMBER 1950)

"I AM COMING to think that the world is too complicated for straight representative government." So a reader of the Easy Chair writes me, calling on me to say where I stand. And a few days after I got his letter, Mr. Joseph Alsop, who was a student of mine when I was a college teacher, alluded in his column to President Truman's "incurable loyalty to the third rate and the natural fellow feeling of so large an element in Congress for whatever is shabby, fraudulent, and political." He concluded, "A Republican leadership that howls against an Acheson while Johnson is almost lovingly embraced [I used to warn you against the passive voice, Joe], a President who seems to take pride in shielding his worst subordinates from the smallest retribution, look like symptoms of decay in our political institutions."

The same symptoms worry my correspondent, who says he is "beginning to wonder whether representative government is really the thing after all." The world, he thinks, has grown too perilous for us to risk Congress and its errors. As an example, "To the extent that Congress has had anything to do with it, our foreign policy has suffered. Everywhere — Europe, China, and the rest." He gives other examples and sums them up, "I wonder if Congress can do anything right."

His next step has been the crucial one as long as men have thought about government. It probably will still be crucial when

Mr. Norbert Wiener's thinking machines have obviated Mr. Wiener's human tendency to commit fallacies. He rejects totalitarianism, for it "seems such a horror." He has "no assurance that 'planning' will stay disinterested for long." And now he is over the cliff, falling like Lucifer son of the morning. "I sincerely wonder if we can give the people much say in policy and survive for long." But, surprisingly, the clincher he submits is this: "I think, for example, a great portion of them [the people] 'think McCarthy has something.' "

(Relevant interruption. Just then I was wrestling with a problem. If you read the symptoms of paranoia in any standard textbook, you will find that they strikingly resemble the behavior of the junior Senator from Wisconsin. I wondered whether, if a Senator should go violently insane, the public had any way of keeping him from influencing policy. So far as I could see, two paragraphs of Section 4, Article I, of the Constitution left the public helpless. It could not require a Senator to appear before a lunacy board. It could not even make good a more important demand, that Senator Taft, McCarthy's licensor, submit to an intelligence test. So I took my problem to an expert in constitutional law, who confirmed me. He describes himself as "a Republican upstate Episcopalian, militiaman, and dirt-roads lawyer." I am a half Mugwump, 60 per cent New Dealer, 90 per cent Populist dirt-roads historian but I found that he and I saw pretty much eye to eye about the state of the nation. Except about McCarthy's results. The constitutionalist thinks that McCarthy has convinced the average man, my correspondent's "people," that Mr. Acheson phones Moscow twice daily for instructions and that the President is surrounded by Russian spies whom he knowingly appointed to key jobs. Whereas I think the average man regards McCarthy as a liar and a Typhoid Mary, the carrier of an infection far more dangerous to our political institutions than any other decay now apparent in them.)

My correspondent is "an editorial writer on a conservative newspaper." He says that he is pretty conservative himself but adds, "I am startled to find that on almost every issue the guy who knows something arrives at an opposite conclusion from the guy who doesn't." He has learned that "the trouble with the press is not cupidity but stupidity." So finally, "If the press is stupid, how can the people be anything else?" Or Congress. If we are to survive, how can we entrust ourselves to either any longer?

The operative phrase is "the guy who knows." It always has been, though in Hamilton's time the guy who knows was also the wellborn guy, the well-placed, the rich, the powerful. The Federalist point of view is immortal. The New England Federalists — Fisher Ames was probably the most persuasive — argued it more cogently and powerfully than anyone has in our time. Their public and especially their private papers would remind my correspondent that the first time representative government failed and the Republic perished was in 1800. The first time, that is, under the Constitution, for that document in itself proved to a formidable company of patriots and thinkers (Luther Martin and Patrick Henry to name no more) that our political institutions had already decayed beyond redemption.

But we need not go looking through history for the Federalist point of view. Implicit rather than formulated, degraded to a vulgar cheapness, it is the point of view of two-thirds of the bankers in my correspondent's city, three-quarters of the newspaper owners in the United States, 85 per cent of the directors of really big corporations, and 90 per cent of our university trustees. It is the dominant point of view of the actual managerial class, as it would be unanimous among the fictitious one that Mr. James Burnham will crystallize out of dream if he can. And with Mr. Burnham we come to the payoff. For it was his point of view while he still consorted with communists, and it abides while all else changeth, it is still his point of view since he crossed over into campground and all the saints shouted hosanna. And with him a large and variegated class of intellectuals and literary thinkers who took the crucial step, fell into the fallacy, faced left, and joined up with the right. It is the characteristic error of those whom my dirt-roads constitutionalist calls "the little liberals."

I like the phrase, which carries a slight taxonomic emphasis on the adjective. We have to have such a label to make clear that we are talking about that species and not the robust and honorable tradition of liberalism. It was precisely when the little liberal of our time repudiated liberalism that he joined hands with Fisher Ames and the enemy. The Federalist philosophy distrusted the people. They were stupid: they would become an anarchy and so bring all down. The little liberal is out of patience with them: they do not do what so obviously would be good for them. Both agree that they must be prevented from doing harm, to others or themselves, and that they are too stupid to be trusted with the government: representative government has failed. I cannot see, however, that if a machine gun, which is the alternative, is to be substituted for representative government, it makes any difference whose finger is on the trigger or which philosophy is lining up the sights. And now that we have a bumper crop of volubly penitent communists, I am unable to see on what grounds we are asked to respect their intelligence, whose sole claim to respect is that they have recanted ideas which only fools would ever have accepted. The point remains the machine gun.

Get down to cases. My correspondent wonders "if we can give the people much say in policy and survive for long." I am not clear who "we" are nor how we are to take away from the people what they now possess and seem unlikely to give up of their own will. Will Congress declare itself inoperative and adjourn sine die? Does the anarchy which the Federalist feared suddenly break out and does the suddenly chastened mob then hand over its sovereignty to the supermen of good will whom the little liberal sees when he dreams? And what happens next?

Back in the blithe days when a handful of unskillful book reviewers were going to make the Revolution before next week's deadline, I used to wonder whom they and the American Communist Party had to run things after it had been made. Staging street-corner demonstrations seemed an inadequate training for running the military establishment, which would still have to be run by somebody. Conspiratorial activities in crepe beards and party names among the revolutionaries of a neighborhood cell would not produce a diplomatic corps that could save the fillings of its own teeth from the pluto-demo-fascist thugs in striped pants. Which treasurer of a local was going to head the Federal Reserve? Was Earl Browder or the movie critic of the *New Masses* going to be Commissar of the Interior? If the thinkers who are now cashing in on their asininity were going to take over, the American Soviet Republic wouldn't last overnight.

So now. Suppose that the seventh trumpet sounds and the massed genius of Inland Steel, Mr. Burnham, and the chorus of recusant little liberals does succeed in extemporizing a mechanism for transferring government from Congress to something or somebody more effective — to whom will they transfer it? There has never been any answer except "the expert." It is spoken in a trance, in a nightmare so frightful that it scares you awake. We can have only one use for the expert — working for us. He can be a fine hired hand but we have paid high to learn that he makes a damned bad boss.

And which expert? We have a body of military experts who seem to rate high in the opinion of everyone except Hanson Baldwin (and, as I write, Ernest Hemingway) but if you want to see Congress illuminated with almost celestial radiance, simply picture turning over appropriations to the generals and admirals. The scientific or technological expert? A lot of scientists are acknowledging their willingness to take over if we will twist their arms a little; they candidly confess that they see no other salvation for us: be science-minded or perish. But there seems to be a tendency for civil and other liberties we still cherish to go out the window when science comes in the door, and big-shot scientists who five years ago were willing to save us unassisted have already begun to warn us against their kind. Congress is keeping an eye on the Atomic Energy Commission for reasons that seem to most of us the worst ones readily available, but we are all profoundly glad to have it watched. And an alliance between the military expert and the scientific expert is terrifying to contemplate.

The consulting specialist, then? He appears to be the commonest hope and has replaced the image of the philosopher-professor-king in many aspiring minds. The vision is of an orderly and untroubled mechanism of government which frees "the guy who knows most" about taxation to work out and decree our tax policy, the guy who knows most about foreign policy (when found) to ordain our foreign policy, and the guy who knows most about agriculture to compel the Farm Bureau, the Farmers Union, the processor of foods, and the consumer to live in amiable co-operation. But that guy doesn't exist whereas the Farm Bureau and the Farmers Union do. If we created him he would have to be a commissar again and one or the other of those institutions, together with a lot of us non-agricultural bystanders, would get shot up.

No, the expert has to be kept on a short rope, which is our present practice. Almost as if they weren't in decay, our political institutions have met requirements of the modern world which the Constitutional Convention did not foresee by developing a lot of semi-independent administrative agencies for which the Constitution did not provide. There and in the Executive departments and bureaus we do use the specialist or the expert. He does his job pretty well, at least as well as he does it in General Motors or the New York Central. Probably Congress and the stupid people keep him from doing it still better, but we have to abide that loss in efficiency in order to keep going at all. Give FCC or ECA or FPC its head, let it operate with full efficiency, without anxiety about Congress or an ear cocked at the stupid people, and we'd be in the ditch before the chairman's term ran out. The expert as specialist has to be subject to the expert in government, and we grow our own. They are in the county boss's office, the state and municipal jobs, or Congress, or trying to get there. They may look pretty bad but we've tried, or seen others try, everything else and everything else has turned out worse.

Mark Twain said, "It could probably be shown by facts and figures that there is no distinctly native American criminal class except Congress." One Congressman has just finished a term in jail, another one is still serving his, doubtless others demonstrably belong in jail, and I can name a number who I think ought to be. Mark Twain also began a speech that hasn't got printed yet, "Once there was a Congressman, I mean a son of a bitch — but why do I repeat myself?" We all feel that way about various Honorables and there can be no doubt that we are sometimes right. As far back as Washington's first term, people were saying just those things about Congress, and sometimes they were unquestionably right.

But it isn't Congress we're talking about, son, it's the people of the United States, who include you and me and the bright guys as well as the stupid. For instance, though it is unsafe to use an absolute superlative, isn't Nevada now represented in the Senate by the worst delegation any state ever had there? Messrs. McCarran and Malone, who speak for a small private fief of big stock companies, big industrial corporations, and big gamblers, cast votes that count as much in policymaking as those of Messrs. Lehman and Ives, who speak for the most populous state and, it may be, the best one. That fact and the fact that each of them equates governmentally with either of the New York Senators and with, say, Senator Vandenburg, Senator Douglas, Senator Aiken, or Senator Fulbright keep a righteous man at a slow burn. I would be almost too busy to protest if some Federalist come from the grave were to propose a Constitutional amendment which would rescind Nevada's statehood and provide a military, judicial, or territorial commission to clean it up and bring it into the twentieth century. Almost but not quite. Our political experiment always was precarious to the very verge of disaster but it remains safer than anything else.

Not Congress but us. It wasn't Congress that brought the boys back in a stampede and opened Europe to the present threat, broke up the defense establishment, made chaos of foreign policy, and brought on the despair of the little liberal, the NAM, Mr. Alsop, and my correspondent. We did it. Congress, a sensitively responsive political instrument, so responsive that the associated garden clubs can scare a Congressman into defying the power lobby, did exactly what we required it to. That's the mold we're cast in, the way the United States operates, the pattern of our society. It's alarmingly loose, wasteful, dilatory, and inefficient, but we're committed to it and there's no way of changing us. If that means we're going under, we will have to go under. But does it? It never has yet. What it has meant so far is that we shake down into adjustment instead of shaking to pieces, and correct mistakes instead of perishing from them. Our system scares any thoughtful man blue, but it doesn't scare him as much as any other system does.

Sure the people are stupid: the human race is stupid. Sure Congress is an inefficient instrument of government. But the people are not stupid enough to abandon representative government for any other kind, including government by the guy who knows. They have just had to fight their worst war to get three such governments out of the way, and may have to fight another one to dispose of a fourth. And bad as our system is, it is more effective than those governments. Their system has been tried repeatedly since Plato (a little liberal who understood that the people are stupid) first proposed it and in the end it never works. They are efficient at starting wars but not much else. I'd rather have efficiency at finishing them, as we have always shown we have, and at keeping the train on the tracks, as we have done. It may be a crude criterion but we are the oldest form of government now operating: we have outlasted every other political system in the world.

Remember, son, that a government which operates with precision straight to the point has to be by machine gun. Such a government would not let you, Mr. Alsop, and me bellyache so much; to do so would be wasteful and ineffective. So go on shooting at McCarthy and cursing Congress. Since I typed the first paragraph of this piece the decaying political institutions have acted on Mr. Alsop's suggestion and harpooned his white whale, the Secretary of Defense. It may be our turn tomorrow; Senator Taft may get alarmed by the trend in Ohio and rise in the Senate to ask if McCarthy is sane. If that happens, how stupid will the people look?

The Case of the Censorious Congressmen

(APRIL 1953)

LAST MAY the House of Representatives became aware that there was one field at which it had not directed its investigatory power. So it appointed a Select Committee, with Congressman Gathings of Arkansas as chairman, to "conduct a study and investigation of current pornographic literature." The Committee has now published its report; it makes interesting reading.

Interesting but difficult, and some day Congress should investigate congressional prose. This report is so ineptly written that in some places I cannot make out what the Committee is trying to say. Thus it declares that the First Amendment "was adopted only after a long and acrimonious debate." And "even as far back as 1789 the idea of granting unrestricted liberty of speech and publication was a moot question of no mean proportions. The founding fathers evidently realized that what was meant to be liberty could readily be transmuted by unscrupulous persons into license."

This drifts unattached in midair — how is it to be construed? Is the Committee saying that the fathers decided this "moot question" wrongly? Did they err when they wrote freedom of the press into the Constitution? I judge that this is what the Committee means. For the burden of what it goes on to say is that we had better put some restrictions on freedom of publication that the fathers refused to.

Does the Committee, then, favor censorship? It says repeatedly that it does not. Thus, page 12, "a practical solution consistent with adequate safeguards against possible violation of the constitutional rights of free speech is the aim of the Committee and never has it entertained any thought of federal censorship of the press." Just as often, however, it entertains exactly such thoughts in the plain view of everyone. Page 17, "It follows logically that any effort by Congress . . . should be directed toward the publishers [of objectionable literature] either from the angle of statutory provisions or through self-imposed control if such is possible." Any effort of Congress from the angle of statutory provisions directed at publishers would be censorship.

Or take this, which immediately precedes the denial I have quoted from page 12. The Committee quotes Mr. Douglas M. Black as saying that the Publishers' Council believes there are enough federal and local laws on the books now to take care of obscene literature if they are properly enforced. Then the Committee says, "This seems to say in effect that if there is a law existing against the commission of a particular crime it is all right to commit the crime, if you can get away with it." I suppose that righteousness exempts the Committee from dealing intelligently with what Mr. Black has said, and even from characterizing it honestly; I suppose the gentlemen do not believe that it is all right to violate the Hatch Act while running for Congress if you can get away with the violation. But I read this as saying that we have not got enough laws to do the job and therefore need additional ones.

The Committee studied comic books, "cheesecake or girlie magazines," and "pocket-size paper-bound books." It heard testimony about the first two evils but devoted most of its attention to the third. Let me say right here that what the report says about pocket books spotlights an embarrassing dilemma: either the Committee is intolerably ignorant or else it is deliberately making intolerable misrepresentations. "This type of writing," the report says, "has now reached a stage where it has become a serious menace to the social structure of the nation." It may be news to you that the blonde in her underwear who adorns the cover of

Silas Marner at the newsstand has undermined American society, but you have worse to learn. The Committee prints an unsigned letter from the combat zone in Korea which says that "most of the reading the Army provides us is filth and adultery." It appears to accept the statement, which must interest the Army, that this filth has "all but destroyed our first line of defense" and the further one, which should interest another House committee, that it has "left us open to dangers far worse than communism."

The Committee says that publishers, meaning chiefly the reprint houses, "are resourceful public enemies, parasites on the free-press privilege." It regards such inflammatory language as justified by the speed with which the parasites have worked their will on us. Mrs. St. George, who lives in Tuxedo and represents the Twenty-ninth Congressional District of New York, "can remember very well that ten years ago so-called smutty literature was unknown in this country." One reason for this swift success is "a general lack of awareness of the problem in its modern form [presumably twenty-five cent books], its scope, magnitude, and techniques." There is a tendency to make light of the problem and to look on those who are disturbed by it as "professional reformists or bluenoses." But we are given leave to hope: various watchers on the walls have recognized the danger and the Committee acknowledges (p. 35) that the most heartening sign so far is the existence of the Committee itself.

But public apathy is not most to blame, we gather from the report; the courts are. The Committee says that they have developed "a new legal philosophy." It "serves as the basis for excuse to print and circulate the filthiest, most obscene literature without concurrent literary value to support it ever known in history." Be damned to such philosophy, and the Committee sets out to undermine the decisions that over the past thirty years have modernized the laws relating to obscenity. Decadence began with Judge Woolsey's decision in the *Ulysses* case, which on appeal was affirmed by Judge Hand. This double charter of obscenity "is as elastic as rubber in its interpretative susceptibility and supplies the purveyors of obscenity with an excuse regardless of what is the degree of obscenity involved, and requires every book to be judged separately, an almost impossible task."

Look at that wretched sentence again; its murkiness conceals the end to which all obscenity crusades come. To judge books separately is an almost impossible task. Then what? Then this: we must legally define a class of books, to wit those that are pornographic, which shall be denied publication and circulation. How, without judging it, can we know that a book is pornographic? Apparently it will be enough if a cop, a district attorney, a "professional reformist," a Congressman, or (in one of the Committee's recommendations) a postmaster — if anyone says that it is. Whether or not the Committee knows it, that is how its thesis invariably works out — except under the court decisions it is trying to overturn. Whether or not the Committee fully means to say it, that is what it says. But, mind you, no censorship.

The Committee moves on to Judge Curtis Bok's opinion in *Commonwealth* v. *Gordon et al.* In the Easy Chair for July 1949 I called it a great document in democracy and a great document in human freedom. The Committee disagrees. "To express it negatively, certainly such a decision contributed nothing whatsoever toward the reduction of the steadily increasing publication of and to [?] the sales of pocket-sized books." It affects "all the elements of our social structure" and sanctions "by negative action the flow of salacious, scatological [no evidence of scatology cited in the report], and suggestive literature, reaching the degree of mass media." So the Committee says it must inquire into the background of the case — meaning Judge Bok's background.

Announcing that it would not dream of questioning his honesty or integrity, the Committee proceeds to slur them intolerably. His family has a large interest in the Curtis Publishing Company, which "owns 42½ per cent of the stock of Bantam Books, Inc." And Bantam Books, Inc., publishes the Committee's abomination, pocket-size paper-bound books. No reflection on Judge Bok — and yet: "It is, however, reasonably possible that having been associated so closely with the publishing business that he became inherently imbued [sic] with a liberal conception of the tradition founded upon the constitutional provision guaranteeing the freedom of the press."

Surely such half-illiterate writing is a greater danger to thought and morals than all the salacious literature ever printed in the United States. But what did it set out to say? This, I think: that we must narrow the First Amendment by repudiating a "liberal concept" and a dangerous "tradition" of freedom of the press. The Amendment says, "Congress shall make no law . . . abridging the freedom of speech, or of the press." The Committee appears to hold that this prohibition in itself does not cover pocket-size paper-bound books, that it has been extended to cover them only by an unjustified concept or a vicious tradition. It implies that Congress *can* make laws prohibiting their manufacture and sale and that it ought to. But, again, no censorship.

The Committee is preoccupied with that alarming phrase, "pocket-size paper-bound books." Would the same content be acceptable in royal octavo bound in cloth? Not necessarily I judge, but it *would* be acceptable at three dollars. This does not mean that obscenity is a class prerogative. The offense is not that obscenity is offered for sale at a quarter, but that at that price it is offered for sale to so many people. The immature, meaning our children, can afford it.

The Committee faces away from the fact that almost all the two-bit books are reprints of more expensive ones that have had a pretty wide distribution in cloth. It conspicuously fails to remind us of another fact: that if twenty-five cent books can be outlawed under the First Amendment, then so can books at any price. And, to make everything clear, the dissenting minority report reveals that the Committee read few, if indeed any, of the books which the majority describe as the filthiest, most obscene literature ever known in history. The hired help and some unpaid volunteers made extracts from various paperbacks, passages which contained "language of the streets" or episodes dealing "with sex and sexual relations." These extracts from a few books are what convinced the Committee that the reprint houses have brought our society to the verge of ruin.

The report ends with three recommendations. One would extend the federal statutes which now forbid common carriers to transport obscenity so that the same prohibition would cover transportation by private truck. The second would liberate the Post Office Department from two existing regulations which prevent it from dealing summarily with obscenity sent by mail. (These safeguards are to be removed because obscene material — the twenty-five-cent book — inflicts "swift and irreparable injury in such a comparatively short time.") Finally, the Committee recommends that publishers purify their output before the public demands *additional federal action.*

In their short but sharp minority report, Congressmen Celler of New York and Walter of Pennsylvania repudiate the methods, findings, and recommendations of their colleagues. They point out that the majority's objections are not confined to the obscenity they set out to investigate but extend to ideas, and that "this comes dangerously close to book burning." The objection to one book is that a passage in it advocates polygamy; to another, that its author does not seem to like law-enforcement officers or "the upper classes." The men who made those objections do not understand, the dissenters remark, that "these are, after all, matters of free speech and free expression."

"It is not the province of any congressional committee," Messrs. Celler and Walter say, "to determine what is good, bad, or indifferent literature." The majority on the Committee have set up their own personal taste as the criterion of what shall be published. Worse still, on the basis of some extracts from a few books, they have "made a sweeping indictment of current literature" — and they have neither official concern with current literature nor jurisdiction over it. The dissenters then move on to defend the reprint publishers, reviewing many facts which are known to everyone who buys books but which the Committee majority never took into account. They end by saying that if obscenity is a problem, there are state laws governing its distribution everywhere except in New Mexico, and Congress is not called upon to act.

The dissenters cover most of the points that must be made about this curious excursion by the House of Representatives.

They do not, however, point out how obscurantist and untrue the Committee's report is. It is not true that today's magazines and paperbacks are the filthiest literature ever known in history. It is not true that cheap reprints are seriously menacing our social structure. It is not true that they are doing irreparable damage. Such statements are mendacious, ignorant, preposterous, and more dangerous in themselves than the sum total of obscenity printed since Gutenberg. Moreover, in all except a minute percentage of the paperbacks there is no more indecency, even casual verbal indecency, than in so many city directories. What does Congress mean by conducting so frivolous an inquiry, sanctioning so flagrant an attempt to frighten the public, and putting its seal on such a bulk of aggressive and irresponsible misrepresentation?

Such ignorance and prejudice as the Committee shows are routine in obscenity crusades, but also there is something new — and evil. The results it reaches are those of any police-court smut snooper; they come down to a wearily familiar demand, "This literature must be suppressed for we don't like it." The report alludes to lurid but entirely hypothetical dangers; not once does it produce or even mention any actual damage to anyone. It tells us that selected passages from some books have shocked it and that is all. A sense of shock is, of course, all that any crusader against obscene literature ever had. But this is not John S. Sumner. It is not a group of professional reformers expressing to a state legislature some professional horror which, they hope, will inspire the regular customers to throw another nickel on the drum. This is a committee of the Congress of the United States, and it feels that the freedom guaranteed by the First Amendment ought to be abridged and believes that Congress has power to act. That is the dangerous novelty.

Are trashy novels, some of which may conceivably offend your taste and mine, a public problem? The occasional irresponsibility or exhibitionism of some Congressmen does not arouse us to crusade for the suppression of Congress. Because a child or an adolescent may buy for a quarter a book which we would just as soon he did not read until he is older and have therefore kept out of his hand at three dollars, we cannot let Congress make it unavailable to adults. We cannot, in fact, permit Congress in any way to censor our own reading or that of our children. What we may care to read is no concern of Congress. Congress has no power and no authority to control it. We are quite free to read anything we may choose to read and Congress can do nothing whatever about it. That's the way things stand now and we intend to keep them that way.

This particular investigation will produce no action, but it is a bad sign and it comes at a bad time. With amazing blitheness a House committee has made another attack on the Bill of Rights that is the basic safeguard of our freedoms. It is no less dangerous an attack for being oblique. The gentlemen have been shocked by some passages in some books. (Though because gentlemen in Congress have stronger moral fiber than the rest of us, they were unharmed by what they feel sure must debauch us.) They propose that such books be heavily penalized. The plain bearing of what they say is that they must go on and forbid the publication of any paper-bound book which they may happen not to like. And we have already slipped so far, impelled mostly by other committees of Congress, that no roar of anger mingled with laughter has rolled across the United States to silence them. The next step is clearly to forbid the publication of any books whatsoever that any Congressman may happen to dislike. In June 1949 Congressman John S. Wood called on some seventy colleges to submit to the Un-American Activities Committee all textbooks and supplementary reading used in all their courses in sociology, geography, economics, government, philosophy, history, political science, and American literature. His obvious intent was to determine what books Congress should permit colleges to use. His colleagues promptly called him off, but that was four years ago. This time Messrs. Velde and Jenner may try to make good on congressional proscription of reading matter.

The new Congress has been asked for an appropriation to continue the investigation begun by the Gathings Committee. Mr. Celler and Mr. Walter could perform no more valuable service than to appear before the Rules Committee and oppose continuation.

Comment on a Technique*

(AUGUST 1953)

THE TWENTY-FOURTH Congressional District of Pennsylvania is in the northwest corner of the state and consists of Crawford, Erie, and Mercer Counties. Topographically it is on the way to becoming Ohio; the landscape is still recognizably Pennsylvania but is less typical than the country just southeast of it. Though defaced here and there by the grime of heavy industry, it is for the most part a pleasant countryside. There is a fine diversity — the Lake Erie shore, a lot of gentle hills and some rugged ones, river valleys, small inland lakes, opulent farms. I have toured it minutely because some of the historical events with which I have been professionally concerned took place there, and it is a rewarding country for tourists. One's notebook fills with good place names, striking individualities in architecture, tangy local idioms, interesting effects in folklore and even costume. If the local cuisine is less spectacular than that of southeastern Pennsylvania, good restaurants are easily come by. Small town hotels tend to be above average, metropolitan ones rather below it. A good country; one wishes it well.

It is depressing to record that this pleasant district had of record last fall 67,790 communists, communist sympathizers, and fellow travelers. After, that is, a manner of speaking. After the

* It seems obligatory to reprint this comment, though it is only half of an Easy Chair. Is is self-explanatory. The rest of the piece was devoted to preparations for a motor trip.

manner of its Representative's speaking.

He is Mr. Carroll D. Kearns. He must be one of the best educated men in the House, formally at least: he is a Bachelor of Science, a Master of Education, and a Doctor of Music. His biographical sketch in the *Congressional Directory* shows that he has had considerable experience as a teacher and a school administrator. He also says that he is nationally known as a concert artist. I assume that he is telling the truth, but does not that fact expose him to the suspicions of his colleague from the Eighteenth District of Michigan, Mr. Dondero? And it might be relevant to inquire into the songs he has sung on his way to a national reputation; have some of them been operatic and can we be sure that all of them have been chaste?

Since in last month's *Harper's* Personal and Otherwise described Congressman Kearns's insinuation about me, I need only summarize it now. He entered in the *Congressional Record* a statement of what he called "activities" of mine which, so he said, "speak for themselves." Citing no authority but his own, he said that I had joined others in signing an ad in the *New York Times* which urged the abolition of the Wood-Rankin Committee and that I am on the council of the Society for the Prevention of World War III, "headed by Rex Stout, former editor of *New Masses*." I signed that ad and I am on that council. (Mr. Stout was never an editor of the *New Masses* and I don't know whether the highly educated Mr. Kearns ever took a course in ethics. He should have told his readers that the Society for the Prevention of World War III, an organization established by former members of the Writers War Board, is concerned solely with preventing the development of another totalitarian movement in Germany.) Mr. Kearns also said that the files of the House Un-American Activities Committee show that an article published in the *New Masses* quoted from the Easy Chair that was called "Due Notice to the FBI." Again I assume he was telling the truth: the article has been quoted in scores of periodicals. He went on to cite the *Daily Worker* as showing that I opposed a proposal to outlaw the Communist Party; in fact he cited it three times to make one act of public protest look like three acts of partnership with the *Daily Worker.* Finally, he cited the *People's Daily Worker,* a publication about which I know nothing, to show that on another occasion I denounced an action of the Un-American Activities Committee.

End of Mr. Kearns's statement of my "activities."

There is a technique here. I did publicly oppose outlawing the Communist Party and I have publicly protested various actions of the Un-American Activities Committee — considerably oftener than Mr. Kearns noted. If those facts interest him, he could have got them from many newspapers, from *Harper's,* or from a number of other magazines. And if he did not care to read my FBI piece in the original, he could have found mention of it in any newspaper in the United States that uses a wire service, for Mr. J. Edgar Hoover went after it with an axe. Only one paper would serve his purpose, however. He used the *Daily Worker* because he wanted to imply that the piece was pro-communist, as the others would show it was not, and that I am a communist sympathizer.

As I have written to Congressman Kearns in reply, my lifelong opposition to communism is part of the history of American journalism and belles-lettres in our time. (I requested him to enter my letter in the *Congressional Record.* As I write this, several weeks later, he has not acknowledged receiving it, though the registry return receipt shows that he did.*) Mr. Kearns must know that quite well. I can only conclude that his defamation of me was not ignorantly irresponsible, but was deliberate and dishonest.

That defamation was Mr. Kearns's response to my criticism, in the April Easy Chair, of the majority report of the Gathings Committee. He was a member of the committee and of its majority. I had criticized one of his official acts: he reached for the most useful six-gun in the possession of public officials. Disagree with a Congressman? — fellow traveler! Criticize a Con-

* He has never acknowledged it. In this instance at least he was a hit and run defamer.

gressman? — communist! The epithet "communist" is intended to make an official immune to criticism; it is meant to be a complete answer to any uncomfortable truth told about him. Maybe it would take the sting out of my criticism, maybe it would scare me into shutting up about the proposed limitations to the First Amendment, maybe it would deter others from criticizing Mr. Kearns or the report of the Committee. Don't tread on Kearns, see, or you'll be exposed.

I don't know whether there are people who believe that it is unpatriotic, even subversive, to criticize what a Congressman does. I do know that a lot of people find it useful to act as if they do. I point out that Mr. Kearns's action "speaks for itself"; it was a specimen of the deliberate terrorism that is the most dangerous force in American public life today. But I can't get steamed up about it, for Mr. Kearns wasn't very expert. His response to what I said about his Committee's report was contemptible but it was also clownish; call it second-rate and let it go. Nuts to this nationally known concert artist. Does he care to say anything in defense of the Committee Report I was criticizing?

I don't know whether the *Daily Worker* carried a story last November about the appalling number of subversives in the Twenty-fourth District. God help Pennsylvania: 67,790 people voted against Mr. Kearns.

Norwalk and Points West

(APRIL 1954)

THE MAYOR's prepared speech told the newspapermen from NATO countries that Norwalk, Connecticut, was "a complete city where men can make a living and live a life." A conducted tour had brought them to Norwalk so that they could see "a typical American city" and "could observe democracy in action." Of the countries they represented five had been subjugated by the Nazis; attempted invasions of two others had failed. All were leagued with the United States against Russian totalitarianism. Except for the years of subjugation those from France, Great Britain, the Netherlands, Belgium, Denmark, and Iceland had always been secure in their persons, houses, papers, and effects; they were accustomed to the unlimited exercise of such rights as, they understood, were guaranteed to Americans by the First Amendment. Perhaps those from Italy and Portugal felt that experience qualified them better than the others to understand the news that broke the day they reached Norwalk. The news was that a committee of the local post of Veterans of Foreign Wars had been making lists of fellow citizens whom it considered subversive and sending them to the FBI.

A former Assistant Secretary of State who last year published an excellent study of intimidation by Congress, Mr. Edward W. Barrett, was assigned to explain this disclosure to the visitors. He was on a hot spot and did not do very well. Such episodes, he told them, showed only that we were a young, spirited, and energetic people blowing off steam; by giving vent to pent-up emotions we were improving our balance and fortifying the cause of true democracy. The newspapermen may have thought this a quotation from George Orwell: we improve our balance by losing it and we fortify the cause of democracy by abandoning its safeguards. One of them remarked to the mayor that if this was democracy in action, then the United States must be a very strange country. The mayor admitted that a bad news break had ruined the glamour of their visit. But he assured them that practically 100 per cent of the people of Norwalk disapproved of the VFW's method.

The visitors would understand that much depends on the accuracy of the mayor's figures. But they must have been further confused by what they learned in the next few days. It became clear that other VFW posts in various parts of the country have had secret committees of proscription for a long time, and so have various American Legion organizations. Boston papers reported that the Massachusetts Legion had just given the commonwealth's Commission on Communism a card file containing the names of more than six hundred "proved Communists, suspects, or left-wing sympathizers" in New England. The file had been compiled by the Legion's security officers, one to each of the 464 posts in Massachusetts. Note: *proved* (by the Legion) communists, suspects (of the Legion), leftwing sympathizers (defined by the Legion). The VFW of Wichita was listing "Communists and subversives"; the Connecticut department was after "Communistic" behavior; the Norwalk post reported on persons who were "Communistically inclined." The visitors would remember that Senator McCarthy has said he is looking not for communists but for "Communist thinkers." Any of these terms may mean anything at all.

The department commander said that the evidence the VFW committee passed on included "attendance at meetings of suspected groups" and "literature found in [a suspect's] home." We have come to understand that a suspected group is a group whom someone suspects; the news here is that the VFW has been spying in private homes. Whether the investigators enter them on ostensibly friendly calls or say that they have come to read the gas meter, the people of Connecticut are not secure from the VFW in their houses, papers, and effects. If Connecticut householders begin to turn their dogs loose on Fuller Brush salesmen, public opinion pollsters, and people making radio surveys, the injured may reflect that some patriots have probably been bitten too.

The post commander said that his committee reported on anyone "suspected of having an interest in activities not related to a strong America." That qualifies the Junior League and the Audubon Society, and the case against them has to pass only a single test, "intelligent suspicion." Admittedly it is a better test than the commonest one today, suspicion without an adjective, and the individual is safeguarded in that the committee will not report him unless three of its anonymous members suspect him.

But, as the Providence *Journal* soon showed, one test leads to another. There was suspicion that the mayor of Norwalk was communistically inclined: he wanted the town to have a playground which was opposed by a man whom he had defeated in the last election. This man, a druggist, discovered after his defeat that a number of names signed to a political advertisement supporting the mayor were suspect, so he sent them to the FBI. It told him, properly, to go fly a kite. Left to his own patriotism, he organized a private spy system and soon found that Norwalk contained "a regular maze" of subversives. His informers are friends, customers, and passers-by who drop into his store and name suspects; the *Journal* reporter observed one in the act of telling the druggist that her husband was a communist. The druggist has a conclusive test for subversive behavior, thinking, and reading: "Boy, when they ask how can you tell a communist, I got one answer — intuition." Though the FBI brushed him off, he lives in hope and is "willing to talk before any public investigating committee."

The Norwalk commander said that he could not understand

why all the fuss was being made — "If someone hasn't got a guilty conscience what have they got to worry about?" It is an inconceivable remark, or would have been inconceivable three or four years ago; it will serve the NATO journalists as a gauge of how far the Bill of Rights has been eroded in our thinking. There is indeed nothing to worry about except that anonymous, irresponsible, privately organized espionage systems which cannot be held to account have been reporting their suspicions to the FBI, or perhaps reporting as suspicion what is actually resentment, envy, jealousy, malice, or business rivalry. Another astonishing comment was made by the President of the United States when he was asked at a press conference about the Norwalk episode. He said that there seemed to be no way in which people could be prevented from sending in lists of suspects, but there were laws against slander and libel and anyone who might be injured by a false charge could hold his accuser responsible.

One of the White House lawyers should tell Mr. Eisenhower how much a suit for libel costs, especially when brought against an organization wealthy enough to fight it through courts of appeal. He should also quote the legal maxim, "No one ever won a libel suit." And this theoretical protection against injury was destroyed when Congressman Velde, eager to get into this act too, invited the veterans to send their lists of suspects to his committee; if a congressional committee makes public a suspect's name, there can be no suit for libel. But does not the President understand that there is no accuser? The accuser is not a person but a number; he is faceless and voiceless; he can never be held to account and the FBI is silent. The anonymous suspicion, or the rumor or the lie, remains in the files. An "intelligent suspicion" reported by a halfwit and okayed by a rumpot and a paranoid could be reported out of file at a congressional hearing (or an election campaign) years later, perhaps after the informers had died or been sent to a sanitarium or to jail. Such possibilities were foreseen, which is why we have the Fourth and Sixth Amendments.

One hopes that the visiting journalists read Mr. David Anderson's excellent stories about the Norwalk incident in the *New York Times*. Mr. Anderson observed that the VFW espionage system became public knowledge during a drive to increase the membership of the post. He reported that both the post and the department commanders were enthusiastic about the result: it looked as if membership would be increased from 350 to 500. The informers did not profit but the post might.

Did the visitors look around Norwalk on their own? If they saw houses with their curtains drawn there was nothing ominous, but representatives of once occupied countries must have remembered windows shuttered and doors locked against the scrutiny of quisling neighbors. A Norwalkian seen to glance over his shoulder was trying to dodge a bore, not a tail, and if talk sank to a whisper or died out when a stranger entered a restaurant it was only by coincidence — and yet the visitors must have felt long inactive reflexes stirring again. They had been told that Norwalk was a typical American town and the mayor said that practically everyone in it disapproved of private and anonymous spying. If they wondered what Norwalk was going to do about it, the local paper ran some sincere expressions of distaste. If they read the *New York Times*, the Providence *Journal*, or the *Christian Science Monitor*, they learned that quite a lot of disapproval was being expressed in various parts of the country. But they must have wondered whether Norwalk or the country at large was going to do anything. As their tour continued, they must have looked for data which would indicate how typical Norwalk was and whether the mayor's figures were trustworthy.

Well, in Salinas, California, there was an effort to keep H. G. Wells's *Outline of History*, Bertrand Russell's *Human Knowledge*, and the new Kinsey Report out of the public library. But this was proscription on a microscopic scale only. In San Antonio there was an effort — defeated by the sensible citizens — to get a label reading "subversive" affixed to more than 500 books by 118 writers, including Thomas Mann, Einstein, and Geoffrey Chaucer. (Chaucer was subversive by association with Rockwell Kent's illustrations.) Texas, which is sometimes advertised as "the State Unafraid," passed a law requiring authors of textbooks to subscribe to a loyalty oath. Alabama was thinking more widely: its law required authors of textbooks not only to state whether or not they were communists but to make the same declaration about the authors of books which their texts cited. The sensitive antennae of Congressman Velde had led him to anticipate them by introducing into the 82nd Congress HR 6636; it would have required the Librarian of Congress to paste a "subversive" label on every one of his library's nine million books in which he could find a subversive passage. Among those whom the bill directed him to consult in order to determine which passages were subversive were " private organizations."

A private organization called Pro-America got references to UNESCO expunged from textbooks used in the Los Angeles schools. A member of the Indiana Textbook Commission demanded that all references to Robin Hood and to the Quaker religion (professed by ex-President Hoover and Vice-President Nixon) deleted, because such references support communism. Responding to public incitation by the Gathings Committee, a number of national organizations and several score local ones were formed to proscribe such books as they or anyone else might not like — to forbid them not only circulation but publication. Their activities were illegal and in some aspects unconstitutional. Police chiefs seized several hundred books, and for a while it looked as if the State of Illinois was going to proscribe 8000.

In their Constellation, between cities, our visitors must have discussed the several hundred instances of which those I have mentioned are fair samples. Did the Americans believe that only by compulsory ignorance and lynch law could they successfully defend their once democratic system? Did they believe that the communist enemy could be fought successfully only in the dark? Besides private espionage and the proscription of books, what else?

They must have discussed such other symptoms as the substitution of ordeal by committee for criminal prosecution, the subversion of due process, multiple jeopardy, and organized and systematic intimidation. Add the scared Minute Women of the U.S.A. Add the prosperous but by no means scared firms that sell lists of names which they call red, leftwing, or merely suspect. At this point one of the journalists may have read aloud the first ten amendments to the Constitution, so that his companions could check examples against them.

Was this just a young and energetic people blowing off steam? Mr. Barrett had said so, but excuse the visitors if they concluded that the most powerful people in the world are also the most frightened people. The Americans call themselves the freest people, one of them may have summed up, but they are not as free as the French, the Dutch, the Belgians, the Danes, the Icelanders, the British, or the Canadians. Nor are they as free this year as they were three or four years ago. No one, the speaker may have added, has taken their freedom away from them, no one except themselves. They have of their own initiative relinquished much of the Bill of Rights — what are we to make of this? Do they now believe that the freedoms which it defends are wrong and dangerous? Do they believe that in order to preserve democracy they must abandon democratic institutions, procedures, safeguards, and immunities?

Elmer Davis' recently published *But We Were Born Free* is the most valuable analysis so far of these phenomena. In the course of it Mr. Davis remarks that if there should be a convention to propose an amendment to the Constitution, any amendment whatever, it probably could not be stopped from proposing others that would abridge the first ten, the Bill of Rights. Last November, in the Lovejoy Lecture at Colby College, Mr. Irving Dilliard of the St. Louis *Post-Dispatch* expressed a conviction that the Bill of Rights could not be adopted today.

"The press," he said, "would not be for it" — would not fight for the freedom of the people or for its own freedom. His weightiest argument rests on the refusal of the fraternity of professional journalists, Sigma Delta Chi, of which he was once president, to investigate the very widespread charge that there was much bias in the handling of the last election, the refusal of the

American Society of Newspaper Editors to rise to the same challenge and conduct the investigation called for, and its decision that Senator McCarthy's assault on James Wechsler did not constitute intimidation of the press.

The newspapers in general have made a creditable fight against censorship, the proscription of books, and both the suppression and the distortion of information. A review of the last year by the American Book Publishers Council which has come in since I began to write this column is a heartening document. In this threatened area the press has achieved notable victories. Even if its behavior in other threatened areas should justify Mr. Dilliard's alarming conclusion, we cannot make the press a scapegoat and ourselves pass by on the other side. The NATO journalists, I believe, would decide that Mr. Davis' conclusion is more fundamental than Mr. Dilliard's and more ominous. For if a convention should succeed in abridging the Bill of Rights, it would be because the American people wanted it abridged. If we have lost much freedom, it has been with our consent. So I repeat that the crucial question at Norwalk was, how accurate were the mayor's figures? What percentage of the people in Norwalk disapproved of the VFW system of secretly reporting "suspects"? How many disapprove it so strongly that they are willing to make themselves felt?

Mr. Davis estimates that between 15 and 20 per cent of the American people are opposed to the freedoms and immunities which the Bill of Rights was intended to protect and which we have in part relinquished. If the estimate shocks anyone, he should consider a paper read at the midwinter meeting of the American Association for the Advancement of Science. Its authors estimated that one-third of the people in the United States do not know what the Bill of Rights is or what its function is, and that another third oppose it.

We have heard much about the Germans who asserted after the war that they had never been Nazis and had never sympathized with the Nazis but pleaded that they were helpless to oppose them. The American press can be no better than the American people; it reflects us just as the government does. Unless we are some day defeated in a war with Russia, the only way in which we can lose the freedoms that have preserved the United States so far is by voluntarily surrendering them — by acquiescing in their destruction. The steady encroachment on the Bill of Rights can be halted, and the charter of our liberties can be restored in full, whenever we may care to call a halt. We can act to preserve our freedom or we can abstain from acting, and it is just that simple for all of us.

Norwalk is a typical American town, it is any stop on the road, it is your home town and mine. The place to stop the erosion of freedom is right here.

Guilt by Distinction

(APRIL 1955)

PARANOIA, the textbook says, is "a chronic mental disorder of insidious development." It is characterized by "persistent, unalterable, systematized, logically reasoned delusions." The text goes on to speak of "delusional beliefs which become the uppermost and guiding theme of the patient's life." No scientist, I believe, has tried to produce it experimentally. But we have seen that it can be grown from seed.

In order to follow the Reece Committee, which was appointed to investigate tax-exempt foundations (all over again), one must do a lot of reading. Its Report runs 432 pages, and there are two volumes of Hearings. The 943 pages of the first volume are mainly devoted to an attack on various scholarly foundations and societies. Some additional material of this kind appears in the second volume, 298 pages long, but most of this volume consists of the statements which a number of foundations filed in rebuttal to the accusations by the Committee's staff and its hand-picked witnesses.

There are some interesting accessory facts about the Report. The minority members of the Committee, Mr. Wayne Hays of Ohio and Mrs. Gracie Pfost of Idaho, announce that they were not consulted during its preparation and say that, so far as they can tell, the majority members were not consulted, either. They add that the staff, which prepared it, altered some portion of the text of the Hearings, "changing the context and meaning of questions by minority members." Also, the report contains a supplementary statement by Mr. Reece vilifying Mr. Hays, which was added to it without Mr. Hays's knowledge.

Finally, there is a remarkable omission, which is connected with some odd behavior by a member of the Committee, Mr. Angier L. Goodwin of Massachusetts. Mr. Goodwin signed the Report, thereby making it a majority report, on December 20, 1954. That is, the Report as printed carries that date. But on December 18 Mr. Goodwin gave Mr. Reece a statement of "Additional Views," which has been mimeographed. A note prefixed to it says that the Report had been filed for printing two days earlier, on December 16. In his statement Mr. Goodwin says that he dissents from the principal findings of the Report that carries his signature. He says that the Cox Committee, of which he had been a member, investigated the same charges against the foundations and explicitly and specifically denied what the Reece Report affirms. He ends the statement, "Nothing has transpired in the proceedings of the present committee to cause me to alter or modify the views expressed in" the Cox Report. Why he signed a verdict which he considered unjustified and untrue is not explained.

Most of the press has shrugged off the Reece Investigation as too idiotic to be taken seriously. I am afraid that this attitude was a mistake. The investigation was a brilliantly planned and executed attack not only on scholarly foundations but on much else besides. The Report is preposterous but it is permanently on record as the findings of a House committee. From now on it will be useful to anyone who may be interested in growing paranoia from seed.

The Cox Committee ended by reporting that the mishmash of accusations about the foundations with which it had dealt were unjustified by the facts. Mr. Reece's motives in procuring another inquiry into the same mishmash may or may not be obscure, but his purpose was clear. In July 1953 he made a speech in the House; rather, he made part of a speech and entered the rest of it in the *Congressional Record.* It was a bill of particulars which set forth the conclusions he was directing the new committee to reach. The dreamlike or phantasmagorical state in which the committee was to operate begins with this speech. It is composed of fantastic allegations presented as facts. Of the ultimate Report the minority says, "Some of the statements of fact and opinion contained in [it] are untrue on their face, others are at best half-truths, and the vast majority are misleading." That goes for Mr. Reece's speech.

Here is a specimen. Mr. Reece alludes to "a grant of $15 million to protect the civil liberties of Communists and to investigate the Congress of the United States," which he says has been made by the Fund for the Republic, an offshoot of the Ford Foundation. A couple of sentences farther on this becomes "$15 million being set aside to investigate the Congress of the United States." To Mr. Reece the grant seems not only subversive but blasphemous, and his outrage was to be faithfully echoed by his staff in the Hearings, but what is he talking about? About this: a grant of $50,000 to the highly respectable American Bar Association, a committee of which was to make seven studies of the state of individual rights under our security system, among them one dealing with "the extent to which Congress should limit the scope and regulate procedures of its investigations." Observe: not investigate but study, not fifteen million but one-seventh of fifty thousand, and not Congress but some of its committee procedures which many other organizations are studying.

The Committee was named and in September 1953 a staff of fifteen was appointed, of whom one, apparently clerical, was assigned to Mr. Hays and Mrs. Pfost. The preparation of an ex parte case occupied them eight months, till May 1954. In May and June twelve public hearings were held. Mr. Reece, Mr. Hays, and Mrs. Pfost attended them faithfully. Mr. Goodwin was present occasionally, the third majority member hardly at all. He was Mr. Jesse P. Wolcott of Michigan, a trance-bound figure whose only contribution to the proceedings was a melancholy assent to the thesis of a witness that Fabian socialism had destroyed Great Britain and was rapidly destroying the United States. "I do not like what I see on the horizon," Mr. Wolcott said. "The sun is not coming up. It is a very cloudy day in America because of Fabian socialism." His and Mr. Goodwin's proxies were in Mr. Reece's pocket, so that the minority could be voted down whenever they tried to bring realism or fairness into the hearings.

There were only twelve witnesses. Three of them were members of the staff and two were officials of the Bureau of Internal Revenue. The latter two had been brought in to represent that the foundations should be denied tax exemption because they were engaging in propaganda and financing subversive activity, but they were much too honest to do so. Six of the remaining seven had been sedulously hunted out, apparently by means of the Cox Committee files, to support the case which the staff had put together — the most bemused of them was the one who saddened Mr. Wolcott by establishing that the downfall of the United States was the work of Fabians. (The Fabians made a "beachhead" here in the early eighteen-nineties. The destruction they have wreaked on us goes back to their first great triumph of subversion, the income tax amendment.)

The other witness was Dr. Pendleton Herring, of the Social Science Research Council. His calm and lucid statement instantly reduced the staff's hurrah's nest to its constituent lies, slander, irrelevance, and nonsense. He was not permitted to complete his appearance and no one else was permitted to testify for the foundations: Mr. Reece called off the hearings. The Report says that the conduct of Mr. Hays had made further ones impossible. It also says that the foundations will be permitted to file statements and that they will thus escape "the embarrassment of cross-examination." (Yes, that is exactly how it reads; see page 2.) All along this had been the staff's idea of how to conduct the investigation. There should be no witnesses, they thought, only "research"; best simply to enter their own paste-up of selected excerpts, assertions, and allegations protected from the embarrassment of cross-examination by Mr. Hays and from any requirement that supporting evidence be offered.

The opprobrious conduct of Mr. Hays consisted of his daily effort to bring out the facts which the staff refused to submit. A witness would make an extreme, ominous, and usually irrelevant assertion of something that was supposed to be fact. Mr. Hays would force him to reduce it to a private opinion, then to a vague suspicion, and finally to mere gas. (Thereupon the Chairman would let the witness proceed on the assumption that his original wild statement had been established incontrovertibly.) Mr. Hays would demand that one or another of the scholars casually maligned by suspicion or slander be brought in and allowed to speak for himself. Mr. Reece or the staff would reply that he certainly would be as soon as the staff's case was completed, but none ever was. Mr. Hays would ask that an issue raised by a witness be explored in the interest of decency; he would be told, "Everything at the proper time," and that was the end of that. The wire services featured his success in getting a member of the staff to identify two excerpts from papal encyclicals as typical of the communist thinking that the foundations are supposed to have succeeded in imposing on our betrayed society. It was a valuable demonstration but it was less important than his obstinate struggle to expose the dishonesty, distortion, misrepresentation, and malice in the testimony that has been printed in the Hearings.

I cannot summarize here nine hundred pages of allegations that are usually crackbrained when they are not dishonest. The staff claimed to have studied only about ten foundations but succeeded in traducing several dozen. Its prime targets were those established by Carnegie, Rockefeller, and Ford money, and great professional and educational organizations to which they have granted funds. These, the case is supposed to establish, have been captured by an "interlock," a managerial caste, which uses them to subvert American scholarship, education, government, foreign policy, religion, morals, family life, and what have you. They are anti-American, international-minded, "globalist," pro-Russian; also collectivist, socialistic, and headed toward communism when not already communist-controlled. Their principal instrument of subversion is the social sciences, most of all sociology. In fact it is the social sciences that have poisoned us. They stand for "moral relativism" and "empiricism." They are subversive and the foundations finance their subversion.

The scarlet thread that unifies this hodgepodge is the theme of conspiracy. Whenever Mr. Hays was able to nail a witness down, he backed away from the word and spoke instead of a "tendency"; but the existence of an active conspiracy is frequently asserted and endlessly implied. We are to believe that a large and growing group of scholars and foundation officials are working to convert the United States into a socialistic if not communistic society, to destroy our political sovereignty, and to force world government on us. (And that many more who do not know what they are doing serve the same ends.) The conspirators have made use of "scientism," the philosophy of John Dewey, the Kinsey Report, progressive education, the New Deal, and every other principle of education or historical event that the staff could lug in. (There was an amusing moment when Mr. Reece, who represents a Tennessee district after all, had to turn a somersault in midair and come up defending TVA, which someone had said was communistic and conspiratorial.) Almost everything that has happened in or to the United States in three-quarters of a century was wholly or in part the work of this conspiracy. Its activities multiply all the time.

This mass of innuendo, insinuation, allegation, and misstatement is too insubstantial to be dealt with critically. But the last few years have made us all too familiar with the methods used to spread it on the record. It is a montage. The staff presents innumerable extracts from books, reports, and other documents wrenched out of context (frequently by elision) and made to say, or to imply or suggest, what they obviously do not mean, often the exact opposite of what they obviously do mean. Many of the assertions and innuendoes that the record contains are of such a kind that they cannot be checked or even analyzed. Many others are absurd and still others are, as the minority says, untrue on their face. The trumped-up case makes use of any material whatsoever that can be made to bring the persons and foundations involved under suspicion, indifferent when one allegation contradicts another one. It contrives to mention accusingly or suspiciously a far larger number of scholars and public figures than any earlier exercise in defamation. Other ventures have tried to defame respectable people by use of the by now wearily familiar principle of guilt by association. But the Reece Committee has created two new categories, guilt by distinction and guilt by advanced education.

And at the end of its Report the Committee draws up a new list of subversives or at least of people who are suspect. It runs 190 pages, it includes many brilliant and irreproachably patriotic people, and some of its tests for guilt are the most frivolous so far. Take the three counts against Henry Commager. He wrote "Who Is Loyal to America?" in *Harper's* and the *Daily Worker* praised it. He wrote for the *New York Times Magazine* another piece which the *Daily Worker* commended. And he was, or so the list says, on a committee of welcome for the Dean of Canterbury. Of the three equally horrifying revelations about George F. Kennan one is "Spoke on Communist China" — end of quotation.

This systematic attack on learning could not have been made honestly by sane minds, and we must not libel the staff by supposing that there was anything wrong with their intelligence. (I would like, however, to see a psychiatrist's report on three of the imported witnesses.) Quite the contrary. The attack was designed to bring into suspicion the learned foundations, the scholars whom they assist and who serve them, and the very spirit of free inquiry itself. It was designed to intimidate scholars and to undermine public confidence in them and their work.

Whether by design or inadvertently, it serves to inflame the anger of all who fear or resent the twentieth century. It is a denunciation of everything that has transformed the United States from a simple society isolated from the other continents into a complex industrial society with a necessarily powerful government and inextricably involved with world events. But its target is neither industrialization nor the process of history: it is those who try to bring intelligence to bear on them. It is an attack on inquiry, on the progress of knowledge, on education itself.

So it will serve even more vicious ends. It implements with free-floating suspicion the mole-like fears and hatreds of Caliban. It appeals to the sickness of our time, the craziness of our time, the craziness in everyone. It will be used to strengthen the neuroses of those who fear reality, fear learning, fear the uses and usages of reason. In this tragic time it is hard enough, God knows, for a stable mind to keep a firm hold on reality, to control the impulses to flee from it that we are all subject to. What about unstable minds? There are those who fear they may be inferior and therefore fear people who they think may be superior to them. There are those who are under almost intolerable pressure to flee from terrifying realities into a fantasy of past time supposed to be safe — to achieve safety by withdrawing from the present and repudiating the necessities of our age. There are those whose judgment has already been impaired by something very much like delusional beliefs — and whose fears can be converted into a conviction that there is directed at them a wholly imaginary hostility of other people, of anyone at all. But especially of a conspiracy.

To create suspicion that a conspiracy is at work is the most effective way to make such fears into "persistent, unalterable, systematized, logically reasoned delusions." We have seen the carefully propagated delusion of conspiracy dissolve away the cements that held other societies together. Here in the United States we have seen many people labor to create in troubled minds a conviction that countless men, institutions, ideas, and events constitute a conspiracy whose aim is to destroy the United States from within. Many of the best and truest among us have been defamed with suspicion for which there was no reason at all. Now the Reece Report has done what it could to taint with the suspicion of conspiracy the institutions of scholarship and learning, and to suggest that colleges and universities are agents of a conspiracy, or when not its agents, then its captives. To suggest that our high schools and primary schools and kindergartens are its victims. That the poisons it spreads are constantly at work among us, our children, our government, our press, and all the other institutions of our society.

The press was right in calling this preposterous but not in dismissing it as only that. It is the kind of nonsense that can be used to make the seeds of paranoia germinate. Is it not, in the most exact sense, subversion?

V

Treatise on a Function of Journalism

The West Against Itself

(JANUARY 1947)

IN Harper's for August 1934, I called the West "the plundered province." The phrase has proved so useful to Western writers and orators that it has superseded various phrases which through two generations of Western resentment designated the same thing. We must realize that it does designate a thing; that, whatever the phrases, there is a reality behind them. Economically the West has always been a province of the East and it has always been plundered.

The first wealth produced in the West was furs, mainly beaver furs. It made a good many Easterners rich. Partnerships and corporations sent technical specialists — trappers and Indian traders — into the West to bring out the furs. No producer ever got rich; few were ever even solvent. The wealth they produced — from the West's natural resources — went east into other hands and stayed there. The absentee owners acted on a simple principle: get the money out. And theirs was an economy of liquidation. They cleaned up and by 1840 they had cleaned the West out. A century later, beaver has not yet come back.

In the early eighteen-forties emigrants began to go west. They leapfrogged over the plains and mountains, which were settled much later, in order to get to Oregon west of the Cascade Mountains and California west of the Sierra. Their settlements were the first permanent local interests in the West and (with Mormon Utah) for decades the only ones. The emigrants expected to stay in the West and expected their descendants to go on living off the country. They made farms and set up local systems of production, trade, export of surpluses, and even manufacture. The interests of these people, the permanent inhabitants, have always been in conflict with the interests of transients, of those who were liquidating the West's resources. Their interests have not been in conflict with those of the East, in fact have been worth more to the East than all other Western sources of wealth put together — so long as the East has been able to control and exploit them, that is from the beginning up to now. The East has always held a mortgage on the permanent West, channeling its wealth eastward, maintaining it in a debtor status, and confining its economic function to that of a mercantilist province.

The development of the mineral West began in 1849. Mining is the type-example of Western exploitation. Almost invariably the first phase was a "rush"; those who participated were practically all Easterners whose sole desire was to wash out of Western soil as much wealth as they could and take it home. Few made a stake. Of those who did practically everyone carried out his original intention and transferred Western wealth to the East. The next and permanent phase was hard-rock mining or mining by placer or dredge on so large a scale that the same necessity held: large outlays of capital were required and the only capital that existed was Eastern. So the mines came into Eastern ownership and control. They have always channeled Western wealth out of the West; the West's minerals have made the East richer. (The occasional Westerner who fought his way into the system — called a "nabob" in his era — became a part of that system, which is to say an enemy of the West.)

Mining is liquidation. You clean out the deposit, exhaust the lode, and move on. Hundreds of ghost towns in the West, and hundreds of more pathetic towns where a little human life lingers on after economic death, signalize this inexorable fact. You clean up and get out — and you don't give a damn, especially if you are an Eastern stockholder. All mining exhausts the deposit. But if it is placer mining, hydraulic mining, or dredging, it also kills the land. Nothing will come of that land again till after this geological epoch has run out.

In witness of what I said last month about the West's split personality, consider this: that in the West no rights, privileges, or usurpations are so vociferously defended by the West — against itself — as the miner's. The miner's right to exploit transcends all other rights whatsoever. Even the national government is unable to effect enough control over mineral property rights to harmonize them with conflicting or even merely different rights.

Oil and natural gas follow the pattern of the mines. Because their development is comparatively recent the national government is able to exercise some control over them in the common interest, by using the lease system instead of the patents which it must issue to miners. But just because that development is recent, Eastern capital has been able to monopolize oil and gas even more completely than ever it monopolized mining. The wells, pipelines, and refineries belong to Eastern corporations. They pump Western wealth into Eastern treasuries. It is possible for a Western independent to make a mineral discovery, finance it, and maintain his local control in defiance of the absentee system; it has happened occasionally in the past and it happens occasionally now. But the wildcatter in oil, the independent, has no chance at all except to submit to the system. He may find oil without its assistance; in fact the system hopes he will. But he cannot refine or transport or sell oil except to the system, on the system's terms.

Western psychology prevents him from desiring to do anything else. Last summer I talked with the manager of a small, locally owned refinery which, with much good luck but mostly because the necessities of war had set up exactly the right conditions, had cleared its debts, secured contracts which seemed to guarantee it permanent independence, and built up an impressive surplus and reserve. It was a minute item of fulfillment of the West's great dream, the dream of economic liberation, of local ownership and control. And what had been done with that surplus and that reserve? They had been invested in Standard Oil of New Jersey.

The West does not want to be liberated from the system of exploitation that it has always violently resented. It only wants to buy into it.

So we come to the business which created the West's most powerful illusion about itself and, though this is not immediately apparent, has done more damage to the West than any other. The stock business. Now there was stock raising along the Pacific Coast before there was American agriculture there, long before there were American settlements. But the cattle business of the West as such has been conducted east of the Cascades and Sierra and in great degree east of the Rockies, and it began when cattle were brought to the open range — first to Wyoming, Montana, and the Dakotas, then elsewhere. Its great era lasted from about 1870 to the terminal winter of 1886–87, which changed its conditions forever. Changed them, I repeat, forever. But the practices, values, and delusions developed in that era, the Cattle Kingdom of romance, dominate the cattle business today.

The cattlemen came from Elsewhere into the empty West. They were always arrogant and always deluded. They thought themselves free men, the freest men who ever lived, but even more than other Westerners they were peons of their Eastern bankers and of the railroads which the bankers owned and the exchanges and stockyards and packing plants which the bankers established to control their business. With the self-deception that runs like a leitmotif through Western business, they wholeheartedly supported their masters against the West and today support the East against the West. They thought of themselves as Westerners and they did live in the West, but they were the enemies of everyone else who lived there. They kept sheepmen, their natural and eventual allies, out of the West wherever and as long as they could, slaughtering herds and frequently herdsmen. They did their utmost to keep the nester — the farmer, the actual settler, the man who could create local and permanent wealth — out of the West and to terrorize or bankrupt him where he could not be kept out. And the big cattlemen squeezed out the little ones wherever possible, grabbing the water rights, foreclosing small holdings, frequently hiring gunmen to murder them. And, being Western individualists and therefore gifted with illusion, the little cattlemen have always fought the big ones' battles, have adopted and supported their policies to their own disadvantage and to the great hurt of the West.

Two facts about the cattle business have priority over all the rest. First, the Cattle Kingdom never did own more than a minute fraction of one per cent of the range it grazed: it was national domain, it belonged to the people of the United States. Cattlemen do not own the public range now: it belongs to you and me, and since the fees they pay for using public land are much smaller than those they pay for using private land, those fees are in effect one of a number of subsidies we pay them. But they always acted as if they owned the public range and act so now; they convinced themselves that it belonged to them and now believe it does; and they are trying to take title to it. Second, the cattle business does not have to be conducted as liquidation but throughout history its management has always tended to conduct it on that basis.

You have seen the Missouri River at Kansas City, an opaque stream half saturated with silt. A great part of that silt gets into it from the Yellowstone River, above whose mouth the Missouri is, comparatively, clear. The Yellowstone is fed by many streams, of which those from the south carry the most silt, the Tongue, the Rosebud, especially Powder River, and most especially the Big Horn. Above the mouth of the Big Horn the Yellowstone is comparatively clear. These plains rivers are depressing and rather sinister to look at, and they always have been helping to carry the mountains to the sea. But one reads with amazement descriptions of them written before the Civil War. They were comparatively clear streams, streams whose gradual, geological erosion of the land had not been accelerated — as it was when the cattle business came to Wyoming and Montana. The Cattle Kingdom overgrazed the range so drastically — fed so many more cattle than the range could support without damage — that the processes of nature were disrupted. Since those high and far-off days the range has never been capable of supporting anything like the number of cattle it could have supported if the cattle barons had not maimed it. It never will be capable of supporting a proper number again during the geological epoch in which civilization exists.

That should be, though it mostly isn't, important to the citizens of Wyoming, whose heritage the West's romantic business in part destroyed. It is directly important to everyone who lives in the lower Missouri Valley or the lower Mississippi Valley, and only a little less directly important to everyone who pays taxes for flood control, relief, or the rehabilitation of depressed areas. For when you watch the Missouri sliding greasily past Kansas City you are watching those gallant horsemen out of Owen Wister shovel Wyoming into the Gulf of Mexico. It is even more important that their heirs hope to shovel most of the remaining West into its rivers.

There remains lumbering. It perpetrated greater frauds against the people of the United States than any other Western business — and that is a superlative of cosmic size. It was a business of total liquidation: when a tree is cut, a century or two centuries may be required to grow another one and perhaps another one cannot be grown at all. Also it killed the land. A logged-out forest does not take so much geological time to come back as a place where a gold dredge has worked but during the generations of men it is even more evil. The effects of denuding a forest extend as far as fire may go and beyond that as far as any of the streams on the watershed it belongs to may be used for human purposes or are capable of affecting life, property, or society.

Lumbering, however, shows several deviations from the Western pattern. First, though the greater part of the timber came into Eastern ownership, with the consequent disregard of Western interests and the usual transfer of wealth out of the West, nevertheless an important bulk of it came into the hands of Westerners. Second, the national government got on the job in time to protect vast areas of forest from liquidation — and to protect the heart of the West from geological extinction. Third, a good many of the big operators got the idea in time and it is mainly they who are now trying to maintain privately owned Western forests as a permanent source of wealth, whereas the drive to liquidate all forests comes most vociferously from small operators, who have neither the capital nor the timber reserves for long-term operation. But with lumbering as with the cattle business we see revealed the psychic split that impels the West to join its enemies against itself.

These then, with power and irrigation which we may skip for the moment, are the businesses founded on the West's basic natural resources. While these businesses were developing, the rest of the West's economic structure, the parts which are like similar businesses everywhere, was also developing. There came to be in the West agriculture, transportation, wholesale and retail distribution, all the multifarious activities necessary to society. As I have already said, they are in sum much more important to the East than the basic businesses it owns — so long as it can control them in its own interest.

II

We lack space to describe the system by which the East maintains the West as an economic fief. It has been described many times and several recent books discuss it in relation to the current Western hope of breaking it up. Mr. A. G. Mezerik's *The Revolt of the South and West* is sound but in some contexts emotional rather than factual and commits the fallacy of assuming that the modern Far West can have the same relation to the South that the Middle West had before the Civil War. Mr. Wendell Berge's *Economic Freedom for the West* is more analytical and much more realistic. Mr. Ladd Haystead's *If the Prospect Pleases* is less comprehensive than either but Mr. Haystead deals with the Western psychology that imperils the Western hope, as Mr. Mezerik and Mr. Berge do not.

The bases of the system are simple. In a striking analogy to eighteenth-century mercantilism, the East imposed economic colonialism on the West. The West is, for the East, a source of raw materials for manufacture and a market for manufactured goods. Like the colonies before the Revolution the West is denied industry. Natural evolution concentrated industry and financial power in the East but the same evolution gave all other sections but the West a sizable amount of both. By the time the development of the West began it was possible to control the evolutionary process — to finance the West in such a way that the growth of locally owned industry became all but prohibited.

The control of capital is, of course, the basic process. There is an amazing spread of interest rates between the East and the West. For such purely individual financing as real estate loans the West pays from two to three times as high a rate as the East. For the ordinary conduct of business it pays exactly what the East cares to charge and always enough to constitute a handicap in competition. But also as Western business becomes large enough to compete the Eastern financial network can either dictate to it absolutely or destroy it. This at the simplest level. Above it is the interconnected structure of finance: the monopolies, cartels, inter-industry agreements, control of transportation, and the many other instruments of power.

Take freight rates. They are devised so that the East pays lightly for the transport of Western raw materials but the West pays heavily for the transport of Eastern manufactured goods — and is prevented from manufacturing its own goods. The cowpoke on a ranch fifty miles from Sheridan, Wyoming, does not wear boots made at Sheridan. He wears boots made of leather from hides shipped from Sheridan to Massachusetts, processed and manufactured there, and then shipped back to Sheridan. The businessman of an Oregon town does not buy a desk made where the lumber is made, but in Grand Rapids whither the lumber is shipped and whence the desk is returned to his home town, paying two freight charges where he should pay none at all. The wheat rancher in Washington or Montana has to buy agricultural machinery made not in rational proximity either to his ranch or to Western deposits of iron and coal but in Illinois, Ohio, or Pennsylvania — and is mentioned here because he pays not only that tax to Eastern control of business but another one, the tariff that protects the manufacturer but builds no wall round the wheat-grower. Finally, the businessman who erects an office building in Denver or the county commissioners who build a bridge in northern Utah may indeed use steel produced within a hundred miles of the operation — but they pay on it, for the maintenance of the system, a tax assessed by the "basing point" principle that makes a satisfactory substitute for the outlawed "Pittsburg plus."

The West is permitted to engage in preliminary operations that reduce the bulk of raw material so that the East can save freight costs in transporting them to the mills where the finishing operations are performed. It is not permitted to perform those finishing operations, to manufacture finished materials into consumers' goods, or to engage in the basic heavy industries which would give it the power to blow the whole system wide open. So far as the West is industrialized, it has a low-level industry. But there are necessarily loopholes in the system: kinds of industry which cannot be prevented from developing in the West. Such loopholes do not disturb the Eastern masters. Control of credit enables them to buy them out or dictate the terms on which they may be operated. Or they manipulate patent rights or trade agreements to the same end. Or they establish a branch plant of their own which cuts the throat of the Western-owned plant. Or they merely mention these possibilities and the Western industrialist, a fiery secessionist in his oratory, joins the system.

The result is an economy bound to the industrial system of the East even where it is not in fact owned and managed by that system. That is to say, the West is systematically looted and has always been bankrupt.

There has never been a time when the West did not furiously resent all this nor a time when some elements in the West were not trying to do something about it. All the furious agitations that have boiled out of the West and terrified Eastern *rentiers* (but have seldom caused the actual engineers of plunder to turn a hair) have had the sole purpose of securing for the West some fractional control over its economic future. None of them have ever succeeded except when they could perform an ancillary service to the absentee system — like the permanently inflated price of silver, as outrageous a robbery of the American people as any ever devised by the steering committee of a patent pool. At most they have got the West an occasional tip amounting to a nickel or a dime, tossed back out of the millions drained eastward. There was never a chance that they could accomplish more. That is, there was never a chance till recent years. But now there is.

The New Deal began it. New Deal measures slowed the liquidation of resources and substituted measures of permanent yield. They operated to rehabilitate depleted resources, halt and repair erosion, rebuild soil, and restore areas of social decay. They eased credit, opened small gaps in the master system, and created much local prosperity. Such things improved the economic system and more important measures widened its base. Public power and rural electrification dented the power monopoly which I have not touched on here but which is a basic tool of the system. A great expansion of reclamation projects increased agricultural wealth and, what is much more important, made a start toward the production of surplus electric power. Finally, with such enterprises as the Central Valley Project and the stupendous, integrated plans for the development of the Columbia River basin, the New Deal laid the groundwork for a fundamental attack on the system.

The West greeted these measures characteristically: demanding more and more of them, demanding further government help in taking advantage of them, furiously denouncing the government for paternalism, and trying to avoid all regulation. But the measures began to make possible what had not been possible before. They would provide electric power so cheaply and in such quantity that great industrial development must follow in the West. The Western economic structure must be revolutionized and reintegrated — which would imply tremendous changes in the national economic structure. And for the first time the West had a chance to seize control over its own economic destiny.

The war came and the process begun by the New Deal was accelerated. Factories of many kinds sprang up everywhere. (Except in Montana, long the private fief of Anaconda Copper and Montana Power, which succeeded in preventing any serious threat to their control of labor and production.) Mr. Berge has shown how, even in the stress of war, the absentee Eastern masters were able to direct much of this development in the old pattern, to restrain it to plants that performed only preliminary or intermediate processes. But not altogether. The West got airplane plants, shipyards, plants that manufactured such complex things as tanks and landing craft, heavy machinery, packing plants, innumerable processing plants. At Fontana in California and Geneva in Utah it got basic steel production. The war also produced something else the West had never had, a large body of skilled industrial labor. Also, by building landing fields and modern airports everywhere it made at least a fissure in the monopoly of transport and took out of transport much of the handicap of time which the West has always had to carry. Finally, it exhausted the new surplus of electric power and so hastened the already contemplated production of more power.

In short, the West now has an industrial plant and the conditions for its use are favorable — and certain to become more favorable. That is the fact on which the reinvigorated dream of economic liberation rests. The plant is too heavily concentrated along the Columbia, Puget Sound, the Willamette Valley, and the Pacific Coast — more so than it would have been if the development had been more gradual — but it does extend through much of the West. And with the production of, for instance, ingots and rolled steel and aluminum, heavy industrial goods, and many kinds of finished consumers' goods, and with the certainty that the production of power will increase, the terms are changed forever. The West can at last realistically envision developing a high-level economy with all that that implies: stability, prosperity, rising standard of living, successful competition with other sections, a full participating share in an expanding national economy.

Realization that the dream can be fulfilled has made the West all but drunk. It is looking forward to the future with hope and confidence. I cannot list here the sectional and interstate associations and committees engaged in implementing the dream, the plans they are working out, the measures they are preparing, or any other specific details that have been born of a strange wedlock — the dynamics of boom which any trigger whatever has always been able to release in the West and the unique opportunity which the last few years have brought about. Enough that the West understands the opportunity, understands the possibilities of success and of failure that are inherent in it, and is taking every conceivable measure to avert failure and insure success.

With a conspicuous exception. The West seems unaware of one possibility of failure, the one that is inherent in its historic psychology.

III

SOME DOUBTS will occur to anyone. Thus if the upheaval should merely transfer financial power from Wall Street to Wall Street's California branch office, the basic system would be changed no more than it was years ago by the entrance of Chicago finance into the Western exploitation that had previously been monopolized by New York and Boston. A coastal dictatorship would merely be substituted for a trans-Mississippi one. Certain assurances will also occur to anyone and of these the principal one is that the Northwest has a better chance of pulling it off than the West as a whole. Its natural resources are more compactly concentrated and have been less impaired. The Northwest is a more self-contained unit with fewer internal frictions and the Columbia system is more uniform and manageable than the Missouri system or any other possible focus of future development. Most important of all, the Northwest seems to have got the idea that sustained use of natural resources — which is to say simply, the future — is incompatible with the liquidation of those resources in the present.

I have described a basic split in the Western psyche. Whether the great dream will fail or be fulfilled depends on how that split works out. Western individualism has always been in part a belief that I stand to make more money from letting my neighbor down than from co-operating with him. Westerners have always tended to hold themselves cheap and to hold one another cheaper. Western resentment of its Eastern enslavement has always tended to be less a dislike of the enslavement than a belief that it could be made to pay.

The oil refinery that invested its surplus in Standard Oil was hardly warring on absentee control and the same thing is to be seen throughout the West. The Wolfville Chamber of Commerce which is campaigning almost rabidly for local investment, local manufactures locally owned, integration of the local commercial system — all surcharged with violence about Wall Street, "foreign" corporations, the freight rates, and the East as such — that Chamber of Commerce is also campaigning by advertisement and paid agents to bring Eastern corporations to Wolfville. At the moment when its rhapsody of insurrection is loudest its agents are spreading out their charts on the desks of Eastern industrial managers. Look, we've got this cheap federal power at Wolfville and a labor surplus, too. The unions are feeble in Wolfville and in fact throughout the state — it's not Paterson, it's not Akron, it's a setup. We'll give you a site free and build your spur. Now as for tax abatement, just what do you need? Just what additional advantages do you need, that is, over the locally owned businesses of Wolfville we are trying to build up in order to break the stranglehold of the East?

The symptoms of the division in the Western mind show more clearly in the Western press, the newspapers, and the specialty journals of mining, lumbering, cattle and sheep growing, engineering. It is, to begin with, an astonishingly reactionary press. The Western radical who occasionally scares the East usually turns out to be advocating on his native plains something a couple of decades earlier than Mark Hanna. An average Democratic newspaper in the West would seem by, say, the advanced liberalism of the Pennsylvania state machine, to be expressing a point of view much too backward for Boies Penrose. A typical Republican editorial page in the West is written out of the economic and social assumptions of avalanche capitalism just after the Civil War. The point is that these conceptions, assumptions, and values are improperly labeled when they are called Democratic or Republican. They are Western.

One image of the West that the East accepts is that of the West not as economic peon but as pensioner of the East, as beggar. The West with its hat held out beseeching the expenditure on its behalf of federal money which must be raised from Eastern corporation and income taxes. Considering how much of that income is plundered from the West, the image is both comic and profoundly ironical. But there are ways in which it is also true. You can hardly find an editorial page in the West that is not demanding as Western right, as compensation for the West, and as assistance toward Western liberation, the expenditure of more federal funds. More government money for public health, hospitals, inspection, treatment; for schools; for service by the Bureau of Mines to the mining industry; for the improvement of Western agriculture, the replenishment of soils, the instruction of farmers; for the instruction and protection of cattle and sheep growers, the improvement of stock and range, quarantine, research; for fire protection in the logging business; for drainage; for reseeding and reforestation of private lands; for roads; for weather service; and always for dams, canals, and the whole program of reclamation.

But at the same time: hands off. The West has been corrupted, its press believes all but unanimously, by a system of paternalism which is collectivist at base and hardly bothers to disguise its intention of delivering the United States over to communism. The second column of the editorial page is sure to be a ringing demand for the government to get out of business, to stop impeding initiative, to break the shackles of regulation with which it has fettered enterprise, to abjure its philosophy of suppressing liberty, and to stop giving money to people who will only store coal in the new bathtub. The editorial is certain to have a few lines about bureaucrats in desk chairs, impractical theorists, probably professors and certainly long-haired, who are destroying the West by interfering with the men who know how. Also it is certain to be horrified by the schools, which the bureaucrats are using to debauch our young people with Russian propaganda.

An editorial typical of scores I read this summer begins, "Next to getting over our complex that we have to appease labor and give it more money every Monday A.M., our next task is to go over to the schoolhouse." It denounces a handful of revolutionary notions, including the dreadful one that "the people should own the water power and the forests," and goes on to suggest measures, of which the first is, "we would call in the principal, or the president of the university, and quiz him on why do his teachers recommend socialism. And if his answer was dubious we would get a pinch hitter to take his place."

It shakes down to a platform: get out and give us more money. Much of the dream of economic liberation is dependent upon continuous, continually increasing federal subsidies — subsidies which it also insists shall be made without safeguard or regulation. This is interesting as economic fantasy but it is more interesting because it reveals that the Western mind is interfusing its dream of freedom with the economic cannibalism of the post-Civil-War Stone Age. It is still more interesting as it reveals the West's attitude toward the federal intervention which alone was powerful enough to save Western natural resources from total control and quick liquidation by the absentee Eastern ownership.

For that preservation the West is grateful to the government. But there was and still is a fundamental defect: federal intervention has also preserved those resources from locally owned liquidation by the West itself. So, at the very moment when the West is blueprinting an economy which must be based on the sustained, permanent use of its natural resources, it is also conducting an assault on those resources with the simple objective of liquidating them. The dissociation of intelligence could go no farther but there it is — and there is the West yesterday, today, and forever. It is the Western mind stripped to the basic split. The West as its own worst enemy. The West committing suicide.

IV

THE NATIONAL PARKS are composed of lands that were once part of the public domain (plus a few minute areas that had previously passed out of it). Exceedingly small in total area, they are permanently reserved and dedicated to their present uses: the preservation of wilderness areas, the protection of supreme scenic beauties, and the pleasure and recreation of the American people. By the terms of the original dedication and by policy so far kept inviolate they are to be maintained as they are, they are not to be commercially exploited at all. But they contain timber, grazing land, water, and minerals. And that, in the West's eyes, is what is wrong with them.

The Olympic National Park contains a virgin stand of Sitka spruce, which yields a wood that was once essential for airplanes. During the war a violent agitation was conducted by logging interests (unobtrusively backed by other interests with an eye on natural resources) to open these forests to logging. It presented itself as patriotism and skillfully assimilated itself to the emotions of wartime. There was more than enough Sitka spruce in privately owned and national forests to take care of any demand but no matter: victory depended on our opening the Olympic National Park to logging. The persistence and power of that agitation and its accompanying propaganda (some of it conducted in the public schools, which are supposed to be poisoned with collectivism) would be unbelievable to anyone who had not looked into them.

The National Park Service, backed by conservation associations and by other lumbering interests which have seen the light, was able to hold fast — the Olympic Park was not logged. But immediately the war ended the same interests, augmented by a good many others, began an even more violent campaign of agitation, commercial pressure, and political pressure. We must now house the veterans and clearly we could not do so unless we opened all the national parks to logging.

That onslaught has been held in check and it will not win this time. But it will be repeated many times and the West intends it to win.

This campaign had nothing to do with Sitka spruce, winning the war, or housing veterans. Its purpose was to make a breach in the national parks policy with the aid of war emotions, and to create a precedent. Once that precedent should be set, the rest would follow. Lumber companies could log the parks. Cattle and sheep associations could graze them. Mining companies could get at their mineral deposits. Power companies could build dams in them, water companies could use their lakes and rivers. Each of those objectives has been repeatedly attempted in the past and the sun never sets on the West's efforts to achieve them. Success would mean not only the destruction of the national parks but, as we shall see, far worse.

The parks are trival in extent, though the destruction of their forests, many of which have critical locations, would have disproportionately destructive effect on the watersheds — the watersheds which must be preserved if the West is to continue to exist as a society. They are trival — the main objectives of the Western assault on the natural resources are the remnants of thc national domain, the Taylor Act grazing lands, and the national forests.

I have heard this assault called a conspiracy but it is in no way secret or even surreptitious; it is open and enthusiastically supported by many Westerners, by many Western newspapers, and by almost all the Western specialty press. Openly engaged in it are parts of the lumber industry (though other important parts of that industry are opposing it), some water users (though water users would be its first victims), the national associations of cattle and sheep growers and a majority of the state and local associations, large parts of the mining industry, the U.S. Chamber of Commerce (some of whose local chambers are in opposition), and those Western members of Congress who represent these interests. Obscure but blandly co-operative in the background are Eastern interests perennially hostile to the West and concerned here because they greatly desire to halt and reduce government regulation and to open additional Western wealth to liquidation — notably the power companies.

Right now the cattlemen and sheepmen are carrying the ball. We must confine ourselves to them and their principal objectives — remembering that the organized assault aims at many other objectives which would benefit other groups. Their limited objectives are:

(1) Conversion of the privilege which cattlemen and sheepmen now have of grazing their stock on Taylor Act and Forest Service lands — a privilege which is now subject to regulation and adjustment and for which they pay less than it is worth — into a vested right guaranteed them and subject to only such regulation as they may impose upon themselves.

(2) Distribution of all the Taylor Act grazing lands, which is to say practically all the public domain that still exists, to the individual states, as a preliminary to disposing of them by private sale. (At an insignificant price. At an inflammatory meeting of committees of the American National Livestock Association and the National Woolgrowers Association in Salt Lake City in August 1946, the price most commonly suggested was ten cents an acre.)

(3) Reclassification of lands in the national forests and removal from the jurisdiction of the Forest Service of all lands that can be classified as valuable for grazing, so that these lands may be transferred to the states and eventually sold. Immediately in contemplation is the removal of all government regulation of grazing in about 27,000,000 acres of forest lands and their distribution to the states — and to stockmen and woolgrowers as soon thereafter as possible.

These tracts compose the Minidoka and Caribou Forests in Idaho, all the forests in Nevada, most of the forest land in the southern half of Utah, and some ten or twelve million acres in Arizona and New Mexico. But that is just a start: a further objective is to wrest from Forest Service control all lands in all forests that can be grazed. And beyond that is the intention ultimately to confine the Forest Service to the rehabilitation of land which lumbermen and stockmen have made unproductive, under compulsion to transfer it to private ownership as soon as it has been made productive again. The ultimate objective, that is, is to liquidate all public ownership of grazing land and forest land in the United States. And the wording of the resolution in which the U.S. Chamber of Commerce came to the support of the program *excepted no government land whatever*. That represents the desire of most of the leaders of the assault.

The immediate objectives make this attempt one of the biggest landgrabs in American history. The ultimate objectives make it incomparably the biggest. The plan is to get rid of public lands altogether, turning them over to the states, which can be coerced as the federal government cannot be, and eventually to private ownership.

This is your land we are talking about.

The attack has already carried important outposts. Regulation of the use of Taylor Act lands, the vast public range outside the national forests, was vested in the Grazing Service. Over the last few years that service was so systematically reduced in staff and appropriations that some cattlemen and sheepmen have been grazing the public range just as they see fit. Violation of the Taylor Act is widespread, flagrant, systematic, and frequently recommended to their members as policy by various local cattle and sheep associations. The Grazing Service was organized to assist grazers and to protect the public interest. When it took the latter purpose seriously it was emasculated and this year has been killed by Western members of Congress, under the leadership of Senator McCarran of Nevada.* But Senator McCarran is by no means so extreme as the majority of the big stockmen whose interests he serves so brilliantly in Washington. His more limited

* See "Notes."

purpose is to get the public lands away from those he calls "the swivel-chair oligarchy," that is, federal officials who cannot be coerced, and into the hands of the states, that is, officials who can be coerced. His model is his own state government, a small oligarchy dominated by stockmen. At the Salt Lake City meeting I have mentioned he warned the associations that demands for private ownership were premature and might embarrass his efforts, and he is understood to have been furious when, after he had left, the combined committees declared for ultimate private ownership of all public lands.

Senator McCarran has been the ablest representative of cattle and sheep interests in Washington, against the West and the people of the United States. But from time to time he has had the help of more than half the Western delegation in Congress — most surprisingly of Senator Hatch — and especially of Congressman Barrett* and Senator Robertson of Wyoming. (New Mexico and Wyoming are the only states whose delegates to the Salt Lake City meeting were unanimous for the program.) Let us look at some of the measures they have proposed.

Senator McCarran has fathered a number of bills aimed at small or large objectives of the program. The one in point, however, is the "McCarran grazing bill" (S 33 in the last Congress) which has now been defeated four times but will certainly be reintroduced in the next Congress. This measure would give present owners of grazing permits in the national forests fee simple property rights in those permits, on the theory that if you have leased an apartment from me (at half price or less) you have become its owner. The purpose was to convert a privilege (and one that is subject to regulation) into a vested right, to confine the use of grazing rights in the national forests to the present holders of permits or those who might buy them from the present holders, and to deny the Forest Service the greater part of its present power to regulate the use of grazing lands.

The Barrett Bill of last session (HR 7638) provided for the sale of disconnected tracts of unorganized Taylor Act grazing

* Now a Senator.

land, up to four sections per tract and to the total of over 11,000,000 acres. Priority in purchase was to be granted to present lessees of those tracts. Its purpose was to let present users of public grazing lands, who pay considerably less than a fair rental, buy that land at less than it is worth — and to get public grazing land out of public regulation and control.

But the most revealing bill was last session's S 1945, introduced by Senator Robertson. The Senator is, it should be noted, the owner of one of the largest and finest sheep and cattle ranches in Wyoming. He holds a grazing permit in his own name in the Shoshone National Forest for 2400 sheep, has a financial interest in an association that grazes 1200 sheep there, and acts in various ways as agent for individuals and associations that graze nearly 8000 more sheep in the same forest. His bill is a sweetheart.

The Robertson Bill would transfer to thirteen Western states all unappropriated and unreserved lands, *including the minerals in them;* all oil and mineral reserves; all minerals, coal, oil, and gas and all rights related to them in the public lands; and all homestead lands that have been forfeited to the United States. It would empower the states to dispose of these lands as they might see fit — that is, to sell them — except that coal, oil, and gas lands must be leased, not sold, and the federal government would retain power to prorate production.

The guts of the bill, however, are the provisions which set up in each state a commission ordered to re-examine every kind of reservation of public land — national forests, national parks and monuments, Carey Act (irrigation district) withdrawals, wildlife reserves, *reclamation reserves,* power sites, and certain less important ones. The commission's duty would be to determine whether parts of the national forests in its state are more valuable for grazing and agriculture (practically no Forest Service land can be farmed at all) than for timber production, and if it should decide that any were, to certify them for transfer to the state for sale — that is, the commission is intended to get forest grazing land into private ownership. The commission's duty in regard to other reservations is to do the same in regard to grazing and agricultural land — and also to determine whether the original purposes of the reserve can be achieved by state ownership or "individual enterprise," and whether the reserves may not have lost their importance or perhaps do not justify national administration.

The Robertson Bill is both transparent and carnivorous. It would liquidate the public lands and end our sixty years of conservation of the national resources. And this single bill would achieve all the main objectives of the whole program of the Western despoilers at one step, except that purely timber lands in the forests would still be protected and would have to be attacked by other means. In some respects it goes beyond anything that had been publicly advocated by the despoilers. Nowhere else, for instance, has it been proposed to turn public power sites or reclamation reserves over to private hands. But it expresses the program.

The public lands are first to be transferred to the states on the fully justified assumption that if there should be a state government not wholly compliant to the desires of stockgrowers, it could be pressured into compliance. The intention is to free them of all regulation except such as stockgrowers might impose upon themselves. Nothing in history suggests that the states are adequate to protect their own resources, or even want to, or suggests that cattlemen and sheepmen are capable of regulating themselves even for their own benefit, still less the public's. And the regulations immediately to be got rid of are those by which the government has been trying to prevent overgrazing of the public range. Cattlemen and sheepmen, I repeat, want to shovel most of the West into its rivers.

From the states the public lands are to be transferred to private ownership. Present holders of permits are to be constituted a prior and privileged caste, to the exclusion of others except on such terms as they may dictate. They are to be permitted to buy the lands — the public lands, the West's lands, your lands — at a fraction of what they are worth. And the larger intention is to liquidate all the publicly held resources of the West.

Everyone knows that the timber of the United States is being cut faster than replacements are being grown, that the best efforts of the government and of those private operators who realize that other generations will follow ours have not so far sufficed to balance the growth of saw timber with logging. Everyone knows that regulation of grazing is the only hope of preserving the range. Open the public reserves of timber, the national forests, to private operation without government restriction and not only the Western but the national resources would rapidly disintegrate. (And presently the government, on behalf of our society as a whole, would have to wipe out private property in forests altogether.) Turn the public range over to private ownership, or even private management, and within a generation the range would be exhausted beyond hope of repair.

But that is, by a good deal, the least of it. Most of the fundamental watersheds of the West lie within the boundaries of the Taylor Act lands, the national forests, and the national parks. And overgrazing the range and liquidating the forests destroys the watersheds. In many places in the West today property in land, irrigating systems, and crops is steadily deteriorating because the best efforts of the government to repair damage to watersheds — damage caused by overgrazing the ranges and overcutting the forests — has not been enough.

Stream beds choke with silt and floods spread over the rich fields on the slopes and in the bottoms, always impairing and sometimes destroying them. Dams and canals and reservoirs silt up, decline in efficiency, have to be repaired at great expense, cannot be fully restored. Fields gully, soil blows away. Flash floods kill productive land, kill livestock, kill human beings, sometimes kill communities.

Less than a month before the joint committees met in Salt Lake City this summer, a hundred and twenty-five miles away in the little town of Mount Pleasant, Utah, the annual parade was forming for the celebration of July 24, the greatest Mormon feast day. That parade never got started. A heavy summer storm struck in the hills and gulches above town and what marched down Mount Pleasant's main street was not a series of decorated floats but a river of thick mud like concrete that, in a town of twenty-five hundred people, did half a million dollars' worth of damage in ten minutes. The range above town had been overgrazed and the storm waters which would have been retained by healthy land could not be retained by the sick, exhausted land. They rushed down over Mount Pleasant, bringing gravel, stones, and boulders with them, depositing several feet of mud, damaging many buildings and much of the town's real estate, leaving much of the grazing land above town ruined and much more damaged and dangerous.

This destruction had been predictable — and predicted; in a small way it had happened before. The government had been working for many years to restore that range but had not been able to begin the infinitely slow process soon enough. It knew and had repeatedly said that such a catastrophe might happen just as and where it did happen.

The same thing has happened repeatedly in Utah, in some places more destructively, in others less so. It has happened and goes on happening throughout the West wherever the grazing land of watersheds has been exhausted or their forests overcut. Mud flows and flash floods are dramatic but only occasional, whereas the steady deterioration of the watersheds and the slow destruction of their wealth go on all the time. Overgrazing and overcutting — and fire, the hazard of which is greatly increased by heavy cutting — are responsible. The program which is planned to liquidate the range and forests would destroy the Western watersheds. Which is to say that it would destroy the natural resources of the West, and with them so many rivers, towns, cities, farms, ranches, mines, and power sites that a great part of the West would be obliterated. It would return much of the West, most of the habitable interior West, to the processes of geology. It would make Western life as we now know it, and therefore American life as we now know it, impossible.

There you have it. A few groups of Western interests, so small numerically as to constitute a minute fraction of the West, are hellbent on destroying the West. They are stronger than they would otherwise be because they are skilfully manipulating in their support sentiments that have always been powerful in the West — the home rule which means basically that we want federal help without federal regulation, the "individualism" that has always made the small Western operator a handy tool of the big one, and the wild myth that stockgrowers constitute an aristocracy in which all Westerners somehow share. They have managed to line up behind them many Western interests that would perish if they should succeed. And they count on the inevitable postwar reaction against government regulation to put their program over.

To a historian it has the beauty of any historical continuity. It is the Western psychology working within the pattern which its own nature has set. It is the forever recurrent lust to liquidate the West that is so large a part of Western history. The West has always been a society living under threat of destruction by natural cataclysm and here it is, bright against the sky, inviting such a cataclysm.

But if it has this mad beauty it also has an almost cosmic irony, in that fulfillment of the great dream of the West, mature economic development and local ownership and control, has been made possible by the developments of our age at exactly the same time. That dream envisions the establishment of an economy on the natural resources of the West, developed and integrated to produce a steady, sustained, permanent yield. While the West moves to build that kind of economy, a part of the West is simultaneously moving to destroy the natural resources forever. That paradox is absolutely true to the Western mind and spirit. But the future of the West hinges on whether it can defend itself against itself.

Sacred Cows and Public Lands

(JULY 1948)

THE CONSTITUTION of the United States does not provide for Congressional blocs, pressure groups, and corporate lobbies but under our unwritten Constitution they have become organic in our government. They are instruments for applying political power in the solution of specific political problems and by now it would be impossible to govern a hundred and fifty million people without them. But their development has given journalism an additional political function, that of keeping their operations publicized.

This article describes the application of political pressure to a specific problem of administration. It shows a committee of the House of Representatives acting in obedient response to a pressure group. The committee is the Subcommittee on Public Lands of the House Committee on Public Lands. The pressure group consists of certain Western cattlemen and sheepmen operating through various of their state associations, their two national associations, a joint committee of the national association, their agents and lobbyists, and their trade press. The immediate objective of the activities described here was to prevent the U.S. Forest Service from making certain reductions in the number of livestock permitted to graze on certain portions of the national forests.

That was the immediate objective but various long-term objectives must be borne in mind. Permits to graze stock in national forests are licenses, not rights, and are subject to regulation, modification, and revocation: for years the pressure group we deal with has been trying to vest the present holders of such permits with permanent rights. It has also been trying to secure such vested rights to present holders of grazing permits on other publicly owned ranges administered by the Bureau of Land Management. Associated with both efforts is a recurrent one to open both kinds of public land to private purchase and to give present holders of permits priority over other buyers, a long period to decide whether or not they want to buy, and the right to buy at the value of the grazing privilege alone, without regard to other uses of the land. In the background are still more astonishing aspirations. The pressure group has periodically undertaken to convert first to state and eventually to private ownership whatever land can be grazed that now belongs to other public reservations, for instance the national parks. It has thereby attracted the sympathy of more powerful interests whose ultimate hope is to destroy the established conservation policies of the United States.

That larger hope interests us here only indirectly. We deal with a small minority group of stockgrowers, with the Subcommittee on Public Lands, and with the hearings which that committee held in the West in August, September, and October 1947. The records of those hearings have been printed. I use ten volumes of them here, two being records of preliminary hearings in Washington in April and May of 1947. I can touch on only a small part of them: eight of the volumes contain more than twice as much reading matter apiece as is printed in an issue of *Harper's*. Some things that happened at the hearings were kept from print by the standard device of declaring them off the record. In addition I suspect that sometimes the printed record may not do the facts full justice. A witness at one of the hearings sent me the part of the typed transcript that contained his testimony: in some respects it differed from the corresponding passage in the printed record.

II

THE PRESSURE GROUP dealt with here consists of only a small fraction of the Western livestock industry. For the most part it consists of large operators who hold government permits to graze cattle and sheep on publicly owned land. By no means all the large operators who hold such permits and only a small minority of the large operators in the Western industry belong to it. The group claims to speak for the industry as a whole but it does not. When you inquire what percentage of Western stockgrowers belong to the two national associations, for instance, you get not figures but polite evasions: it is a small percentage. Many local cattle and sheep associations have officially repudiated the objectives of the group, asserting that they were not consulted about the pressure campaign and have had no part in it. Since the ultimate objectives of the group were publicized in the early part of 1947, the number of stockgrowers who had opposed them has steadily increased.

The group claims that the entire livestock industry of the United States is in deadly peril because the Forest Service is reducing the number of stock grazed in national forests. Well, all told something more than a third of the sheep raised in the United States and about one-seventh of the cattle are raised in the West. Of these by far the greater part are not grazed in the forests at all: 91 per cent of the cattle and 73 per cent of the sheep. Those that are grazed there spend, on the average, less than four months of the year on forest ranges. In other words the national forests supply a little more than 2 per cent of the grazing for Western-owned cattle and a little less than 7 per cent of the grazing for Western-owned sheep. And of these small numbers only a microscopic fraction are affected by the Forest Service reductions that produced all the uproar.

Grazing in the national forests is wholly permissive. You and I as co-owners license stockmen, for ridiculously small fees, to graze their herds there subject to the regulations of the Forest

Service. Moreover, grazing is a subsidiary use of the forests, which are dedicated by law primarily to the production of timber and the protection of watersheds. Timber production is much more important than grazing, especially in view of the growing timber famine, but watershed protection is more important still. The stock business of the West, its agriculture, its mining, its industry, and its community life all depend on the healthy condition of its watersheds.

The basic fact is that in many places the national forests have been dangerously overgrazed. Early practices of the Forest Service were in part to blame. Scientific range management has developed only in the twentieth century: the Service has had to learn from its own mistakes and in the beginning authorized more grazing than, as the outcome proved, the range could stand without deteriorating. More important, however, was the overstocking of the range during the First World War, when public demand for increased meat production forced the opening of the forests to much greater numbers of livestock than they had ever carried before. Widespread damage resulted, to the forest ranges, to the forests, to the vital watersheds they contain. Ever since then the Service has been working to repair the damage and to reduce grazing to a safe amount. It has not yet succeeded and many forest areas are still being overgrazed, with continuing damage to the range, the forests, and the watersheds. In some places this damage has become critical, in a few it has come close to the edge of disaster.

And there is another equally important fact. Some of the grazing ranges in the national forests had already been very seriously damaged by overgrazing when the forests were established.

The pressure group has consistently opposed regulation of grazing by the Forest Service but most of all it has objected to the reduction of the number of cattle and sheep permitted in the forests. (There are still more cattle in them than there were in 1905.) Meanwhile unregulated grazing on other public lands has damaged them far worse. By 1926 the forage value of 84 per cent of the unreserved public domain had been cut in half. By 1932 further depletion of these ranges, plus the anarchy of the stock business, forced stockgrowers themselves to demand government regulation. Under the Taylor Act most of the remaining public domain was organized and turned over to a new agency, the Grazing Service. When the Grazing Service undertook to reduce overstocking of ranges and to raise grazing fees to a respectable fraction of what the grass was worth, it was marked for destruction. Senator McCarran of Nevada obliged. After a three-year campaign he succeeded in getting the Grazing Service merged with the General Land Office to form the Bureau of Land Management. Then he got the new agency's appropriations reduced to the point where it was administratively impotent, a captive of the stockmen it was supposed to regulate.

It was during the final stages of the attack on the Grazing Service that plans for a similar attack on the Forest Service were matured. The Forest Service program for reducing the number of stock grazed in the forests was continuing. The need for it had become more urgent because in some places the deterioration of the range had become critical, because the wartime increase of population in the West necessitated a higher land-use policy, and because that increase also necessitated every possible measure that would develop, conserve, and protect the water supply which absolutely conditions Western life. The reductions in permitted grazing made by the Forest Service have been smaller than impersonal regard for public policy would require, they have been gradual, and except when an emergency situation called for drastic action they have been made with extreme consideration of the stockgrowers whose permits were being cut. They have been made only after discussion with the permit holders, usually after consultation with specialists and the local advisory boards, and always with complete freedom of appeal through the administrative channels of the Service up to the top. All these facts are brought out by the printed record.

Necessarily, however, some reductions bore severely on individual operators, and no stockman who does not see the wisdom of protecting the future of his own grazing can rejoice in any reduction of his permit. The pressure group, in whose eyes no land that can be grazed has any other value, was angered and alarmed. Something had to be done about the Forest Service. If the advisory boards which consulted with the Service could be given administrative power, then stockgrowers themselves could control grazing in the forests. If grazing permits could be given the status of legal rights, then reductions could not be made. Better still would be to get the grazing areas out of the jurisdiction of the Forest Service and into that of the Grazing Service. A number of bills providing for such measures were introduced or prepared for introduction in Congress and the propaganda arm set up a vociferous advocacy of them or, alternatively, for such as could be effected by executive order. But best of all would be to turn all publicly owned grazing lands in the United States over to state ownership, as a step toward private sale, or to open them directly to private sale.

It was here that the pressure group attracted the support of interests far more powerful. But it was here too that trouble began. Too many stockgrowers and their local associations were opposed to such a program. Too many other interests would suffer from it — agriculture, mining, industry, power, villages and towns and cities, hunters and fishermen, dude ranchers. Too many conservation organizations and too many newspapermen found out what was being planned. Too great a national interest was at stake.

A tentative formulation of plans was made in August 1946 at a meeting in Salt Lake City of the Joint Committee on Public Lands of the American National Livestock Association and the National Woolgrowers Association. In *Harper's* for January 1947 I described those plans and during the next few months other writers described them in other magazines and newspapers. There has never been any refutation of what we said about them. There never will be — stockgrowers who oppose the plans and conservation organizations have transcripts of the Joint Committee's meetings. And in the Denver *Post* for February 2, 1947, the Vice-Chairman of the Joint Committee published an article which verified what we had said.

This premature publicity stopped the program in its tracks. Public opinion in the West was so instantly outraged, so many organizations began to protest, so many Western newspapers lined up in opposition that the program had to be — temporarily — abandoned. Bills implementing it had been prepared for introduction in the new Congress. They were never introduced — and various Congressmen hurried home to explain to angry constituents that it was all a mistake, that they had been cruelly misunderstood. There is no chance that, in the immediate future, any effort will be made to open the public lands to sale. The program has been laid away for future use; at present the issue is too hot for anyone to touch.

But, as the pressure-group press pointed out, there are various ways of skinning a cat. There was the immediate problem of halting the Forest Service cuts in grazing permits — it was too late to stop them for 1947 but how about 1948? There was the continuing problem of bringing the Service to see things as the pressure group wanted it to — by means of threat, by intimidation, by defamation. Stockgrowers' publications were filled with denunciations of the reduction program as unnecessary, unjust, and arbitrary. Stock associations memorialized Congress, accusing the Forest Service of despotic and illegal administrative policies, and demanding an investigation. The legislature of Wyoming demanded an investigation and suggested that it be made by the Public Lands Committee of the House or the Senate. The legislature also pointedly alluded to Forest Service appropriations, and this club — such a reduction of appropriations as had hamstrung the Grazing Service — began to be brandished in the trade journals with increasing frequency. Demands for the dismissal of forest rangers, forest supervisors, and regional foresters were made. A college professor who had discussed the proposed landgrab in a radio broadcast was prevented from repeating his talk. The mail of Congressmen was filled with complaints against the Forest Service, so similar in phraseology that a common source was indicated.

Seldom has so much noise been made about so small a matter. Remember that all told the forest ranges supply only two per cent of the grazing for Western cattle and only seven per cent of that for Western sheep. Consider too that the proposed cuts for 1948 would reduce sheep grazing in the forests by only two-tenths of one per cent and cattle grazing in them by only three one-hundredths of one per cent. It was in order to prevent this minute reduction that the pressure group organized its campaign. It concentrated on a proposal that no reductions in grazing permits be made for three years and that during this "test period" an investigation be made to determine whether any reductions whatever were needed.

This is the pressure to which Congress and its committees yielded. It yielded all the more rapidly because the election of 1946 had made Congress Republican and so had given the Republicans the chairmanships and the majority representations in congressional committees. On February 4, 1947, the House Committee on Public Lands resolved that its Subcommittee on Public Lands would hold public hearings on the grazing policies of the Forest Service. On April 17, 1947, the House of Representatives authorized such hearings with House Resolution 93.

Before the House Resolution was passed, the April issue of the *American Cattle Producer* published a "Notice to Forest Permittees," signed by the executive secretary of the American National Livestock Association. The same "Notice" was published by the *Record Stockman* and the *New Mexico Stockman* and by other trade periodicals. It announced that hearings were to be held in the West and called for letters of complaint against the Forest Service, "in order to furnish this [the Congressional] committee with as much background material as possible." It listed seven kinds of complaint that would be most helpful to the committee. Its final paragraph thanked the prospective complainants for their help and remarked, "Generally speaking, it is the complaint of forest users that the Forest Service is judge, jury, and prosecuting attorney, all in one. In other words, it is a law unto itself." At the hearings so many witnesses faithfully parroted those words that they became embarrassing.

III

The House Committee on Public Lands, of which Congressman Richard J. Welch of California is chairman, consists of twenty-five members of Congress and the delegates from Hawaii, Alaska, and Puerto Rico. Under the Reorganization Act it is charged with duties formerly distributed among six committees. Twenty-two of its members besides the three delegates compose the Subcommittee on Public Lands, of which Congressman Frank A. Barrett of Wyoming is chairman.* It was the Subcommittee that held the hearings. The number of its members who attended them varied; so far as I can make out from the record no more than nine were ever present at one time; ten signed the letter addressed to Secretary Anderson when they were over. Since the touring Congressmen were members of other subcommittees that had work to do in the West, some of the hearings did not touch on the Forest Service.

The Subcommittee had already scheduled hearings on Congressman Barrett's annual attempt to abolish the Jackson Hole National Monument. They were held in Washington April 14–19, 1947, and the printed record contains some illuminating items. Mr. J. Byron Wilson, chairman of the legislative committee of the National Woolgrowers Association and a registered lobbyist for the industry, indeed one of the most skillful lobbyists who have ever worked in Washington, appeared as a witness favoring the abolition of the Monument. The testimony of such a person about such an issue would seem farfetched and irrelevant if it were not obviously part of a pattern. The pressure group is interested in undermining all federal authority over any part of the public lands, and to abolish one national monument would create precedent for further inroads. The same reason explains the appearance of the U.S. Chamber of Commerce. The manager of its Natural Resources Department testified in person and a

* Under a later reorganization the parent committee has become the Committee on Interior and Insular Affairs.

telegram from a member of its Natural Resources Committee was entered in the record. They were speaking officially for one of the larger interests which I have said feel an affinity for the pressure group's ultimate aims. At that time it was standing on a platform for distributing the public lands to private ownership more extreme than any other that has been acknowledged in public. A year later, however, in May 1948, it retreated from that extreme and revised its statement of public lands policy, which is now rather mild.

Congressman Barrett's bill for abolishing the Jackson Hole Monument would have transferred some of the land in it from the National Park Service to the Forest Service. The record, therefore, strangely shows Mr. Wilson, the lobbyist, and Mr. J. Elmer Brock, the Vice-Chairman of the Joint Committee, praising the Forest Service for efficiency, co-operativeness, administrative skill, and expert knowledge. Other stockmen even praised its grazing policies. And with this praise Congressman Barrett found himself in generous agreement. Since he was harrying the Park Service, the Forest Service seemed to him, by comparison, a superb organization. The same oddity was to be repeated later in the year. When Mr. Barrett staged his production in Wyoming, Colorado, and Utah, the Forest Service was staffed with incompetents, petty tyrants, swivel-chair bureaucrats, and impractical theorists. But when the committee moved to Lake Crescent, Washington, where there was a proposal to detach a large tract of timber from the Olympic National Park and turn it over to the Forest Service, for two happy days the Service found itself admirable and expert again.

The committee held a preliminary hearing on Forest Service policy in Washington on May 12, 1947. The only witnesses were officials of the Service, who described the grazing policies and the multiple problems they involve. Chairman Barrett, a lawyer by profession, had prepared the pressure group's complaints with admirable thoroughness and put them on the record like a lawyer's brief and pleadings. The tone for the hearings that were to follow was set right there. Mr. Barrett's arraignment was hardly a foundation from which a fact-finding inquiry could be conducted. He was not going to be judicial; to use the language of the "Notice to Forest Permittees," he was going to act as prosecuting attorney on behalf of the pressure group and against the Forest Service. As such, he conducted this hearing very ably and with frequent cinematic effects.

Mr. Barrett is a very intelligent man. So are most of his fellow committeemen, though I confess that I cannot follow with full understanding the excursions of Mr. Lemke's mind — present at only a couple of hearings, he seemed to be principally interested in providing booster advertising for the State of North Dakota. Both their impartiality and their competence to make such an investigation as they were about to embark on are, however, another matter. Chairman Barrett, Congressman Robert F. Rockwell of Colorado who played the second lead, and Congressman Wesley A. D'Ewart of Montana are all stockgrowers. The last two hold grazing permits on the national forests. Congressman A. L. Miller of Nebraska, who understudied Mr. Barrett and Mr. Rockwell, revealed at Lake Crescent that he could not recognize a burnt-over area in a forest. (He wondered if those blackened snags might not be the "over-mature" timber that lumbermen were so passionately eager to cut down for the common good.) Since no one who knows anything at all about forests can fail to identify the marks of fire, a faint doubt of his qualifications for judgment rises in one's mind.

The record is upholstered with stately congressional courtesy, committeemen's ornate praise of one another as "your distinguished Representative," and topical references to "this great State." One who reads it comes to see that Congressman Peterson of Florida, who did not go West but attended the Washington hearings, wanted to bring out the facts. So did Congressman Crawford of Michigan, who attended in Washington and got back from an official trip to Alaska in time for some of the Western hearings. So especially did Congressman Fernandez of New Mexico, who frequently pinned down outrageous statements by witnesses, forced equivocation into the open, and drew out facts that except for him would have been buried under abuse. Mr. Fernandez, in fact, is the only member of the committee who seems to have been actively interested in giving the Forest Service a hearing. But the necessity of all congressional committeemen to play ball on one another's home lots was dominant. This was Chairman Barrett's show and he must be allowed to stage it as he pleased. Mr. Rockwell supported him brilliantly. Dr. Miller (he is a Fellow of the College of Surgeons) backed them up well and, at Rawlins, went farther in attacking a witness than anyone else did anywhere. He was, however, obviously astonished to learn how small were the fees charged for grazing in the forests. His repeated elicitation from witnesses of the fact that they paid the Forest Service only about one-fourth of what grazing cost on the privately owned ranges of his home state was a discordant note.

The first hearing in the West was held at Glasgow, Montana, August 27, 1947. It was concerned with engineering projects and some public lands under the jurisdiction of the Soil Conservation Service; Forest Service matters were not mentioned. They were first taken up at Billings, Montana, on August 30. And here, if I read the script correctly, the performers went up in their lines. Mr. Barrett indulged in some of the blustering accusations of the Forest Service that he was to make much more prodigally later on, but the audience did not respond. For Montana was not answering the "Notice to Forest Permittees"; Montana was, on the whole, well satisfied with the Forest Service. A few officials of stock associations made complaints but they did not follow the outline of the "Notice" and seemed to be merely *pro forma.* A few individual stockmen expressed grievances, but these proved to be trivial and mostly irrelevant to the inquiry. Whereas a large number of individuals and associations, stockmen, chambers of commerce, veterans organizations, civic and sportsmen's societies, labor unions, and others had turned up to testify in favor of the Forest Service. The meeting had certainly not been planned as a vindication of the Service but it certainly turned into one. Moreover, as many as twenty-nine individuals (including the Governor of Montana) and organizations made it clear that they knew of plans to turn the grazing lands of the forests over to other agencies, to the states, or to private sale. They made it clear too that they were violently opposed. It was here that Chairman Barrett and Senator Edward V. Robertson of Wyoming — whose reason for sitting with a House committee and cross-examining witnesses is not clear — began to assert that they had never favored any such measures and in fact had never heard of any.

The assault on the Forest Service, then, made no headway at Billings. It is easy to see why. The Service completed its adjustments of permitted stock to the carrying capacity of its Montana ranges twenty years ago, and the stockmen are fully satisfied with them. Those ranges are now sound and healthy — the Montana forests are the only ones of which this is wholly true — and the resultant benefits to stockmen and public alike are fully evident. No one would dream of suggesting that greater numbers of stock be grazed on them. The Billings performance was a bust.

On September 2, however, the road company moved to Rawlins, Wyoming. This is Mr. Barrett's home state and in a couple of Wyoming forests the critical condition of watersheds had made some of the proposed cuts in grazing permits very large. "The hearing as I understand it is for the stockmen," a witness remarked. Though Mr. Barrett hastened to cover that break by pointing out that they were for the general public, the witness was telling the obvious truth. The hall was packed with an uproarious audience of stockmen, who had obviously assembled on call. They yelled, stamped, and applauded; the pressure group's witnesses and the active committeemen, the Chairman and Messrs. Rockwell and Miller, played up to them. Moreover, the oversight made at Billings was corrected. Forest Service witnesses, witnesses who wanted to testify in their behalf, and witnesses appearing for conservation societies were held to very short periods, mostly at the end of the day. Most of their formal resolutions and statements were not read but only entered in the record for later publication. At the end of the day Congressman Miller spoke of the hearing as a "spanking" of the Forest Service and the word is mild. "I have sat through dreary hours," said Mr. Charles C.

Moore, President of the Dude Ranchers' Association, "listening to repetition, testimony of personal problems, testimony filled with useless verbiage; of the approximate fifteen hours of testimony, less than one hour and one-half was accorded our side for discussion of matters supposed to be taken up by [the] committee." Mr. Moore made a formal protest and added, "Never in all my experience have I attended a meeting so one-sided and unfair, so full of bias."

Mr. Moore's judgment must stand. Comparatively few specific complaints against the Forest Service were made. Some of them were quite footless, others consisted of accusations for which no supporting evidence was offered. For practically all the others the Forest Service had factual and unanswerable rebuttals in its records of the cases, which show misrepresentation by the complainants or completely just and judicial handling by the Service. Most of these case histories, however, were not entered in the record till later: the audience did not hear them and the committee could not have seen them when it made its recommendations.

The committee was willing to listen to wholly irresponsible accusations. Hostile witnesses, for instance, charged the Service with the intention of eventually eliminating all grazing of livestock from the forests. This is an accusation circulated by the pressure groups in order to arouse the fears of stockgrowers; it is untrue and absurd. The Service has invested fifteen million dollars in range improvements (on behalf of the very men who were lying about it), extensive programs of range development are under way, and the demands of witnesses that these programs be speeded up sufficiently revealed that they knew they were lying. Equally vicious was the repeated statement that the Forest Service had destroyed its own ranges. Again, one witness said, "The forests of the West furnish the major portion of the summer pasture used by its stock," and this clear falsification (I have given the true figures above) is typical of much reckless testimony. Its purpose must have been either to inflame public opinion or to set up a drawing account of propaganda to be used later on.

The intention to discredit the Forest Service showed clearly in the testimony of officers of state and national stock associations. What they had to say was extremely generalized. The proposed reductions in grazing permits, they said, were unfair, arbitrary, and quite unnecessary. There was no need for reduction. The ranges were not in bad shape. Forest Service scientists did not know what they were talking about, they did not know how to manage ranges, their researches and experiments were silly and their reports wrong. Besides, only stockgrowers understood range conditions and no stockgrower would ever overgraze a single acre. Again, the Service was heavily overstaffed — the threat to get its appropriations cut down glints here. Again, it was not spending enough money for range improvements. (It is spending all it can get from Congress. And the state of mind from which these complaints issued is revealed in the bellyache by one witness that the Service was heinously squandering public money in building forest roads for fire protection). Again, it was spending taxpayers' money for propaganda against stock interests. (This means that the Service, in its regular publications, has reported that some of its ranges are in bad shape and that there is opposition to its repairing them by reducing grazing. It is required by law to make such reports. In 1947 its total expenditure for education and information, including all bulletins and reports on all the manifold activities of forestry, was less than one-half of one per cent of its appropriation.) And, the accusation ran, the Service had incited attacks on the stockgrowing industry by foreign, that is to say Eastern, journalists. This also is entirely untrue; since it involves me I am discussing it in this month's Easy Chair.

The printed record shows Congressmen Barrett, Rockwell, and Miller acting as open partisans and shows their more than occasional belligerence toward Forest Service officials and witnesses who wanted to testify in the interest of conservation. At the end of the evening Mr. J. Byron Wilson, the lobbyist, made his inevitable appearance and got consent to enter a statement for the record. It skillfully summarized all the accusations that the hearing had produced and it ended by calling for a congressional investigation of the Forest Service. The Service, Mr. Wilson said, had grown so powerful that it was no longer accountable to Congress and an investigation would disclose that all the nonsense spouted about it at Rawlins was true. That demand for an investigation was not there idly or by chance: it was helping to lay some groundwork.

At Rawlins Chairman Barrett told the two highest Forest Service officials present that they were in for a tougher time at Grand Junction, Colorado, and he knew what he was talking about, he had advance information. A larger, more noisily contemptuous audience had been assembled there, and the "Notice to Forest Permittees" had been well implemented. A mimeographed broadside had been prepared and copies of it were distributed to everyone who entered the room. A quotation will be instructive.

> *The Forest Service is a child of Congress, grown up without parental discipline or instruction, an arrogant, bigoted, tyrannical off-spring, the same as any off-spring reared in the same manner, void of respect of law or customs of our land or the rights or feelings of other people.*
>
> *We now demand the Congress to accept the responsibility of this outrageous off-spring and put the restraining hand of parenthood to guiding it in the straight and narrow way before it runs afoul of some sterner justice.*

The reader will observe an interesting resemblance to Mr. Wilson's formal statement at Rawlins, though Mr. Wilson writes more suavely and grammatically. He will also observe the threat of mob violence in the second quoted sentence, another revelation of a state of mind. Let him remember that what the Forest Service is here accused of is action to protect the national forests from damage by improper grazing. Our forests and our children's.

The hearing at Grand Junction was better stacked than the one at Rawlins. Witnesses were required to sign cards and specify the subject they wanted to speak about. By a selective use of these cards, the testimony of conservationists, water users, city officials, and representatives of protesting organizations was kept to a minimum. (They were booed by the audience.) Almost all of them were limited to five minutes apiece, though there was as much time for complainants as they wanted. The Forest Service officials, who had been grouped together like prisoners, were not asked to make an answering statement until the evening session. Then Mr. Barrett announced, "I thought . . . we should give Mr. Watts and Mr. Dutton or any of their subordinates about fifteen minutes or more to answer any of the charges that were made here today."

So far as those charges were specific, they were practically all trivialities, distortions, or misrepresentations. The factual reports of the Forest Service disprove and dispose of them step by step — and reveal their reckless malice. But again those reports were entered in the record later on. They were not heard by the audience and could not have been consulted by the committee before it made its recommendations.

If the witnesses were out of bounds, so were the active committeemen. This is from the *Record Stockman,* which highly approves the behavior it is describing: "His [Chairman Barrett's] arms waved; he pointed an accusing finger at the Forest Service section of the huge, tense crowd. As he finished, his voice quaking with emotion, a large majority of the crowd rose to its feet, applauded, and hurrahed." This is from a report by the chairman of an Arizona conservation group: "Representative Barrett did all that he could to undermine the authority of the Forest Service, to belittle the scientific work that has been accomplished by some of the leading experts of our country, to discredit its employees from the Chief of the Forest Service . . . down to the Supervisor and Rangers." This is from a report by a representative of the Izaak Walton League: "Rep. Frank A. Barrett . . . launched into a shouting, fist-clenching outburst that was intemperate in language and at times reached screaming intensity." There are other eyewitnesses' descriptions of Mr. Barrett's passion and the record shows that Mr. Rockwell was not far behind him. It also shows that, almost at the end, a stockgrower from "the same [national forest] where Bob Rockwell runs cattle" testified that we haven't much to complain about in our neighborhood and we are getting along all right with the Forest Service."

It was gaudy, gorgeous, and inflammatory. But it was a tactical mistake. Officials of cities whose water supply had been acutely endangered by overgrazing and especially a representative of the Colorado State Planning Commission got into the record factual descriptions that turned a bright light on the folly of the complainants. Other conservationists, among them cattlemen and sheepmen from the ranges under discussion, in the brief time allotted them controverted and rebutted much of the testimony that had been so noisily presented. A representative of the Farmers Union who had been gagged by the five-minute rule wired to Speaker Martin of the House that the committee's "firing-squad hearings" were "a shocking exhibition" and "a reflection on the dignity and decency of the House of Representatives." And a large part of the Colorado press began to protest. The Denver *Post* spoke of "Stockman Barrett's Wild West Show." The Gunnison *Courier* used stronger language in editorials too long to be quoted here. The *Daily Sentinel* of Grand Junction, a town whose water supply was in danger, said in a blistering editorial that the committee was "weighted in favor of one side and presided over by a chairman, also a party to the controversy [he was not a party directly], missing no opportunity to denounce the other party in the dispute, which was given limited opportunity to present its case." And so on — the surge of public opinion was like that which had followed exposure of the land-grab scheme earlier in the year.

There were prompt reactions. The committee called off the hearing it had scheduled for Phoenix, presumably because conservation societies in Arizona were organizing to receive it. And when it moved to Salt Lake City, on September 8, things were different. The same kind of witnesses (sometimes the same witnesses, in fact) began the familiar act. But they ran into the mobilized opposition of a state which had been alarmed by repeated catastrophies resulting from overgrazing ranges, which understood that only by protecting its water supplies could it survive, and which knew that the one realistic hope of protecting them lay in the Forest Service and its co-operation with other government bureaus that direct conservation. Mayors of cities, representatives of many civic and labor and veterans organizations, stockmen, sportsmen, farmers, engineers, plain citizens forced their protests into the record. The pressure group had run into the hard fact of higher land use and its spokesmen were stopped cold.

On September 20, after hearings elsewhere on other subjects, the committee was in Redding, California, dealing with the Forest Service again. The "Notice to Forest Permittees" was doing its stuff, and to a reader of the record the mob spirit makes the Redding hearing seem uglier, more reckless and sinister, than any other. But also the demonstration seems fantastic and it was certainly futile. Then, after hearings on unrelated subjects in California, the committee moved on October 4 to Ely, Nevada. Here something exploded in its face.

A member of the Joint Committee presented a long, well-argued, brilliantly written summary of the theses and arguments on which the pressure group stands, with their single-minded concentration on grazing interests to the exclusion of all others and their plain distortion of the realities. He was arguing for transfer of the forest grazing lands to the emasculated Grazing Service (now the Bureau of Land Management) which, as I have said, is helpless to oppose the will of stockgrowers. Also he permitted himself a kind of talk common among his colleagues but heretofore sagaciously kept out of their testimony before the committee. The power of the government to regulate grazing, he said, "seems more nearly modeled on the Russian way of life" and though we are opposing Russian autocracy, in government regulation of the range we are building "that very same system." To protect the ranges, the forests, and the watersheds is communism.

But Nevada is a desert state and life there, even more straitly than elsewhere in the West, is a function of the water supply. So something like the breaking of a dam occurred. Beginning with the mining industry, the most important one in the state, and running through practically every other way of life, witness after witness repudiated as unsafe the proposed transfer of forest grazing lands, denounced proposals to sell the public lands, and backed the Forest Service to the hilt. As the flood rushed on, the congressional attorneys for the prosecution were uncharacteristically silent. The hearing turned into a rout, and a couple of days later the member of the Joint Committee who had testified was writing to Nevada newspapers, explaining that what he said had been horribly misinterpreted.

IV

THE COMMITTEE had visited only one of the forests whose condition it had undertaken to investigate. (That trip occupied only part of one day and the range visited was not one of those whose deterioration the Service wanted to offer in evidence.) It had not seen the reports of the Forest Service which replied to the complainants it had listened to. But, though it did not report to Congress under whose Resolution it was acting, it was willing to make recommendations. It made them in a letter to Clinton P. Anderson, the Secretary of Agriculture. That letter is dated October 8, 1947, four days after the Ely hearing, and it is signed by ten members of the committee. But by October 4 the committee had already begun to disperse and go home: the printed record and the local newspapers show that only five members were present at Ely. The letter must have been written in California before the hearings ended. What it said might just as well have written in Washington in April.

The letter made six recommendations about Forest Service administration of grazing. Five of these recommendations were pure smoke screen — they dealt with practices effectively in operation already or with procedures which anyone would favor. The sixth recommendation, number two in the letter, was the payoff, the one for which the entire campaign had been conducted: "Effective immediately and extending for a three year 'test' period there shall be no reductions made in permits."

Conceivably pressure-group propaganda and the violent emotions encouraged at the hearings might have created a force which the Secretary would have found too great to resist. But the hearings had gone too far — their excesses, their partisanship, and the resulting misrepresentations were obvious — and so he was able to stand firm. In a letter to Congressman Barrett dated January 13, 1948, Mr. Anderson accepted the five immaterial recommendations but rejected the one on which everything pivoted. He accompanied his rejection with a detailed analysis that disposes of the charges so tiresomely repeated at the hearings. He demonstrated that the cuts made in grazing permits were not unnecessary or unduly large or arbitrarily imposed, that Forest Service administration is not capricious or biased, that its officials and representatives are not ignorant of the stock business but in the main know it through long experience, that its experts are not impractical theorists but scientists standing on the irrefutable findings of their science, that the Forest Service is doing justice to stockmen and protecting both their interests and those of the public. His letter makes mincemeat of the propaganda.

The Secretary's letter was just, courageous — and final. The hearings of the Subcommittee on Public Lands had failed of their immediate purpose. The three-year "moratorium" on cuts in grazing permits had been killed.

But those who watch over the interests of a pressure group neither slumber nor sleep. Though the hearings failed of their immediate purpose, they got said and printed a great deal of stuff that may be useful for the long haul. The demands for a congressional investigation of the Forest Service and other government bureaus that deal with the public lands, which were made repeatedly, were made with an eye to the future. They can be used in the effort to force the Forest Service to accept dictation from the pressure group: they add teeth to the threat to get its appropriations cut down. What is more important still, they are an open bid for the support of stronger and wealthier interests that would profit from any change in conservation policy, from any loosening of government regulation of the public lands, and especially from extinction of the public-lands reserves.

Such threats, always dangerous, are especially so in an election year. In March 1948, a pressure-group spokesman testifying before a subcommittee of the House Appropriations Committee proposed just such an investigation — and Congressman Barrett, appearing before the same committee, backed him up. Congressman Engle, a member of Mr. Barrett's subcommittee, has called for "an impartial study" — and the phrase always means a study which will find that the ranges are not overgrazed. General Patrick J. Hurley, campaigning for the Republican senatorial nomination in New Mexico, has pledged his "support to a thorough investigation" of what he calls the Forest Service's "unreasonable domineering bureaucratic management" of "grazing rights." (Complete adoption of the propaganda: there are no grazing *rights* in the forest: there are only leasehold permits.) Mr. Harold E. Stassen has adopted not only the pressure group's position but that of the landgrabbers at large and has called for "a major revision of public-lands policy." No major revision of public-lands policy is possible except one that would put an end to the public lands. And though Governor Dewey promptly attacked Mr. Stassen's position, he did so in words that made conservationists shudder and suggest that the public lands would by no means be safe in his hands.

There are other straws in the wind. In the May Easy Chair I called attention to a resolution by the New Mexico Woolgrowers Association which demanded a reduction of Forest Service appropriations in order to bring the Service to heel. Since then the same resolution has been adopted by the cattlemen's association of the same state and equivalent ones have been adopted by other state associations. Both of the national associations and various of the state associations have increased their publicity funds and begun a campaign "to neutralize unfavorable publicity against the cattle [and sheep] industry" — that is, to neutralize such articles as this one. Pamphlets, canned news stories, and press releases carrying the pressure-group message are now in full production. Two weeks before this was written an article clearly inspired by the pressure group and packed with obvious untruths appeared in a magazine of national circulation. (Mr. Kenneth A. Reid has already exposed the misrepresentations it contains, but his detailed analysis is not likely to be circulated on the same scale.) Various professional writers have been approached about presenting "the stockgrowers' side." (None I know has yet accepted.) An earlier agitation by the national associations to present that "side" is shaping up as a guided tour for editors, reporters, and feature writers through the Western stock country.

Even the landgrab is stirring again, though, as I have said, there is at present no chance that it can get congressional support. Since the committee hearings, some of those who testified that they had never heard of it have come out in favor of part or all of it. At its annual convention in January 1948, the National Woolgrowers Association resolved that national parks and monuments (our wilderness and scenic reserves) ought to be opened to grazing and that "all lands not of timber value" (including watersheds) ought to be removed from the jurisdiction of the Forest Service. A month earlier the Secretary of the Wyoming Stockgrowers Association asked that those same lands be given "public domain status for ultimate State or private ownership," and he said the same thing more guardedly at the convention of the Izaak Walton League in February. In November 1947 the Farm Bureau Federation of Wyoming officially demanded that *all* the public lands except national parks and monuments eventually be turned over to private ownership. (There go the forests and, when someone remembers them, the graves of the Seventh Cavalry.) The pressure-group press alternates between declaring that no one has ever made such proposals and demanding that they be put into effect at once.

By itself, the pressure group cannot succeed in any of these attempts. In a fighting speech Secretary Anderson asked the New

Mexico Cattle Growers Association, "If there is going to be a battle, who has the most votes — the livestock ranchers or a combination of conservationists, game protective associations, public power enthusiasts, and the water users? Who is going to come out second best?" This small minority of Western stockgrowers, with their refusal to take into account any interests but their own immediate ones, their ignorant and arrogant rejection of scientific knowledge, their noisy but so far inept propaganda, will always lose out as long as they do not get allies.

But there are two dangers. The attack on the Forest Service is only one part of an unceasing, many-sided effort to discredit all conservation bureaus of the government, to discredit conservation itself. It is a stubborn effort to mislead the public. Conceivably it could succeed. And it could produce formidable combinations. Ever since the public lands were first withdrawn from private exploitation the natural resources they contain have been a challenge and a lodestar to interests that were frustrated when the reserves were made. Those interests are much more powerful now than they were then. The natural resources husbanded for the common good have enormously increased in value. The consumption of natural resources not publicly reserved has astronomically increased the lust to get at those that have been saved. If the interests that lust to get at them should form an effective combination they could bring the United States to the verge of catastrophe in a single generation.

The danger is not Western; it is national. Fifty per cent more saw timber is cut every year than is grown to replace it — what would happen to our future wood supply if the national forests should be turned over to private ownership? The widespread impairment of range lands is a naked fact and our tariffs amount to a subsidy to stockgrowers to destroy them — what would happen if government regulation of the publicly owned ranges should be ended? East of the Sierra and the Cascades, Western agriculture is absolutely dependent on irrigation — can the United States at large afford to let dams and irrigation systems silt up and cropland deteriorate because of unwise grazing and lumbering that destroy watersheds? Business, industry, population growth, and life itself in the West are absolutely dependent on the fullest possible production of water — can the United States carry eleven states bankrupted by floods, a falling water table, and the destruction of land, business, and wealth that results from them?

These overwhelmingly important questions are given a sharp irony by the fact that they must be asked at a moment when a new era in conservation is beginning all over the world. Awareness of the necessity of protecting natural resources is now more widespread than it has ever been before, and in the United States, the first nation that ever made conservation a public policy, the happiest omen is that this awareness has spread not only among the public but among scores of nationally important businesses and industries as well. But at the same time the acknowledged goal of other businesses and industries is to put an end to conservation forever. That is what gives national significance to a minute fraction of the cattle and sheep growers of the West who are hammering away at the program here described. We must keep an eye on them, inconsiderable as they are. But it is infinitely more important to make sure that no support of their program by anyone else goes unobserved.

Statesmen on the Lam

(JULY 1948)

I WANT to treat at greater length several topics merely glanced at in my article about the hearings before the Subcommittee on Public Lands. The first of them is what Senator Robertson of Wyoming, at the Billings hearings, called "the biased and prejudiced articles which have been appearing in weekly papers and monthly magazines." He and Congressman Barrett, at Billings and again at Rawlins, were referring to articles by Mr. Arthur H. Carhart, Mr. William S. Voigt, Mr. Kenneth A. Reid, Mr. Lester Velie, and me. The articles of Mr. Reid and Mr. Voigt have appeared mostly in publications of the Izaak Walton League. Mr. Carhart, for years a specialist in wildlife management, has written for various magazines. Mr. Velie is an editor of *Collier's* and in the summer of 1947 published there two articles that dealt primarily with the efforts of the pressure group I have described to get hold of the public grazing lands. His articles and the one I published in *Harper's* for January 1947 were the ones most often referred to at the hearings.

Both Senator Robertson and Congressman Barrett accused the Forest Service of "collaborating" in articles about the attempted landgrab. No, let's speak as cagily as a politician who is mending fences. They insinuated that the Forest Service had done so. Senator Robertson "came to the conclusion" that an Izaak Walton League pamphlet had been worked out in collaboration with the Forest Service and had been printed in the same shop as Agriculture and Interior Department pamphlets, which could only mean the Government Printing Office. (Whether he meant to imply that Forest Service funds had paid for it is anyone's guess.)* Congressman Barrett said, "I don't know whether the Forest Service has collaborated with some of these writers in these magazines or not. I have reason to believe it has; I'll say that much, I'm not charging you with it but I really feel deep down in my heart that you have."

The Forest Service has never asked me to write anything, has never suggested that I write anything, has in no way collaborated with me in anything I have written. It has volunteered no information to me. It has given me no information except at my request and the information it has given me is only of the kind which it is required by law to give to anyone who asks for it. Senator Robertson's toes were pinched by my having published in *Harper's* the number of sheep for which he held grazing permits in a national forest. I knew that he held grazing permits, I had asked the Forest Service for the exact figures, and I had got them. At Rawlins he asked Mr. Lyle Watts, the Chief of the Forest Service, "Information as to individual permits of permittees, is that given out by the Forest Service to these writers?" Mr. Watts replied to the Senator that when anyone wants to know how many stock anyone runs on a forest under permit, the Forest Service would tell him. "That," Mr. Robertson said, "would be Mr. DeVoto as well as Mr. Velie." It would be Mr. DeVoto; by law it would be anyone who might ask. The privileges of a Senator do not extend to keeping his grazing permits secret.

More interesting are Senator Robertson's and Congressman Barrett's efforts to dissociate themselves from proposals to open the public lands to private purchase. At Rawlins Mr. Reynold A. Seaverson, the President of the Wyoming Woolgrowers Association, read a long statement. At the end of it Senator Robert-

* The Senator knew that the Printing Office could not possibly print anything for private parties and that Forest Service funds could not possibly be so used.

son said, "I do not see any recommendation at all that the lands comprised in the national parks and monuments, the national forest lands, or the reclamation withdrawals should be sold to individual stockmen. You make no recommendation such as that, do you?" Mr. Seaverson said no. Mr. Robertson: "You never have?" Mr. Seaverson said no. Senator Robertson: "Speaking as president of the woolgrowers, you would definitely say that such a statement made by Mr. DeVoto, or Mr. Velie, or any of the Izaak Walton leagues, or any dude ranches in this country, to the effect woolgrowers advocate such a purchase by private individuals is absolutely without foundation, would you not?" Mr. Seaverson: "Yes, Senator, without foundation whatsoever."

The impression created here is that Senator Robertson had never heard of any such proposals, that none had ever been made, and that Mr. Velie, other writers, and I had malignantly invented the notion in what Mr. Barrett called our "scurrilous articles." Well, on March 14, 1946, Mr. Robertson had introduced into the Senate his bill S 1945, which I described in one of my scurrilous articles. This bill, if it had passed, would have granted to the states all the organized Taylor Act grazing lands, lands to be eliminated from various other public reserves, and "all lands eliminated as hereinafter provided from national forests, national parks or monuments . . . " It would have made mandatory the creation of state commissions and the elimination from national forests of any lands which those commissions should find "to be more valuable for grazing [in whose eyes?] or agriculture than for timber production." And it provided that all these lands and all other lands which under its terms were to be granted to the states, "shall be subject to lease, sale, or other disposition as the legislature of such State may determine."

At Rawlins, Senator Robertson was strikingly ignorant of the provisions of his own bill. True, he did not write it but he must have read it and there can be no doubt that he discussed every item in it many times with many people. Moreover, in his official statement Mr. Seaverson had recommended that lands "suitable only for grazing" [who decides?] be eliminated from the forests.

This, of course, is not a recommendation that they be sold, though such a recommendation usually accompanies that proposal. Conceivably, except in private discussions, neither Senator Robertson nor the witness had heard of the many proposals to open Taylor Act land and forest grazing land to sale that had appeared in the stockgrowers' press, or of the twenty-nine protests against them made at Billings three days before, though the Senator was present there. Conceivably they had heard none of the repercussions of the article by the Vice-Chairman of the Joint Committee in the Denver *Post* which said that "as a first step toward acquiring ownership of the land they use" the stockgrowers proposed that "the government be required to offer [the Taylor Act lands] for sale" and went on to admit that "stockmen hope" eventually to get into private ownership "some tracts now in national forests" and others "which never should have been included in national parks."

Conceivably. But the record shows that Senator Robertson was present at the opening of the Rawlins hearing at which he later questioned Mr. Seaverson. It seems odd that he did not hear the acting clerk of that hearing, at Mr. Barrett's direction, read a statement by the Governor of Wyoming, the Honorable Lester C. Hunt. Mr. Hunt's statement, so short that I think most people could keep it in mind, ended with several recommendations. The fourth one reads, "That the Federal Government either dispose of these forests (*a*) to private ownership, or (*b*) to the respective States in which they are located." For a few minutes, one would think, the Senator must have known openly about some of the proposals which his bill would have enacted, if only inadvertently, into law.

Congressman Barrett said at Glasgow, "So far as I know, no one in Congress ever advocated granting the forest or the timberlands to private ownership." At Rawlins he dissociated himself from such proposals and told a witness that Senator Robertson's bill, of which by then he *had* heard, was dead. Its spirit was not dead in November 1946, when a convention of the Wyoming Woolgrowers Association was discussing one of the bills which my articles mention as having been in preparation when the landgrab scheme was publicized. The Casper, Wyoming, *Tribune-Herald* for November 14, 1946, reports Congressman Barrett's speech at that convention. It quotes him as saying that 51 per cent of the area of Wyoming belongs to the federal government and then going on, "We must work out a plan whereby the eleven public land States of the West can grow, develop, and promote their own economy on a free and equal basis. The problem is to work out a plan for returning these millions of acres to the States. If such a plan is evolved, I believe we can sell the plan to the whole Congress . . . "

Finally, it is worth noting that, after Mr. Velie's articles and mine had been thoroughly denounced by Mr. Barrett and Mr. Robertson at Rawlins, Mr. Charles C. Moore asked that they be entered in the record. Page 219 of the record at Rawlins, Mr. Barrett speaking: "We will consider it; there has been objection by the committee; Dr. Miller has objected." They were not entered in the record.

Observe that Mr. Barrett speaks of "returning" the public lands to the states. The pressure-group press habitually speaks of "returning" them to the states or to private ownership. This is high-quality dust for throwing in the eyes — or should I say wool for pulling over them? True, the public lands contain some microscopic tracts that were once state land: mostly they represent either even-up exchanges or purchases of land that had been forfeited to the states for nonpayment of taxes. There are also microscopic tracts which were once privately owned but for which the government exchanged equivalent tracts, usually agricultural, from public reserves. There are other tracts, agricultural land abandoned as submarginal or cutover forest land, which the federal government bought from private owners for purposes of conservation. The total area of all these tracts makes only an infinitesimal fraction of the public lands. Except for that minute fraction it would not be possible to "return" the public lands to state or private ownership. They never belonged to the states or to individuals. They have been publicly owned ever since their acquisition from France, Mexico, and Great Britain.

By the acts of admission the Western states were granted various tracts of the public land within their borders, to support education and for other purposes; these are the state lands. By their constitutions the states renounced forever all claim to the remaining public lands. These lands, the public domain of the United States, however, remained open for entry by individuals under the Homestead Act, various grazing and timber and irrigation acts, the malodorous Timber and Stone Act, and others. But from time to time parts of the public domain were closed to private entry and as "reserves" dedicated to the common good and benefit of the United States: the national forests are one such reserve. They are exactly what the term says and what they have been from the beginning, public lands. When the propaganda talks about "returning" them to the states it is talking nonsense. When it talks about "resuming the historic land-ownership policy of the United States," it is talking about a policy from which the public reserves were excepted, exempted, and withdrawn. (And one which failed tragically in the arid West.) When it draws analogies between these lands and lands in the East to which the original states had a more or less undefined claim, which they relinquished to the federal government, and which were then opened to private entry — it is perverting historical fact. But all this is grist to the mill. The idea is to set up a specious claim that the Western states have been robbed of their heritage. The further idea is to demand the Western public lands if Hawaii and Alaska are granted parts of the public reserves when they are admitted as states. But the basic idea is to get the forests and grazing lands of the West that are now a common possession of the American people into private hands.

The state of mind behind this agitation is sometimes grotesque. The Vice-Chairman of the Joint Committee on Public Lands of the two national stockgrowers associations is testifying in favor of abolishing the Jackson Hole National Monument — now composed of land always under federal ownership to which Mr. John D. Rockefeller, Jr., has been trying to add as a gift land which he has bought. "First of all," he says, "I deny that the federal government has any right to that land. It has no right by its treaties of acquisition. It has no right for the proposed retention of those lands, which are now outside its constitutional limitations of land ownership . . . To me when you get a lot of federal bureaus operating and managing lands which are not the proper function of government provided in the Constitution, it is nothing more or less than a mild form of communism. And that malignant growth in the West is almost destroying the American form of government . . . There is an arrangement [for?] taking our lands away from us, in violation of constitutional limitations and our act of admission as a State." Here the gentleman seems to be saying only that to reserve lands for national parks and monuments is communism. But in his article in the Denver *Post* two months earlier he had said flatly, "Federal ownership or control of land is a form of communism."

His constitutional argument is based on the clause in Section 8 of Article I of the Constitution, which confines to areas ten miles square the legislative authority of Congress over tracts granted by the states to the government for governmental use, the authorization of the District of Columbia. Few constitutional ideas so absurd have been aired in public since 1787 but this sort of thing, if not accepted by his associates, is nevertheless useful to their purposes. The gentleman lives in Wyoming: one wonders what authority he accepts as guaranteeing his title to the land he owns there. And one is reminded of a suggestion made some years ago by a writer who had been studying the cattle-baron state of mind that germinates such arguments. Over its history, he said, under stockgrower control, Wyoming had failed to develop the mature responsibility for self government that statehood requires, and he saw no plausible evidence that it ever would develop it. He proposed that Wyoming be returned to territorial status so that it could be governed responsibly.

Such curiosa, however, are harmless. A really dangerous irresponsibility is the refusal of such stockgrowers as the Joint Committee represents to admit that overgrazing damages the forage, the land, or the watersheds. The record of the hearing is spotted with assertions that the results of overgrazing were in fact not due to it at all. The heaped-up, irrefutable findings of many sciences and many scientists — in various government bureaus that deal with land, in state and private universities, in private foundations, in experiment stations, in similar institutions all over the world — are ignored, denied, or ridiculed. I have space to mention only one example, the common denial that natural processes of erosion are speeded up — and unnatural erosion caused — by the deterioration of plant cover which occurs when an area is grazed too heavily. No fact that science deals with is more firmly established, but the pressure-group propaganda — and as I showed here last year, that of the U.S. Chamber of Commerce — challenges and denies it.

Some members of the Subcommittee were willing to support that denial. At Rawlins Mr. Barrett said, " . . . it seems to me that the Forest Service ought to make a little study of this thing [erosion — the service has been studying it intensively from the beginning] and be a little honest about it, and say here 'This thing has been going on for centuries; it was going on before there was a cow in Wyoming; that it was going on before there was ever a white man in Wyoming . . . ' Why blame it on the poor sheepherder and the little old cowboy that's trying to make a living here on these hills?" There are places in Wyoming where the poor sheepherder and the little old cowboy have accelerated erosion several hundred thousand per cent and permanently impaired the range, but science does not impress Mr. Barrett. And the jocose Mr. Rockwell at Ely: "Geologists [scientists who apparently can be trusted about the condition of the land millions of years ago but not today] say the original height in my State of Colorado was 36,000 feet. It has now gone down to 10,000 feet. I wonder what the Forest Service would have done to prevent that loss, had they been in service at the time." An entire psychology is compressed in that arrogantly ignorant sneer. At Grand Junction Mr. Rockwell had listened to scientific evidence which proved that the water supply of that and other Colorado towns had been endangered by erosion resulting from overgrazing. At Salt Lake City he had heard how erosion resulting from overgrazing had brought an entire Utah county to the brink of catastrophe — and how scientific measures to arrest erosion and repair the damage it had done had saved that county. But that was the talk of long-haired scientists and only a practical stockgrower, such a man as Mr. Rockwell, is qualified to judge the condition of a range.

Against such a state of mind as this only the force of the ballot can defend the public interest. Argument, demonstration, proof, considerations of higher land use, of long-term values, of any values except the immediate ones of the pressure group cannot alter it in the least. I come back to Secretary Anderson, asking a secessionist group of cattlemen who, if it should come to a battle, had the most votes. It may come to a battle — it could come as early as the appointment of Republican Secretaries of Agriculture and the Interior.

If the West cannot control the exceedingly small number of people whose program would destroy it, the rest of the country will have to control them for the West's sake and its own. Up to twenty Western votes in Congress might be swung to support that program, and such a bloc might be enough to hold the balance of power. But your Representative has a vote that counts as much as any other. Better make sure that he does not cast it on this issue in ignorance of what is at stake.

Two-Gun Desmond Is Back

(MARCH 1951)

THE HUMBLE sheep-walker has come down from the rocks and the bronzed horseman rides again. They are after the national forests in thirteen Western states; they have been for years. They tried to steal them in 1947, together with all other public lands that could grow a little grass, but they got stopped. They decided that they had been trying to get away with too much at a time, so now they will settle temporarily for control of the forests, with some additional tricky stuff thrown in. Understanding that the methods they thought up for themselves in 1947 were too crude, they have hired some brains to brush a little suavity and finesse over the steal. You have got to know about it because it is your property they want to alienate.

As I said in *Harper's* at the time, if the 1947 effort had succeeded it would have been the biggest landgrab in American history. All the public lands that could be grazed at all were to undergo forced sale to stockmen. Those that were being grazed at the time were to be sold to the stockmen who were using them, sold at a rigged estimate of the grazing value alone without regard to other uses or values, and the happy beneficiaries of their own thrift were to have up to forty-five years to pay the gratuity. Any public land that wasn't being grazed but had some grass on it was to be sold on the same terms to the queue of stockmen lined up for it, and presumably anybody who could graze a cow in

Yosemite Valley or on the lawn in front of headquarters at the Custer Battlefield could bid it in. The plan had the simplicity of the pastoral mind. But it was barefaced fraud and the pastoral mind did not get away with it. It endangered so many Western and national interests, private as well as public, that as soon as the light was turned on it public opinion killed it. The bills that had been written were never even introduced into Congress; as one of the Congressmen who had been detailed to smooth the way remarked out loud, once the public found out about them they became too hot to handle.

But, again as I pointed out in *Harper's*, there are many ways to skin a cat. The boys got out a different skinning knife and went to work on the Forest Service. The idea was to bring it into disrepute, undermine public confidence in it by every imaginable kind of accusation and propaganda, cut down its authority, and get out of its hands the power to regulate the grazing of stock in the national forests. The last has always been a major objective, not the ultimate objective but one that is a prerequisite for everything else in the plan. The Forest Service is the federal agency charged with administration of the national forests on behalf of the public. Grazing is only a minor, subsidiary, and contingent use of the forests, and the Service has to regulate it in accordance with a safe and equitable balance of all other uses. To regulate it, especially, to prevent stockmen from overgrazing the forest ranges, impairing or even destroying them, and gravely endangering other and more important forest values.

Precisely that is what the stockmen want to prevent. They want to get the power to regulate grazing taken away from the Forest Service and turned over to the stockmen who use the forest ranges. Everybody who has ever looked into the matter knows what that would mean.

Let's be clear about something else: this is not the Western stock business as a whole. About nine-tenths of the Western cattle business and about three-fourths of the Western sheep business never touch the national forests at all. The pressure campaign is conducted by a joint committee, now called the Grazing Committee, of the two big trade organizations, the American National Livestock Association and the National Wool Growers Association, working with various state organizations and a variegated assortment of other helpers. A good many of the small local stock associations and a good many Western stockgrowers as individuals oppose the campaign but they seem unable to make their opposition count. Don't ask me why the bulk of their Western colleagues simply stand by and let things slide; I have never understood why. One does not suspect them of undue saintliness and yet with amazing disregard of self they unprotestingly accept the handicap of the preferential treatment which their competitors who use the forest ranges get from the Forest Service and the public.

As taxpayers they help subsidize that preferential treatment—and so do you. For every dollar a stockman pays to graze his stock on national forest land, one who leases privately owned grazing land pays at least three dollars, sometimes as much as six dollars. The public, including you, pays the difference; it subsidizes the user of forest ranges by writing off two-thirds of his grazing fee. It then spends part of what it does get improving the range for him.

You and the lessee of privately owned grazing, however, take a worse beating than that. A lot of publicly owned land, the remnants of the Public Domain, was organized into grazing districts under what is known as the Taylor Act, districts which are administered by the Bureau of Land Management, Department of the Interior. (The Forest Service is a bureau of the Department of Agriculture.) For reasons and by methods which I have several times explained here, the local stockmen soon got effective control of the Taylor Act lands. So where a holder of a Forest Service permit pays a dollar for grazing, and where the lessee of private land pays at least three dollars, the Taylor Act licensee pays at most twenty-five cents. (Currently there is a move on—it probably originates in Moscow—to raise this to about twenty-nine cents.) The subsidy here is eleven-twelfths. You are paying it. The legislation which the Grazing Committee has worked up proposes a study of grazing fees on forest ranges with a view to revision. Guess what "revision" means.

As co-owners of both the Taylor Act lands and the national forests, you might require Congress to see to it that your licensees get their hands out of your pocket and pay the market rate for grazing, and I don't say that wouldn't be a good idea. Or if your heart bleeds for the sunburned supplicant for your bounty — how long since you could afford a sirloin? — you might at least require him to bid competitively for the privilege of using your ranges. When someone wants to cut timber in your forests he has to enter a sealed bid against all others who want to bid and can make the required guarantees. Not the cowboy and the shepherd, types who are always bellyaching about bureaucratic tyranny.

The national forests are the property of the American people. By far their greatest value, Western and national, is the preservation and protection of watersheds. The West is arid country; not only its solvency but its very survival depend on its water supply. On the safeguarding of that water supply and the utmost possible production of water the expansion of industry in the West depends, and the expansion of Western industry may be a matter of life and death to the United States if full-scale war comes. Any future expansion of Western agriculture also depends on water production. Vital parts of every important watershed in the West are in national forests — and stock grazing is a threat to a watershed the moment it becomes overgrazed. Many watersheds have been damaged by overgrazing, and the efforts of the Forest Service to reduce and repair the damage — in large part by reducing the number of stock grazed in areas that have deteriorated — have always met with truculent opposition by the stockmen. A prime objective of this campaign, as of all its predecessors, is to end the power of the Forest Service to reduce the number of stock in overgrazed areas. To prevent a public agency, that is, from administering the public land for the public benefit.

There is no legal right to graze public land. The stockmen have long been trying to create such a right by legislation, to make it adverse to all other forest uses, and to vest it in the present holders of grazing permits — thus handing themselves a fine capital gain at public expense. Grazing on the public lands is a privilege and the man who holds a grazing permit is a licensee. In the forests, moreover, grazing is a subsidiary use, subsidiary not only to water production but to other uses which are worth more to the public and to the balance of properly managed land units as a whole. The forests are after all forests, not primarily grazing areas. They contain the only federally owned merchantable timber, federal reforestation is conducted on them, and they are the basis of the national forestry program. And they have many other uses. In the Western forests to which the proposed legislation is to apply there were just under 17,000 grazing permits last year. There were about 35,000 "special use" permits, ranging from private summer camps through commercial recreation enterprises and on up to prospecting and mining. There were 15,000 revenue-producing timber sales. And more than 16 million people used these same forests for recreation. The proposed legislation undertakes to subordinate all such uses to stock grazing and then to take the regulation of grazing away from the Forest Service.

I have space to mention only some of the proposals; I will return to the subject some months from now. Most of them are familiar and all of them are aimed at the constant objectives of the stock associations. They undertake to give local boards, composed of the stockmen who use the ranges they are to pass on, the administrative power that is now vested in the Forest Service, ultimately that of the Secretary of Agriculture. The regulation of grazing, that is, would be vested not in the representatives of the public but in the grazers. On their consent all other uses of grazing areas would depend. Any kind of emergency action in the public interest would be impossible. If drought, fire, flash floods, a bad winter, or one of the sudden lapses from productivity to which overgrazed land is subject should threaten the water supply of a Western town or irrigation district, no action could be taken unless the local board of licensed grazers should, as the proposed bill puts it, "concur."

Even if the board should concur, no holder of a permit could be required to make any changes in less than five years, by the end of which irreparable damage might be done to the range, to the public interests, and to other private interests.

The proposed bill provides that no holder of a grazing permit can have it canceled, or the number of stock it licenses him to graze reduced, if he has borrowed money on it. Nothing is specified about these immunity-producing loans except that they be "bona fide." If I lease a store building from you, that is, I can force you to extend the lease indefinitely and on the original terms so long as I can get someone to lend me money on it. No amount or percentage specified; just legal tender.

The bill also provides that if land for which a grazing permit has been issued is turned to some other and higher use, or if the number of stock it licenses is reduced, then the holder of the permit shall be "compensated" to the extent of the "damage" he may suffer. Damage not to private property, that is, but to the subsidy he gets from the public. If you want to change the terms of the lease I hold for your store building when renewal time comes, you must pay me damages. Nice going. No miner, prospector, water user, timber cutter, or dude wrangler — no other user of the forests supposes he is entitled to a bonus.

These are some of the proposals the stockmen intend to make for getting administration of the national forests into their own hands and cutting themselves a melon. There are others, including a tricky one that would change the basis of investment in home property by which many grazing regulations are now scaled. They add up to the old game with a new backfield formation. But the proposed legislation contains a more dangerous threat to the national forests, the public lands in general, and the national stake in conservation. It is worded to take advantage of any possible change in public-lands administration and it seems to favor unification of land-management policy. That is a very pious idea — or would be if the plain intent of the whole game were not to bring the regulation of grazing in the national forests under the Taylor Act, and if this wording were not aimed to bring it under the Taylor Act if the Executive Departments of the government are reorganized.

The possibility that precisely this might be tried has kept a lot of conservationists from favoring the establishment of a Department of Natural Resources, as a task force and a minority report of the Hoover Commission proposed to do. We foresaw as all too easily possible what the stock associations are in fact now trying to bring about: the degradation, rather than the improvement, of public-lands management. Unification of grazing land under one bureau would indeed be desirable — if certain fundamental principles were applied to it and if certain fundamental values were safeguarded. One absolute consideration is this: the national forests are multiple-use lands and grazing in them will always be a minor use, whereas the Taylor Act lands are primarily grazing lands and have only minor value for other purposes. For reasons repeatedly explained here it will not do to concentrate the management of public grazing land under the Bureau of Land Management as it is now set up. The former is what the present stock-association campaign is trying to do immediately, and the latter is what the phrasing of its proposed legislation is designed to insure.

You had better watch this, now and from now on. The landgrabbers are on the loose again and they can be stopped only as they were before, by the effective marshaling of public opinion. Your property is in danger of being alienated, your interests and those of your children are threatened, and your money is to be used to subsidize a small percentage of the Western stock business while it makes further inroads on the public wealth. If the proposed legislation has not been introduced in Congress by the time this column is printed, it soon will be. The only question is whether the boys will try to do it by a series of first downs or with a touchdown pass that puts everything in one bill. You had better make sure that your Representatives and Senators understand quite clearly what is going on and where you stand. Then if you don't belong to one of the conservation societies, join one and keep in touch.

Another thing. The landgrabbers have a habit of talking loudly and indiscreetly. Loud talk in a hotel lobby in Salt Lake City, one summer evening in 1946, was what enabled a reporter to dig out the record of a secret meeting of the Joint Committee, publish the carefully guarded plans for the landgrab, and so touch off the public outcry that stopped it. Right now the stock associations are claiming out West that this time they have got the Department of the Interior on their side. They are saying that the Bureau of Land Management and the Bureau of Reclamation favor their proposed legislation.

This cannot possibly be true but the cowboys can gain a lot of ground merely by claiming that it is. For people remember occasions in the past when parts of Interior have lusted to get back jurisdiction over the lands that were withdrawn from it when the Forest Service was created. The plausibility thus traded on ought to draw a flat declaration from Director Clawson and Commissioner Straus that they do not favor the legislation and that no one under their authority will be permitted to assist it.

For there could be no better way to divide the forces of conservation than to let that old issue be revived even in appearance, and no better way of assuring the victory of anti-conservation forces than to increase or create rivalry among the federal bureaus that are charged with conservation. The public needs a solid front, absolute co-operation among those bureaus, and the bureaus need the united support of all conservationists. The brains the cowboys have hired are trying to serve their clients by the old and formidable game of dividing the opposition. We have all got to be on guard, to walk the bounds and keep our eyes peeled, and that goes for your representatives in Congress.

Billion-Dollar Jackpot

(FEBRUARY 1953)

THREE WEEKS after the election the Denver *Post* ran an editorial pointing out the necessity of maintaining "the public's right to protect its own land." It did not know, the *Post* said, whether the incoming Administration would retain or replace a U.S. district attorney who had filed suit against two Colorado ranchers for grazing sheep on the public lands without a permit, but in either event the suit must be fought through. For its outcome might well determine whether the benefits received from nearly half a billion acres of publicly owned land "shall go to the people who own the land or to those who, under any other name, may still be classified as trespassers."

In short, could the public continue to control the use and prevent the abuse of its property? "We favor," said the *Post*, which, I point out, is a soundly Republican newspaper, "we favor the maximum beneficial use by the people of the lands and forests they own, particularly in the Western states, but we do not favor a few of the people being able to commit abuses or to establish a profitable monopoly in such lands under false pretenses or by absolute illegality." The land involved in this particular suit was grazing range administered by the Bureau of Land Management, but the principle supported by the *Post* applies to all categories of public land. The public-lands policy which the editorial expresses is both typically Western and national as well.

A policy the exact opposite of this is the one expressed in some resolutions adopted by the Wyoming Farm Bureau Federation at about the same time. We are going to hear a lot of talk about the public lands from this and related points of view during the next few months, while alert special interests try to impose on a Republican Congress that will take a little time to learn its responsibilities. So the Federation's language is worth scrutinizing.

One of the whereases speaks of the public lands which are located in Wyoming as being "claimed by the federal government." Note: *claimed.* The notion that the United States never owned any land and has held the public lands unconstitutionally or illegally shows up in Wyoming now and then. Supporters of the idea cannot have reflected that their title to any land they may hold is no better than the "claim" of the United States. Title originates in a patent from the United States, whether direct to an original homesteader or purchaser, or at one remove through such a grantee as the state itself or a railroad company. If the United States did not own the land it granted, the present holders of it do not own it, and presumably they are liable to ejection, dispossession, alienation, and action for damage.

A related and more popular absurdity speaks of "returning" the public lands to the states in which they are situated. With the exception of a few minute areas which the government has acquired by exchange or purchase, it would be impossible to "return" any public land to the states, for it was never theirs. So long as it has been American it has belonged to the federal government, that is to the people of the United States.

Another of the Federation's whereases says that since the public lands are not on the Wyoming tax roll, land taxed by the state is under a double burden. This is a very ancient bouquet of horse feathers. Much of the public land in the West is desert that could never in any circumstances be taxed. As state officials well know, from practically all the rest of it, except the national parks, the Western states receive from the federal government payments in lieu of taxes at least as large as taxes would produce — greater, in fact, considering the additional benefits tied in with these payments.

The whereases lead to a thunderous conclusion. The Federation resolves "that all public lands and all minerals on or under said lands [oil rates as a mineral] claimed by the federal government should become the property of the State of Wyoming." It endorses "any steps necessary to attain this goal" and declares that legislation which will attain it should "be tied onto the Tide Lands Bills."

This is one version of a proposal that is going to be made in various forms and to various degrees, as desirous groups experiment to see how far they can get the new Congress to go. (The groups are numerically small but powerful, and after all there was that public-lands plank in the Republican platform; you will remember that I predicted just this in the October *Harper's.*) It is aimed at the most valuable publicly owned natural resources: oil and coal and natural gas reserves now worked under lease, other reserves such as phosphates and oil shale, power and irrigation sites, the mineral and water resources of the national parks, and the timber and grazing ranges of the national forests. It has some implications that should alarm all the West but the predatory groups.

Thus Montana would find itself the proprietor of the Custer Battlefield National Monument, including the national cemetery. The upkeep is considerable and the Montana taxpayer probably would not assume an expense that is now borne by the Americans at large. Unless some way of making it an amusement park for tourists could be found, it would have to be abandoned. (Leased for grazing, as the Wyoming cowboys have proposed, it might bring the state from $30 to $60 a year.) Wyoming could not possibly assume the expense of maintaining and operating Yellowstone and Grand Teton National Parks. The power potential of Jenny, Jackson, and Yellowstone Lakes is negligible but they could be sold to irrigation companies. (This one was actually tried in the nineteen-twenties.) The gold that is supposed to be "locked up" in Yellowstone Park could be sold, though only at a trivial price, for trying to find it would be a highly speculative enterprise. The timber in the parks could be sold and such scenery as might survive the construction of mining, dredging, and irrigation works could be sold to resort corporations.

Perhaps, once the foreground has been made hideous by irrigation developments, Wyoming would be willing to divert to the maintenance of Teton Park some of the money to be obtained by selling the national forests. But since they can be sold only once, the state must set up a trust fund and run the parks on the income from it. It won't be large: the idea is to dispose of the forests at fire-sale prices.

When the Western states get the forests they will be acquiring a big future expenditure. Once the grazing ranges have been worn out, as those now owned by the states mostly are, and once the timber has been clear-cut, silt from the resulting erosion will soon fill power dams, irrigation systems, and municipal reservoirs. The upstream states will find themselves defendants in damage suits brought by irrigators, cities, factories, and the corporations which by then will have bought the dams. Sometimes these suits will run to many millions of dollars, as when Los Angeles or the Pacific Gas & Electric Company sues Wyoming for loss of water and power caused by the destruction of Bridger National Forest. Since the forest will have ceased to be national, the damage can be assessed only against Wyoming taxpayers. If the Federation expects Vermont to pay damages, it had better inquire into the nature of Yankees.

The states are also going to lose a lot of income which they now get from the national treasury and only their own taxpayers can make good the deficit. They will have to build most of their own roads, for instance. Because they have got public lands within their borders, the federal government contributes considerably more for road construction than it does to states that haven't got them, and that benefaction will end. They will also have to raise their own tax funds for fire protection and fire control in the once-national forests and for the 50 per cent cut that the Treasury now pays for the same work in private and state forests. California might be able to do this, if its taxpayers should consent, but none of the other states could. Insect control, wild-game management, construction of recreation facilities and fire- and access-roads, and maintenance of roads and trails within the forests — these too will be a charge on the local taxpayer. So will reforestation and the reseeding of forest grazing ranges and those now under the Bureau of Land Management. Most research in forestry and related sciences, land management, power transmission, gas, petroleum, mining, and the like will have to be paid for by the states as soon as they and corporations get the public lands. The big-income states — New York, Pennsylvania, Massachusetts, Illinois, Texas — pay for most of it now, and all the states pay their proportionate share, simply because these *are* public lands, the property of all the people. But there is no reason why Pennsylvania should pay a dime to maintain an Oregon (or a Weyerhaeuser) forest, a Nevada (or P. G. & E.) dam, or a Wyoming grazing range. And why should Pennsylvania pay for any of the other direct or indirect subsidies the West now receives because of the public lands? Pennsylvania Congressmen have to get re-elected and will not appropriate federal funds for private profit or state graft in the West.

Another gimmick is being hopefully set up because of some incautious Republican speeches during the campaign. It will cost, say, three hundred million dollars and upward to build a power project on any of the remaining sites. A percentage of this cost, under the present system, is charged against reclamation (and ultimately against the taxpayer by way of relief bills), and a larger percentage is written off as "non-reimbursable" because of flood protection, recreation, and native American piety. Three hundred million dollars is a large sum for even the biggest power company to raise by bonds. So the hope is that Pennsylvania can be persuaded to build the project, write off the percentages aforesaid, and either give it to Oregon (which pays one per cent of the federal income tax) or sell it at some agreeable valuation to a public utility. Well, the Western bloc was able to put over a series of silver-purchase acts but they were small potatoes. A stop-the-music program with a billion Pennsylvania and New York dollars in the kitty would be different.

In connection with these grabs and giveaways we are going to hear a lot about something else worth noting here, the wail that the Western states never got a fair cut of the national domain and ought to be given the public lands as an apologetic tip. This is simply a request that they be given free what everybody else had to pay for. Connecticut and Virginia did indeed receive (from the area that is now Ohio) some land and some warrants to buy land, to satisfy bounties promised their Revolutionary veterans. (They got them in return for turning over to the national government their ancient grants of far larger areas.) All states carved out of the national domain received Section 16 of every unsold township for the support of public education. After the passage of the Morrill Act in 1862 additional small areas were given to the states for the support of agricultural and mechanical colleges, and those that had no national domain within their borders were allotted their proportionate share from the sale of the national domain. Payments to land-grant colleges ceased to be made from land sales in 1907 and they are now made direct from the Treasury. Last year they totaled $48,000,000. The West got its cut.

The total area of all these grants was infinitesimal compared to the portions of the public domain that were granted to the eleven Western states. They were given land for common schools, normal schools and colleges, internal improvements, various state institutions, state parks, and other purposes. Nevada, which received the smallest area, got just under three million acres—more than the total combined areas of Rhode Island and Delaware, neither of which ever got an acre of public domain, plus a third of Connecticut. New Mexico got most, just over ten million acres, almost twice the area of Massachusetts, more than twice that of New Jersey, neither of which, again, received any of the public domain. Eight Eastern states, in fact, are smaller than the area of public land granted New Mexico or that granted Arizona. California, Utah, and Oregon each got an area larger than Maryland; Montana an area larger than New Hampshire; Colorado, Idaho, and Wyoming each an area larger than Connecticut. Most of this land is still in the possession of the states. If, when the states ask for Boulder Dam and Yellowstone Park, Congress will inquire into the condition, uses, finances, and management of these state lands, as the Denver *Post* did last spring, it will find some shocking conditions. Montana and Idaho have managed theirs with considerable wisdom, Washington pretty well, and the others with various degrees of venality, including the highest possible degree. But I will discuss state lands at another time.

The public lands are public property which Congress long ago decided to preserve and develop in the common interest. The new Congress would be wise to recall the reasons that made conservation a national policy. The reservation of the public lands was the outcome of the realization that much of our heritage of natural resources had been wasted, that much of what remained was impaired, and that all of it was in grave danger of being exhausted. The objectives were the controlled use of nonrenewable resources, the preservation and scientific development and increase of renewable ones, and the protection of watersheds, especially in the arid West. The great achievements of our conservation policy have been in the twentieth century but its roots go back almost to the Civil War. One remembers the pioneers, the prophetic genius John Wesley Powell, such scientists as Charles Sargent and Nathaniel Shaler and Othniel Marsh, such statesmen as Carl Schurz, many other scientists, public officials, industrialists, business men, and the National Academy of Arts and Sciences and the Association for the Advancement of Science.

The new Congress will note that those I have named were all Republicans; down to 1932 practically all the achievements of conservation were the work of Republicans. The word "conservation" itself was given its present meaning by W J McGee, a Republican. The first reservations of public land were made by President Benjamin Harrison and the biggest ones by Theodore Roosevelt, who also established the Forest Service and procured the passage of the Reclamation Act. The Carey Act, the Withdrawal Act, the Weeks Act were Republican measures. The Inland Waterways Commission was a Republican creation and so were most of the national parks, the mineral and oil and coal and water-power reserves, the licensing system under which they are used, and the reservation of Muscle Shoals. If Franklin Roosevelt is one of the three greatest names in conservation, the other two, Theodore Roosevelt and Gifford Pinchot, are Republican. Finally, it was a Republican who phrased the policy under which the public lands have been administered: "the greatest good of the greatest number in the long run."

From this well-established point of view, safeguarding the future has always been more important than enriching small pressure groups at public expense, the nation more important than two per cent of the West, and the public interest in publicly owned resources more important than the private interests that coveted them. This view has always been under attack and will now be under very hopeful attack by groups, hitherto frustrated, who hope they can induce Congress to undo the great work that has been done. They are the same interests they have always been, and they constitute the same threat to the future of the West and of the United States. They are using the same pressures, arguments, lies, and fraud that they have been using for more than fifty years. In the twentieth century they have won only one victory, the annihilation of the Grazing Service expertly perpetrated by Senator McCarran.

Senator McCarran's technique is in their minds as they prepare now for what they hope will be the kill. As I have been pointing out here at intervals ever since the January 1947 issue of *Harper's*, their first objective will be the Forest Service; if they cannot wreck it as completely as the Grazing Service was wrecked, depriving it of its regulatory power would do almost as well. Beyond the Forest Service are oil and oil shale, phosphates, water power, and the hope that Massachusetts can be induced to build dams for Utah. They will be stopped again unless they carry it with the first rush, for Western and national public opinion will, as always, solidify against them. But there is that first rush. When it begins, Congress should remember three things: that the public lands belong to the citizens of forty-eight states and not to two per cent of the citizens of eleven states, that impairment of the public lands would arrest progress in the West and ultimately make the region a charge on the rest of the country, and that the public lands are the only responsibility of the government besides atomic energy about which Congress could make an irretrievable mistake, one that could not be corrected later on. For if the public lands are once relinquished, or even if any fundamental change is made in the present system, they will be gone for good.

The Sturdy Corporate Homesteader

(MAY 1953)

IN A HAPPIER time, so a U.S. Chamber of Commerce speaker tells us, the government used the public domain to "give every man a chance to earn land for himself through his own skill and hard work." This is the sturdy homemaker sob with which the air will presently resound when this gentleman's associates get to work on Congress. He may have been thinking of the California redwood forest. It was so attractive a part of the public domain that in this generation we have had to raise millions of dollars from rich men and school children to buy back a few acres of it here and there for the public.

Under a measure called the Timber and Stone Act, a homemaker who had his first citizenship papers could buy 160 acres of redwood forest from the government for $2.50 an acre, quite a bit less than a panel for your living room costs. Agents of a lumber company would go to a sailors' boardinghouse on the waterfront. They would press a gang of homemakers and lead them to a courthouse to take out first papers. Then they went to a land office and each filed claim to 160 acres of redwood: a quarter section whose number the lumber company had supplied. At a lawyer's office they transferred to the lumber company the homesteads they had earned by skill and hard work, received $50 for services rendered, and could go back to the boardinghouse. "Fifty dollars was the usual fee," a historian says, "although the amount soon fell to $10 or $5 and eventually to the price of a glass of beer."

Under this Act four million acres of publicly owned timber passed into corporate ownership at a small fraction of its value, and 95 per cent of it by fraud. Under other Acts supposed to "give every man a chance to earn land for himself," enormously greater acreages came to the same end with the sturdy homemaker's help.

The laws stipulated that the homemaker must be in good faith. Erecting a "habitable dwelling" on his claim would prove that he was. Or if it was irrigable land, he had to "bring water" to it, for a homemaker would need water. Under a couple of dozen aliases apiece, employees of land companies or cattle companies would file claim to as many quarter sections or half sections of the public domain and after six months would "commute" them, get title to them, at $1.25 per acre.

The sworn testimony of witnesses would prove that they had brought water to the claim; there was no reason for the witnesses to add they had brought it in a can. Or the witnesses swore that they had "seen water" on a homestead and so they had, having helped to throw it there cupful by cupful. Or to erect a "twelve by fourteen" cabin on a claim would prove good faith. Homemaker and witnesses neglected to mention that the size of this "habitable dwelling" was twelve by fourteen inches, not feet. Alternatively, a "shingled residence" established that the homemaker intended to live on his claim; one could be created by fastening a couple of shingles to each side of a tent below the ridgepole. Sometimes a scrupulous corporation would build a genuine log cabin twelve by fourteen feet, mount it on wagon wheels, and have the boys drive it from claim to claim, getting the homemaker a lot of public domain in a few hours. In a celebrated instance in Utah the efficiency of this device was increased by always pushing the truck over the corner where four quarter sections met.

In six months the homemakers, who meanwhile had been punching cows or clerking in town, commuted their two dozen parcels of the public domain. They transferred them to their employers and moved on to earn two dozen more quarter sections apiece by their skill and hard work. Many millions of acres of publicly owned farmland and grazing land thus passed economically into the possession of corporate homemakers. If the corporation was a land company it might get half a million acres convenient to a railroad right of way or within a proposed irrigation district. Or a cattle company could thus acquire ten thousand acres that monopolized the water supply for miles and so graze a hundred thousand acres of the public domain entirely free of charge.

Lumber companies could operate even more cheaply. Their employees need not pay $1.25 per acre or wait to commute their claims. They could pay a location fee, say $16 per 320 acres and the company could forthwith clear-cut the timber and let the claims lapse. At twenty cents an acre virgin stands of white or ponderosa pine, Douglas fir, or Norway or Colorado spruce were almost as good a buy as some of the damsites which, our propagandist hopes, will presently be offered to the power companies.

These are typical, routine, second-magnitude land frauds in the history of the public domain out West — to describe the bigger ones would require too much space. Enough that in the golden age of landgrabs the total area of the public domain proved up and lived on by actual homesteaders amounted to only a trivial fraction of the area fraudulently acquired by land companies, cattle companies, and lumber companies. Among the compelling reasons why the present public-land reserves had to be set aside was the headlong monopolization of the public domain that was threatening the West with peonage. Those reserves were also made to halt the waste of natural resources which the United States has dissipated more prodigally than any other nation. They had to be made so that a useful part of our national wealth could be preserved, developed, wisely managed, and intelligently used in future times. They had to be made so that the watersheds which control the destiny of the West could be safeguarded. But no one should forget for a moment that they were, besides, necessary to prevent Eastern and foreign corporations from taking over the whole West by fraud, bribery, and engineered bankruptcy.

The land frauds and the landgrabs compose the shabbiest chapter in our history. We have had seventy-five years now of conservation as a government policy, of husbanding, developing, and using the publicly owned natural resources for the public benefit. So we have grown used to believing that such corruption, such raids on the treasury, such blind imbecility were ended for all time. But at this moment some powerful interests are preaching that what was intolerable corruption on a scale of half a million acres becomes wise public policy if you up the scale to half a billion acres. They are calling on Congress to legalize a final, conclusive raid on the publicly owned resources of the United States.

This one would be for keeps and it would put the government itself into the land-fraud racket. Officials of the government, true enough, were sometimes in that racket in the past, from two-dollar-a-day deputy clerks in the General Land Office on up to Senators and Secretaries of the Interior. Always before, however, the government regarded them as common criminals. It threw them out, sent to jail those it could get the goods on, and did what it could to repair the damage. Now Congress is asked to legitimatize and legalize what it used to make them felons for trying to do. It is asked, with an effrontery so great that it has not yet been widely perceived, to perpetrate by its own deliberate act a land fraud beside which any in our shameful period would appear insignificant.

As I write this, at mid-March, we have not learned by what means the citizens of forty-five states will have their property alienated on behalf of three states. Senator Holland's bill to convey to Texas, Louisiana, and California the publicly owned oil under the marginal sea has had slow going. The Attorney General has perceived some impairments of sovereignty and some administrative difficulties that were not visible when the tidelands were a bait for votes. There has arisen the interesting possibility that Rhode Island or some inland state which owns part of that oil may bring suit on the ground that Congress has no constitutional power to give it to any state. At least a part of the Administration is showing some regret for its campaign commitment. But it is committed and we may assume that the Supreme Court will find some opening through which it can follow the election returns.

So be it, but let's be clear about the tidelands episode. There has never been any doubt that the natural resources thus handed over to three states belong to the public, to the people of all the states. The Supreme Court has three times declared that they do; indeed in one of the cases which the Court was adjudicating, the State of Louisiana stipulated that they do. What we shall see, then, will be governmental conversion of public property. That the raiders were three sovereign states does not alter the fact that this is a successful raid on the public heritage.

So, with that precedent, what next? Senator Butler of Nebraska, the Chairman of the Senate Committee on Interior and Insular Affairs, has announced that when the tidelands business is finished his committee will take up proposals for still more important attacks on our property. First the Committee will deal with proposed measures to turn over the public lands to the states, then with similar measures to turn over the public power installations. This means, as the tidelands bills do not, the sale of public property to private corporations — the only reason for giving the public lands to the states is that the states will sell them. Unable to buy the public heritage from the federal government, corporations will be able to buy them at fire-sale prices from eleven Western states. They belong to the people of forty-eight states, the people of the eleven states have borne maybe two per cent of the cost of protecting and developing them, patriotic private enterprise can bid them in cheap, and everybody should be happy, more or less.

Among those who testified on the tidelands question before Senator Butler's committee was Mr. Oscar L. Chapman, lately Secretary of the Interior. He was afraid, he said, that the tidelands action would "establish the pattern for the greatest giveaway program in the history of the world." He added, "For years powerful pressure groups have been attempting to raid various parts of the public domain. They are now redoubling their efforts."

Mr. Chapman was entirely right. He mentioned the U.S. Chamber of Commerce. In 1947 it supported the notorious effort of stockgrowing interests to grab (at a few cents an acre) large areas of the national forests, the national parks, and other public reservations. Public opinion stopped the stockmen cold and scared the Chamber into reversing its stand for a while. Now it is again agitating for the sale of public lands to private (that is, corporate) parties and is broadcasting remarkably misleading propaganda. The National Association of Manufacturers has lined up beside it, with propaganda equally mendacious and much subtler. For the first time in a generation big lumber interests are supporting the raid. As always the stockmen are out in front, happily carrying the ball for stronger and cannier groups that happily let them carry it. Previously circumspect power companies have come out from behind their public relations programs and various granges and farm bureaus have signed up.

In short, desirous ears have heard the sound of a great Perhaps which they hope they can convert to the great Amen. The day of jubilo may be about to dawn. The federal government's seventy-five years of fidelity to the public interest, the millions of dollars of public money spent to maintain and develop the public lands, the long husbanding and use of them for the benefit of all the people — this is acknowledged to have been a memorable and splendid thing. For lo, this policy has multiplied the value of the public assets a thousandfold — and now the harvest can be reaped by those prepared to cash in on it. A business administration means business, doesn't it? Prolonging federal protection of this public interest would be bureaucratic tyranny and inefficiency, wouldn't it? There is so big a melon to be cut that not to cut it would be creeping socialism — let's go. Or, wheresoever the carcass is, there will the eagles be gathered together.

It is quite a carcass. Mr. Chapman told Senator Butler's committee that the public lands "contain an estimated 4 billion barrels of oil, enough oil shale to produce 130 billion barrels of crude oil, 111 trillion cubic feet of gas, and 324 billion tons of coal." These are sample figures; Mr. Chapman said nothing about timber, grass, electric power plants, sites for future ones, irrigation and other water potentials, precious metals, other minerals, and the rest of the miscellany now owned by the public — by everybody, including you. He said that a rough estimate of their value in the United States, not counting Alaska, made it "well over a trillion dollars." Nobody can think of a trillion dollars; the sum is only a symbol. But it gives the scale of the proposed operation of transferring publicly owned property to the states, so that whatever corporations may prove to be in the best position can buy it for a fraction of what it is worth. Every bill that Senator Butler's committee will proceed to take up could be titled, An Act to Enrich Stockholders at the Expense of Taxpayers.

In the cruder age there had to be a pretense that the homemaker was to benefit but there can't be now, for no land suitable for homesteading is left. Instead, the public lands are to be disposed of on the sound business principle that they are a storehouse of raw materials of value to corporations. The great stands of timber will go to Big Lumber, oil and oil shale to Big Oil, minerals and chemicals to Big Mining, public power plants and sites for future ones to Big Power. Nor is there any pretense that the desirous Western shibboleths will be regarded: the local enterprise and home rule that were to emancipate the plundered province from absentee ownership. The power company that is prepared to build an installation in Hell's Canyon which will generate 40 or maybe 60 per cent of the power the government planned to is not an Idaho corporation. It is not even a Western corporation: it is chartered in Maine and largely owned by investment trusts.

The landgrabbers of the golden age were small-time. A cattle company's two hundred thousand acres of public grazing land at $1.25, a lumber company's half-million acres of publicly owned Douglas fir at $2.50 and a glass of beer — they are police court stuff compared to a political job that undertakes to knock off half a billion acres of public land in a single session of Congress. This proposed steal is so large that its size is counted on to conceal it — like ultraviolet light and supersonic sound it is to escape attention. But it is under way. The bills are drawn, Congressmen have been found who will introduce them and direct their course, and Senator Butler has agreed to clear the decks.*

Mr. Chapman told the committee that the estimate of a trillion dollars was only a rough guess, was in fact much too low. And, he said, "if this Administration is intent upon following a give-away policy, the people are at least entitled to know what and how much is being given away." So he proposed that a commission be established to inventory and appraise the public property that is to become corporate assets. It is an excellent suggestion. We are being told every few minutes that business is on trial now, that this Administration will give business its chance to prove itself, and everything ought to be done on the best business principles. Establish the commission and have it hire Price, Waterhouse.

The trouble is that such a study would put an end to Operation Götterdämmerung on the public lands. Publication of its results would instantly blow this culminating land fraud sky high. As a matter of fact that is going to happen anyway. The script is OK but the casting is wrong: it calls for the public to be docile and for Congress to be fools.

A very distant association with the Credit Mobilier — railroad-land fraud — kept James G. Blaine, and it may be Schuyler Colfax too, out of the White House. There was William Lorimer of Illinois: expelled from the Senate for corrupt practices rooted in timber-land fraud. There was Senator John Mitchell of Oregon: found guilty of timber-land fraud but dying before he could serve his sentence. Albert B. Fall, Secretary of the Interior, went to jail — oil-land fraud. Richard A. Ballinger, Secretary of the Interior, left a blasted name to history — coal-land fraud. A lot of lesser names have disappeared from the newspapers but not from memory. When you hear them or look them up in books they give off, after all these years, the odor of corruption. Land fraud always did and it always will.

* As it turned out, the syndicate in part learned discretion and in part lost its nerve. Only a handful of the prepared bills were introduced in the 83rd Congress and of these only two were stubbornly pushed. Both were beaten.

The Sturdy Corporate Homesteader (May 1953)

The redwood forest deals, the Oregon timber frauds, Teapot Dome — they were peanuts, birdseed, compared to what this crew of blue-sky pitchmen are asking Congress to slip over on us now. But the stench still rises from them and drifts down history and over Capitol Hill. Congress will sit this one out, the carefully planned agenda notwithstanding.

Heading for the Last Roundup

(JULY 1953)

THE MOST EFFECTIVE disseminator of propaganda is the man who spreads it innocently. It is possible that some of my readers took part in the radio program which I proceed to describe. It is certain that almost everyone who took part in it spoke the lines provided for him in good faith, trusting the organization which had provided them. He would not voluntarily have used his position as a leader in his community to support a series of misrepresentations and misstatements. But that is exactly what the organization in question beguiled him into doing.

That organization is the U.S. Chamber of Commerce. Its Radio-Television Section sends to local chambers scripts to be broadcast in a weekly program called "The Business Viewpoint: A Radio Report to the Community from its Business Men." On March 10, 1953, it thus sent out its Series A, Program 56, "The Public Lands." The program is in the form of a dialogue between two businessmen, and has blanks at the proper places so that the right local names and allusions can be inserted. Thus the local chambers would be led to co-operate in the campaign I have frequently described here: to turn over our publicly owned natural resources to exploitation by private parties.

A small but powerful group of Western stockmen have taken the lead in this campaign and their prime objective is the Forest Service. They hope, first, to deprive the Service of its power to regulate their use of the public grazing ranges and, ultimately, to buy at two cents on the dollar such national forest lands as they may want. This would so breach our long established conservation policy that private interests would forthwith be able to get hold of the far more valuable publicly owned timber, oil, minerals, and hydraulic power. And that shining vision explains why the U.S. Chamber of Commerce has put its power and prestige at the service of the stockmen's propaganda. It has elaborated and reissued the stockmen's misrepresentations in a series of press releases. It has reproduced them in an official pamphlet, "Policy Declaration on Natural Resources." They appeared in a much publicized speech by its president, from which I quoted when I discussed land frauds in the May *Harper's*. Observe that this speech was an official address by the President of the U.S. Chamber of Commerce — since then his term has expired — and that he was voicing the propaganda line of the livestock pressure group.

Perhaps he was voicing it not altogether altruistically: he is himself a stockgrower. He is vice-president and director, and his brother is president, of a large New Mexico stock company which uses public grazing ranges. His company holds grazing permits from the Bureau of Land Management for 3000 cattle, 10,000 sheep, 250 horses, and 165 goats. From the Forest Service it holds grazing permits for 180 sheep, and crossing permits, spring and fall, for 3000 cattle and 10,000 sheep. A big operator.

The canned radio speech is a rehash of these familiar distortions and misstatements. It is misleading throughout but for the most part too puerile to deceive anyone who has the slightest acquaintance with the facts — as of course neither the local speakers nor their audiences would be expected to have. I select from it a few statements that will be endlessly repeated in the developing, post-tidelands attack on the public lands. Remember that the operation against the Forest Service is the key to the whole campaign. If "a larger measure of local control" can be achieved by turning the national forests over to the states for private sale, then all the other public reserves will follow as a matter of course.

The voices of our radio dialogue open with a standard gambit.

They are shocked by the large amount of land in the United States which is in federal ownership, and by the fact that the states in which that land is located collect no taxes on it. Revealing that their target is the Forest Service, they say that the federal government owns 91 million acres of timberland. They say that this amounts to 40 per cent of all commercial standing timber. They compare this shocking figure with "a country where socialistic ideas are popular," Sweden: there, they say, in spite of socialistic ideas only 25 per cent of the timber is publicly owned. Here one of the voices should be fed through a patch-board to the echo effect, so dire is its message: "Some of the Western states are owned almost lock, stock, and barrel by the government. . . The national government owns 87 per cent of all the land in Nevada."

Sensation! In Nevada, perceive, socialism has ceased to creep; it has broken into a gallop and will ride us down. The audience, its fear of Big Government aroused, is to envisage six-gun bureaucrats wrenching the state away from its citizens.

Thus an innocent local speaker is induced to mislead an uninformed audience, and we may call this lying by intimation. The basic reason why 87 per cent of Nevada is in public ownership is that more than 70 per cent of it is land which the government was unable to give away. When the national domain was virtually closed, in 1934, three-quarters of the state was still open to entry under the various Acts of Congress designed to give it to settlers. It had been thus open for many decades but no one had homesteaded it. It is the very dregs of the public domain, waterless and sterile. It could not be given away now, and if someone could be induced to take it, it could not pay a tax. Such land constitutes nine-tenths of the federal holding in Nevada. The Chamber's propagandists could hardly have avoided knowing as much. But Nevada's creosote-bush desert may serve to help them get a loop on publicly owned timber, oil, minerals, and power elsewhere.

Scrutinize the rest of that preamble. The Chamber plucks its statistics from the air and must be flunked in arithmetic: I can find no tables that give the areas it cites and its percentages are in error. Actually there are 74 million acres of commercial timberland in the national forests, 16 per cent of the total in the United States. How did the Chamber arrive at its 91 million acres? Is it adding in timberland on Indian Reservations? That is private property. Is it including state, county, and municipal forests? They are publicly owned but not federally owned. And if the total is 91 million acres, however arrived at, then it constitutes 20 per cent of our commercial timberland, not 40 per cent. (Double by inadvertence?) And by the way, the less socialistic Sweden imposes government regulation of cutting and a good many other scientific forestry practices on private forests, none of which are enforced on private operators here.

When technicians of political distortion say that public lands pay no local taxes they are telling the truth, but not enough of it. This half-truth will be hurled at Congress innumerable times, as the technicians work to get the public storehouse of natural resources knocked down to desirous corporations. What the Chamber of Commerce neglected to mention to its uninformed audience was the payments made to states and counties by the federal government in lieu of taxes, and the revenue-sharing payments that are the same thing under another name.

These payments vary from class to class of the public lands. The national forests pay 25 per cent of their gross receipts to local communities. Lands under mineral lease pay 37 1/2 per cent of royalties received. Land-utilization projects of the Soil Conservation Service pay 25 per cent of net receipts. Federal Power Commission projects pay 37 1/2 per cent of the license fees of power sites. Wildlife refuges pay 25 per cent of net receipts. Grazing districts under the Bureau of Land Management pay 12 1/2 per cent of gross receipts, lands under the same bureau not in grazing districts, 50 per cent. There are some lump-sum payments, such as the $300,000 paid annually to Arizona and New Mexico by the Hoover Dam Project. Perhaps a few exceptions are theoretically conceivable, but a generalization will hold: if these properties were in private ownership they could not pay anywhere near so much in taxes to local governments.

In 1952 Forest Service payments to Idaho from timber sales

were three-quarters of a million dollars, to Washington almost three million, to California more than three million, to Oregon more than four million. In 1951 Wyoming got four million dollars from mineral leases, Colorado nearly two million dollars, New Mexico one and three-quarters million.

There are also indirect benefits in cash. The federal government shares the expense of fire protection in state and privately owned forests. In 1951 the State of Washington received more than half a million dollars for this purpose, Oregon just less than three-quarters of a million. Federal highway aid is paid at a higher rate in the public-land states than in the others, and this too is in lieu of taxes. Mention of such facts, however, would have spoiled the propaganda effect.

Next the radio voices profess to be alarmed by the additions that are made to the public lands, purchases by a land-hungry, tax-obliterating centralized bureaucracy. One of them says with horror that since the turn of the century "the government has added 45 million acres to its holdings — and has consistently been trying to acquire more." You can see the Forest Service fairly pushing New York City into the Hudson.

Here are some classes of federal acquisitions: dustbowl and other submarginal land that had to be retired from cultivation; tax-delinquent lands bought in other forms of local relief; lands acquired by gift, such as the Rockefeller donations to the national parks; lands bought by towns to protect their water supply and given to the government for protection; similar tracts bought at the solicitation of threatened communities. The Chamber of Commerce also neglects to say that its total includes large areas bought for military and atomic installations — to mention them would have impaired the picture of the Forest Service as out of control and dangerously encroaching on our liberties. For the same reason it neglects to say that by far the largest part of its total actually attributable to the Forest Service consists of purchases made under two acts of soundly Republican Congresses, the Weeks Act and the Clark-McNary Act. One authorizes the Service to buy land for the protection of watersheds, the other to buy it for reforestation and the establishment of forests.

The Forest Service conducts this activity under the direction and supervision of a body set up by Congress, the National Forest Reservation Commission. It includes representatives of both houses of Congress and the Secretaries of the Army, Interior, and Agriculture. It has long been engaged in a scientific program which has given the South and the East the national forests they so greatly prize — before it there were national forests only in the West. Purchases under these Acts in the West have been negligible, 8000 acres in Nevada, 22,000 acres in Utah, and in most of the other states none at all. Whereas purchases amount to more than a million acres each in Arkansas, Michigan, Minnesota, Mississippi, Missouri, North Carolina, Virginia, and Wisconsin; to more than half a million acres each in Florida, Georgia, Louisiana, New Hampshire, South Carolina, Tennessee, Texas, and West Virginia. Weep for the disappearing West.

These forests are among the finest achievements of our conservation policy, a vital step toward reducing our serious scarcity of wood, invaluable for recreation in the heavily populated East and for the protection of its watersheds. Most of the land that was bought for them had been logged and was tax-delinquent; eroding, a fire hazard, it was a public danger; it was good for nothing except to grow trees. The Forest Service has changed it from a public liability to a public asset of constantly increasing value. And note this, which the Chamber of Commerce fails to point out: every purchase was consented to by the state involved. Otherwise not an acre could have been bought.*

So far the program has confined itself to distortion and misrepresentation; now it experiments with falsification. One of the voices says that the government has its eyes on 35 million acres of private (it should have said, non-federal) timberland, which it wants to add to the national forests. That is true; the figure was proposed by a study of future needs and ways of meeting them. The voice goes on to imply, however, that the Forest Service is

* This program has been halted by the Bureau of the Budget in the Eisenhower Administration, a munificently spendthrift form of economy.

going to take this land by some kind of seizure, by somehow forcing it out of the hands of its helpless owners. The speaker describes the system by which the Service sometimes exchanges tracts of timber for other tracts or for cutover land — but describes it with stark dishonesty. He intimates that the Service forces private owners to make exchanges, that it does so in avoidance or defiance of congressional intent, and that by so doing it defrauds the U.S. Treasury. And he says in a remarkable fabrication, "the idea has not been to save the taxpayers' money. It has been to increase the size of United States forests and decrease the taxable lands from which they have been taken." The bureaucracy wants to bankrupt the states: I conclude that here one of the cowboys took over from the professional script writer.

What are the facts? Practically all the timber sales which the Forest Service makes are for cash, after competitive bidding. Sometimes, however, it exchanges mature timber for immature timber, which it will scientifically husband for future use, or tracts of timber for tracts of logged-out land which it will reforest.

These are comparatively small transactions, and *almost all of them are initiated by the timber operators who profit from them.* If there was no profit for the operator, there would be no exchange; no one is pointing a gun at him; usually, if he did not dispose of his land in this way, he would let his title lapse by nonpayment of taxes. Sometimes, however, there are value-for-value exchanges, from which the Forest Service profits directly as well as the operator. The Service makes an exchange to consolidate isolated small holdings or rationalize forest boundaries, to conserve scenic or recreational values, or to protect threatened portions of watersheds. No coercion is possible. No private owner is compelled to make an exchange and it is safe to say that none does unless he profits by it.

Look at the program's total, 35 million acres of contemplated future acquisitions. Of this, 23 million acres were long since approved for purchase — approved not by the ravenous Forest Service but by the body I have mentioned, the National Forest Reservation Commission — and this entire area is in the East.

Not an acre is in the West which the Chamber of Commerce represents as being everywhere reduced to the helplessness of any clump of sagebrush in Nevada. The remaining 12 million acres are a small total, when you consider that they are spread over all the national forests, the forests which are and must always be the foundation of our entire conservation program, and when you consider what the future is going to demand of them. Sometime I will describe here the purpose of the contemplated acquisitions.

The rest of the Chamber's dialogue consists of repetitions of the stockmen's propaganda assertions, even more childish than the one I have just discussed. No one who knew anything about the subject could take it seriously. The point is, however, that it was written to be broadcast to a public which was assumed not to know anything about the subject and therefore, so the Chamber hoped, could be induced to support the attack on the public-lands system, the attack on the public's own property.

Just how does the U.S. Chamber of Commerce get that way? It is entitled to adopt any public-lands policy it may desire to and to advance that policy by any honest means. But it is not, I think, entitled to mislead and misinform its member chambers, the private persons whom it thus uses as stooges, and the public at large. The Chamber has lost status, it has become suspect.

This, however, is only a specimen of tactics that can currently be observed in many places. They are deliberately dishonest tactics. You will hear many repetitions of them; you will hear them, especially, repeated in Congress, as the bills to make corporate property of the public lands are taken up. See to it that no one is allowed to get away with them. See to it that no one imposes them on your Congressman.

Conservation: Down and on the Way Out

(AUGUST 1954)

AN APHORISM of the Chinese philosopher Mencius declares that the problem of government presents no difficulties: it is only necessary to avoid offending the influential families. In January 1953 the Business Administration in Washington took off from a related premise: that it was only necessary to get along with the trade associations.

This article deals with public power and the public lands, other natural resources, and the national conservation policies which have been developing for three-quarters of a century. In dealing with them the Administration had to convert into concrete measures the generalizations of the Republican platform and campaign promises. It had no program when it took office. It was promptly handed one specific program, which the electric power companies had worked out in anticipation of a Republican victory in 1948. It has improvised several others, playing by ear. On several problems, it apparently is not concerned with programs; it has simply drifted downward.

Perhaps I can formulate the campaign generalities as working principles. In fields where private enterprise could operate at a profit, the Administration would try to reduce government operations. In fields where private enterprise could not make profits, it would maintain government operation up to the minimum political necessity. In both areas it would try to provide "a greater measure of local participation and control," greater co-operation between federal and local governments, and "a friendly partnership" with private business. It would try to "decentralize" federal administration, and it would — in an even more opaque phrase — "operate at the grass roots."

There was an inherent weakness in these working principles. They would throw the gates wide open to the boys in the back room unless the Administration could get in first with programs of its own. It did not and the boys — the trade associations, the lobbies, the special interest groups — rushed in with a loud whoop. During the campaign Mr. Eisenhower once remarked that he would not interpret his election as a mandate to preside over the liquidation of the publicly owned natural resources of the United States. Others *have* so interpreted it, however; a considerable liquidation has been effected already and much more is in the works. Eighteen months have made clear that the Executive departments and the independent agencies will go much farther than Congress in alienating public property — but not (except perhaps in the Department of the Interior) as far as the boys have in mind.

They pin their hopes to the new Hoover Commission. The first one worked out intelligent plans for reorganizing the Executive departments in the interests of efficiency and economy; but the second one is clearly intended to slay Mr. Hoover's white whale at last. It is to erase twenty years of infamy, root out all remnants of the New Deal, and turn the clock back to 1928. There are those who regard 1928 as practically a pinko compromise: the clock should be turned back somewhere beyond Theodore Roosevelt.

II

IN THE Departments of Agriculture and the Interior the businessmen whom the Administration summoned to government promptly displayed the political ineptness visible in other departments. One reason may have been the sources of information which it was natural for them to rely on. A Congressman who wants a quick check on what the folks back home are thinking is apt to telephone to a local editor or political figure, or the head of some local labor or farm organization. From the top offices of Agriculture and Interior, however, the phone calls went instead to a chamber of commerce or to the Washington office of a trade association. The information available there being of a radically different kind, there followed such miscues as Secretary McKay's nomination to be Director of the Bureau of Mines of an open and recorded enemy of the services he would have to direct.

Top officials were also unable to recognize public opinion as a political force. Congressmen saw a clear portent in the widespread opposition to the Tidelands Bill — and in the public outrage when the Assistant Secretary of Commerce tried to discharge the Director of the Bureau of Standards for affirming that the addition of a laxative to a storage battery would not improve it. But to the Businessmen in Office these were unrelated and meaningless phenomena, just one of those things. The Department of Agriculture revealed this state of mind in its handling of the reorganization of the Soil Conservation Service. There could be no more local an organization than a Soil Conservation District; more than 2500 of them cover the country and they are literally of the grass roots. But they were not consulted about the reorganization of SCS and indeed could not find out what was going on till it was completed. In Administration semantics, "local participation and control" had become "fiat by Washington." The districts were enraged; they still are.

This reorganization, an aggrandizement of the land-grant colleges and the Extension Service at the sacrifice of conservation values, was typical of the new order in several ways. SCS had originally been organized on the basis of state units but had evolved a much more effective organization in a series of regions, each with its own headquarters, specialists, and technicians. The reorganization plan proposed to dissolve the regions and substitute state units for them. The heart of SCS assistance to farmers was its six technical services; four of these were to be abandoned and the specialists of the other two were to be distributed among the land-grant colleges (so far as the colleges had jobs for them) and the Washington headquarters. For the immensely successful program of SCS, forty-eight fractional and necessarily unharmonized programs were to be substituted; and these were to be administered from Washington. Decentralization had worked out in the semantics as greater centralization. Incentive to local conservation practices was to be provided by decreasing appropriations. And with technical service reduced, much research was to be abandoned.

But opposition to Tidelands and the firing of Dr. Astin had *not* been just one of those things, and nation-wide opposition to the new scheme forced the Department to reverse itself in midair. A new system of regional offices, under a different name and with headquarters in different cities, was extemporized. (In the semantics, A ceases to be A when you rename it B.) The technical services were retained, though in a more cumbersome and more expensive form.

As I write, SCS is half flux and half chaos. The technical teams have been broken up. Their invaluable pool of common experience at working together has been dissipated. This drastic impairment of professional skills is typical of the administration of public resources in the new order. So are the increased expense, delay, red tape, and inefficiency. So is the destruction of morale in a career service. Promising young men have left SCS in droves; promising young men who might have sought a career there are notably failing to join it. An Administration fetish whose name is Management-Practice Improvement has had its paper tribute, but a straitjacket of mediocrity has been forced on public administration. And a damaging blow has been struck at the conservation of American cropland and rangeland.

The Department of Agriculture, however, appears to have taken instruction from the public reaction. Evidently it has abandoned some reactionary changes which it had in mind a year ago and has narrowed the scope of some others. Not so the Department of the Interior. The boys have practically taken it over; the predicted giveaways are in progress. There is a cynicism in Interior which reminds observers of the aromatic days of the General Land Office. Yet some things that look like cynicism may be mere ineptness. Thus Secretary McKay at a moment when all the conservation organizations in the country — national, nonpartisan, and representing hundreds of thousands of votes — were denouncing his recommendation of Echo Park Dam. Seeking for *le mot juste* to characterize conservationists, he came up with "punks."

III

The top officials of SCS have been put on Schedule C; so have those of all other conservation bureaus in Agriculture except (as yet, perhaps) the Forest Service, and all those in Interior except the Geological Survey. Schedule C is a classification withdrawn from Civil Service protection which permits discharge at the will of the Secretary, without regard to merit. It has a twofold purpose: (1) to provide jobs; (2) to substitute a pliable sycophancy for professional judgment in the making of policy. Promotion according to merit is abandoned for the spoils system, and career services become political footballs. The effect on the conservation agencies has been disastrous; it had not hitherto been supposed, and it cannot be supposed now, that the publicly owned resources could be administered on any basis except a purely professional one. These bureaus first introduced into the American government the concept of a professionally expert civil service. Staff them with spoilsmen, and the public resources must begin leaking away.

The Administrator of the Rural Electrification Administration is appointed to serve ten years. It was therefore a tipoff wher the White House requested the resignation of Mr. Claude Wickard two and a half years before the end of his statutory term. Rural electrification and federal power can be treated together here, and several facts which are tirelessly misrepresented must be noted. The electric power generated at public installations runs between 13 and 16 per cent of the national total, never more. In spite of nationwide propaganda by the utilities (paid for out of tax money and rate increase), unalterable natural circumstances make it certain that the percentage will decrease as time goes on. Furthermore, the consumer co-operatives which REA serves are strictly private enterprises, locally owned by their members and locally managed. They pay interest on the loans which REA makes them; they pay off the loans; they pay local taxes. They are "socialistic" only in the new semantics: in that they are not owned by the utility companies and they sell power to consumers so cheaply that their rates serve as a yardstick by which the rates of the utilities — a natural monopoly — can be regulated. Finally, most of the power they sell is bought from the utilities.

They constitute an area of private enterprise which the utilities had refused to pioneer or develop. In 1935 when REA was established, about 11 per cent of the farms in the United States had central-station power; in 1952 about 90 per cent had it. This constitutes an agricultural revolution even greater than that effected by SCS; it has transformed agricultural production, farm labor, and rural living. REA and the co-ops have greatly increased the business done by the utilities and very greatly increased that done by manufacturers of electrical equipment and appliances.

A multiple squeeze has been put on co-ops and REA. The Administration's first budget request drastically cut REA funds. Its power-generation program, and therefore its bargaining power with the utilities, would have been destroyed. Its ability to accommodate new co-ops and the ability of the co-ops to serve new customers would have been drastically reduced. Congress refused to go so far and saved much of the program by increasing the appropriation far above the request. But Congress did not vote an increase over the Budget's allotment for technical service. Thus the theme of SCS is repeated, for the abandonment or even any serious reduction of REA's technical service to the co-ops would be a serious blow, to some of them a fatal blow. Small co-ops, unable to afford such a technical staff as a utility company maintains, have been able to get their problems solved cheaply by REA. Moreover, the Power Use Section of REA was cut down, and the auditing services were abolished, thus increasing the financial hazards of the co-ops. A related but unsuccessful move was the attempt by Congressman Kit Clardy of Michigan — an old and dear friend of utility companies — to double the rate of interest which REA charges on loans to the co-ops.

Meanwhile what amounts to a rewriting of the Federal Power Act, supplementary acts, and even the Reclamation Act has been achieved by administrative action. The utilities would be glad to have the government build the large and expensive control dams — because they make private downstream dams efficient — provided they could buy the power generated at them on their own terms and could control its distribution. But they have always rebelled against the "preference clause." This clause — which in essence goes back to the earliest conception of public power in Theodore Roosevelt's first administration — is a provision that public bodies and co-operatives shall have first call on the power generated at federal dams. ("Public bodies" means primarily municipally owned systems and such organizations as the power districts of Oregon and Washington.) The ordinary growth of such systems was provided for by selling the rest of the power to utilities on short-term contracts only. By abandoning this practice, the Administration is in effect discarding the preference clause.

In the Northwest, utility contracts, previously short-term, now run twenty years. This limits the growth of co-ops, denies them new customers, and rations the power used by their present customers. A similiar change in the Missouri Valley has been held up till after the November election. The co-ops have been faced with an impossible choice. Either they must forfeit their preference privilege, thus arresting their own growth, or they must contract for power far in advance of their needs and so pay a ruinous bonus for power which they could not use and which would have to be resold to the utilities at dump prices.

The utilities have fought the construction of steam-generating plants by REA to firm the power produced at government hydroelectric plants, a frequently necessary measure because of seasonal fluctuations in stream flow. And the low rates charged by the co-ops have always harrowed them, for the differential is all too visible. There would be no reason for co-ops if they could not pass on to their members the savings they effect, and Assistant Secretary of the Interior Aandahl announced the answer. Federal power rates, he said, would be raised to the point where there would be no incentive to continue REA or establish co-operatives. Here is one form of private business with which the Administration will not enter into a friendly partnership — and, as Senator Murray remarked, here is a negative yardstick for the power industry.

As for the generation of power, the Director of the Budget announced that there would be no "new starts" — no additional federal power projects — till arrangements had been made with local (which here means large-scale and absentee) interests to install the generating facilities.

He thus proclaimed publicly a policy which some members of the Administration were simultaneously denying. It is significant that of the twenty-three new starts so far made by the Corps of Engineers, none are multiple purpose and none include power. And it seems likely that the Engineers will be favored over the Bureau of Reclamation in such new projects as are authorized. They are far friendlier to the utilities, they can legally assess against the taxpayers a larger percentage of the costs, and they are able to circumvent painful provisions of the Reclamation and Power Acts.

The program drawn up by the utilities in 1948 has not been carried out in full. But the process of strangulation that has been applied to REA should kill it in another two years. The co-ops will be withdrawn from competing with the utilities and furnishing data for the regulation of their rates. It would take considerably more than two years to get a wall round federal generation of power.

Secretary McKay's abandonment to the Idaho Power Company of the Hell's Canyon site — the greatest remaining one in the country — was geared to this policy. In the current semantics a consumer co-operative, owned and operated by farmers unable to get electricity except by their own efforts, would not be local enterprise; but Idaho Power is.

Idaho Power is a Maine corporation and holds its annual meetings across the continent from the Snake River. It is like any big utility company, which means that its policies are banker-directed, which means in turn that they are Wall Street policies. It belongs to all the institutes and associations, national and regional, that tie utility companies together. But its stock setup is such that statements about ownership have to be made with great care. A vigorous selling campaign in the last few years has distributed its preferred stock widely through the West; in fact 60 per cent of it is held in the intermountain West. Moreover, the preferred stock has voting rights and each share carries five votes whereas the common stock has only one vote per share. Yet the common stock has senior voting rights. And the thirty largest stockholders own 30 per cent of the common stock; most of them hold large blocks of preferred stock as well. Of these thirty all, except Harvard University and the Commonwealth Fund, are insurance companies or security companies or investment trusts; all but two are east of the Mississippi and those two are insurance companies. The company is no more local enterprise than Western Union or the New York Central is.

Secretary McKay also withdrew government opposition to the Pacific Gas & Electric Company's proposed developments on the North Fork of the King's River — developments made possible by existing facilities built at public expense. As I write, his assistants are constructing what they frankly call a "detour" round the basic Reclamation Law so that users of water from a federal project on the Kern River will not be subject to the 160-acre limitation. Bills to make the branch official in large areas have been introduced in Congress but are not likely to pass.

But much as Eastern-owned Western utilities respect the spirit of private initiative, the West needs dams and wants payrolls. The relinquishment of federal reserved sites and the no-new-starts policy caused uneasiness, and there was November to think of. So the Upper Colorado Storage Project was taken out of mothballs and nearly a billion dollars' worth of construction was recommended. (It will cost at least twice that; for obvious reasons, Bureau of Reclamation estimates are poetic conventions.) Its political feasibility is obvious but its economic and social justification is open to the most serious doubt. Worse still, the plans for it are part fantasy and have been changed so often and so capriciously that no one knows to what extent its engineering is sound. But it satisfies the requirements. No corporation would ever want to build dams on this stretch of the Colorado, so there is no competition; but the promise of the Budget Director would attract corporate investment in the generating facilities, since the public would be paying all other costs.

The recommendation of this project breaches the basic national parks policy: one of the dams it includes, Echo Park, is to be built in Dinosaur National Monument. (Later, another dam is to be built in the Monument.) The dam will destroy the beauty of spectacular canyons of the Yampa and Green Rivers. There was a peak of cynicism in Mr. McKay's promise to spend $21 million of Bureau of Reclamation funds to build the roads now denied the Monument and to construct "recreational" facilities at the fluctuating, unsightly reservoir which the dam would create. This sum is equal to four-fifths of the drastically cut 1955 appropriation for the entire National Park Service.

The progressive impairment of the parks by budgetary bloodletting is a national disgrace — but it is a smaller evil than Mr. McKay's approval of Echo Park Dam. Opening the parks to exploitation by the Bureau of Reclamation — which in the semantics is "co-operation between federal and state governments" — makes only a matter of time their exploitation by any corporations which may want their water, water power, timber, minerals, or grass, and which have sufficient capital to impress a businessman in office.

Conservation: Down and on the Way Out (August 1954)

Many trial balloons about TVA have been sent up. The refusal to reappoint Mr. Gordon Clapp as its director made clear that career-service administration is not desired. His successor will need only a single qualification: a distaste for socialistically increasing private business in the Tennessee Valley by providing cheap power. Several other trial balloons from Interior are significant, such as suggestions that the tremendous Central Valley Project might be sold to the State of California. At the right price it would make a happy deal: the big corporate farms would get the water denied them by the 160-acre limitation they have been fighting since 1902 and P. G. & E. would get the power facilities. This clue is underscored by a recent announcement that the utility companies of the Northwest are forming a syndicate capable of taking over all the federal dams and power plants on the Columbia River, the projects that brought industry and boom times to the Northwest.

If the Central Valley and the Columbia Basin projects should be handed over to utility corporations, how will flood control, erosion control, and the other conservation functions of federal projects be carried on? The utilities could not possibly assume them. Indeed a corporation has no proper concern with them, and no state has ever done an even passable job at any of them. Nevertheless, the clues suggest that the groundwork is being laid for the property evaluators, rate specialists and constitutional lawyers of the new Hoover Commission to propose that all federal reclamation and power projects be sold.

IV

Both the platform and the campaign had promised to take care of the small but influential group of Western stockmen who ever since 1946 have been trying to gut the Forest Service and get hold of the grazing ranges in the national forests. A bill embodying as much of the malodorous "Stockmen's Proposal for an Act" as it seemed cagey to put in one package was sponsored by Senator Barrett of Wyoming — who as a Congressman had spearheaded the attempted landgrab of 1946–47. He has great parliamentary and backstage skill; but his sole victory with this bill was his success in keeping the Secretary of Agriculture's adverse report on it from reaching the House Subcommittee on Public Lands.

At the public hearing Western spokesmen — water users, sportsmen, wildlife specialists, hydrologists, city engineers, individual stockmen, small stock associations — ripped the bill to shreds. The Denver *Post* attacked it repeatedly; so did such other prominent papers as the Salt Lake *Tribune*, the Portland *Oregonian*, and the San Francisco *Chronicle*. More striking was the opposition of many small newspapers, even in Wyoming, which had always before supported the plans of the stockmen's lobby. Whereas the attempted landgrab of six years before had to be stopped by the East, this time the West itself prevented a shameful raid on the public resources. Senator Barrett — seeing that the bill would be defeated if it came to a vote — maneuvered to keep it in committee and to prevent publication of the testimony at the hearings.

But something had to be done for the stockmen and so the Hope-Thye-Aiken Bill was made an Administration measure. Bad to begin with, it was rendered truly vicious by amendment; it has been passed by the Senate but as I write has not yet been taken up by the House. That such sound conservationists as Senator Aiken and Congressman Hope have been lined up behind so reprehensible a measure shows the formidable pressure that the U.S. Chamber of Commerce and other allies of the stockmen's lobby have succeeded in bringing to bear on the White House. Long since, Senator Aiken should have been attacking his own bill.

The bill would achieve three major objectives of the landgrabbers. It would give present holders of grazing permits in the national forests two kinds of property rights in those forests, thus impairing the public title and in part alienating public property. It would enable the present permit holders to sell the permits at will and without reference to the Forest Service, closing the ranges to newcomers and making monopolization of them certain. It would permit them to construct permanent improvements on the public ranges, further alienating public property and enabling the permit holders to tie up the public lands indefinitely with lawsuits. Finally, it would cripple the regulatory power of the Forest Service by permitting appeal to the courts on various kinds of purely administrative decisions. It is a raid on the public-lands system and its passage would seriously undermine our conservation policy.*

The House of Representatives stopped something even worse, a bill by Representative Ellsworth of Oregon, long a congressional spokesman for big lumber interests. It provided that when the government acquired privately owned timberland, as for the reservoir of a dam, which a timber operator had under sustained yield (that is, cutting only in step with replacement by natural growth), the operator would have the option of being paid in cash or by the transfer to him of publicly owned timberland of equivalent value. This meant the national forests or the far smaller forests administered by the Bureau of Land Management — and in committee it was extended to include the forests in the national parks. Proof of operation under sustained yield was not stipulated and there was no guarantee that it would be used on the land to be acquired. The government bureau which must provide the timberland was given no control over its selection, and no power to require any kind of protection or conservation.

Barefaced as these provisions were, however, they were unimportant compared to the central fact: *ostensibly a measure of relief for suffering corporations, the bill provided for the direct transfer of portions of the permanently reserved public lands to private ownership.* Enemies of the public-lands system have been trying to achieve precisely that fundamental step ever since the first reserves were made in Benjamin Harrison's time. The Hope-Thye-Aiken Bill would open fissures in the foundation of our national conservation policy — but the Ellsworth Bill would have shattered it.

* It was defeated in the closing days of the session.

The Secretary of Agriculture drew up an adverse report and this time it reached the committee. Normally this is enough to stop a bill. He was, however, prevailed on to withdraw it. No notice of the public hearing was given except the routine listing in the *Gazette;* conservation organizations and interested Congressmen did not know that it was to be held. It was attended only by representatives of the Department of the Interior, who had been instructed to think highly of the bill (one who wasn't thinking highly enough on the witness stand was called away by telephone), and of the Department of Agriculture, who had obviously been instructed not to think ill of it but to try to get it softened nevertheless. The committee reported it out and by a tricky lateral pass in the Rules Committee Mr. Ellsworth cleared the way for an attempt to slip it over on the House in the closing days of the session. Chance discovery at the last moment, however, scared him into holding it over till the next session.

By then the bill was in the open and it was murdered. The quarterbacking on the floor of the House was by Congressman Metcalf of Montana, who was making a distinguished record in his first term. His Democratic teammates were Madden of Indiana, Price of Illinois, and Brooks of Texas, with McCarthy of Minnesota, Magnuson of Washington, and Hays of Ohio assisting at critical junctures. A striking development, however, was the co-operation of four Pennsylvania Republicans who were well acquainted with the issues at stake — Messrs. Gavin, Saylor, Fulton, and Mumma. Mr. Gavin's role in the debate was especially informed and expert. This extemporized coalition drew the bill's teeth with amendments and then, when the strength of the opposition became manifest, Mr. Metcalf moved to recommit it. His motion carried on a roll-call vote of 226 yeas and 161 nays — a brilliant victory for the freshman Congressman, who is not even a member of the relevant committee.

Perhaps a few other Republican Congressmen, who were active in opposition to the grazing bill, can be added to what looks like a conservation bloc. If the Republican Party retains control of the House in November, this bloc will be important. For it is clear that if any of our historic conservation policy is to be saved, it must be saved in the House. Senator Langer opposed some anti-conservation measures but no other Republican Senator did. Senator Aiken, who devised the strategy for many earlier victories over anti-conservation forces, has now put his great prestige at the service of the attack on the Forest Service. The Independent Party, Senator Morse, has been magnificent, making an all-out fight against every anti-conservation move.

V

The Forest Service may also serve to illustrate dangers latent in other Administration fetishes — reorganization, consolidation, and that cant phrase from schools of business administration, "management-practice improvement." If consolidation and reorganization are the first recourse of a management engineer, they can serve more devious ends and become the last one of a lobby or a landgrabber.

The Forest Service has always been decentralized. It began with a regional organization, to prevent the delays and rigidities that half paralyzed the General Land Office. There are now ten regions, each with headquarters and specialist staffs. Differences in terrain, climate, forestation, methods of lumber operations, and other complex variables make this the only kind of organization that could conceivably be efficient. To consolidate the regions, reducing them to four or even two, as has been proposed, would greatly increase expense and greatly reduce efficiency. It would increase travel, paperwork, and red tape. It would slow up administration and all field operations. It would make the specialist and scientific activities of the Service more cumbersome and expensive. *In all these ways it would add to the costs of the private businesses that use the forests.* But the notion is attractive to the managerial mind. You consolidate the Omaha and Denver offices of Continental Gadgets; why not, then, consolidate Nebraska and Colorado?

There is a more sinister aspect. Weakening professional and administrative efficiency by such a consolidation of the regions would favor both the special-interest groups which want to exploit the national forests and those which want all federal regulation everywhere undermined. Also it would greatly reduce such ability as the Service now has to resist the attacks of its enemies. That is one of the ends in view.

All these hazards would be increased by the unbelievably idiotic plan, which has also been proposed, of abolishing the regional setup and achieving "local control" by grouping the national forests — which disregard state lines — in state units. Neither a forest stand nor the watershed of a river will stop short at a state boundary on Executive Order. But the thirty-eight miniature Forest Services thus created — in ten states there are no national forests — would be easy prey for the local special-interest groups. The Administration fetish which dreams of reorganizing federal conservation activities on a state-wide rather than a regional basis is a victory for the propaganda which represents issues as a conflict between local interests and Washington — when in fact they are conflicts between one local interest and all the others; that is, between a special interest and the public interest. In every aspect of conservation this kind of "local control" must inevitably mean local vulnerability, local manipulation, and local intimidation.

All research in the Department of Agriculture except that of the Forest Service has been grouped under one bureau. In some respects the results have been of no particular importance, in some others they have reduced expense and increased efficiency. But also in some instances they have reduced efficiency and increased expense. It seems likely that the eye of the management-improver is on the Forest Service research, and that his table of organization calls for transferring it to the central bureau. To do so would be a truly stupendous blunder. Forest Service research created scientific forestry in the United States and is now the foremost in the world. It is so organically related to the field activities and daily jobs of the Forest Service that it could be dissected out only at the cost of permanent damage. The damage would increase geometrically in the future.

And one wonders. The Forest Service, always the cornerstone of our national conservation policy, is the most vigorous of the conservation bureaus. That is precisely what is wrong with it in the eyes of the landgrabbers, the cowboys, the U.S. Chamber of Commerce, and its other organized enemies. It is threefold: it consists of the national forests, its agencies which assist and supervise and co-operate with state forestry and private forestry, and its research programs and experiment stations. The effort by the Bureau of the Budget to abolish two of its co-operative programs suggests an intention eventually to amputate one full third of the Service. Removing its research to another bureau would also lop off a third. Reduced by two-thirds, it would be weak, ineffective, easily preyed upon, immensely less valuable to the American future. Is that the end in view? At any rate, in their most arrogant moments the landgrabbers never dreamed up so promising a way to make it impotent.

VI

In a year and a half the businessmen in office have reversed the conservation policy by which the United States has been working for more than seventy years to substitute wise use of its natural resources in place of reckless destruction for the profit of special corporate interests. They have reversed most of the policy, weakened all of it, opened the way to complete destruction. Every move in regard to conservation that the Administration has made has been against the public interest — which is to say against the future — and in favor of some special private interest. Most notably, too, every one has been in favor of some big special interest and against the local small ones. The friendly partnership with business has turned out to mean only some kinds of businesses, the bigger the better.

More important still is the appointment of officials friendly to the enemies of the public interest, for this is preparation for the future. Judicious selection of a director could doom TVA, for instance, and no doubt will. The utilities plan to "get the government out of the power business altogether," with all that that implies in destruction of resources and exploitation of consumers. Many other corporate plans look to getting hold of publicly owned resources and converting them to dividends. Under Secretary of the Interior Tudor has announced that his legal staff is rewriting contracts for the water from federal dams in such a way that the 160-acre limitation can be "by-passed"—which means that the government will connive at breaking the fundamental Reclamation laws. Assistant Secretary Lewis has said that he looks forward to the time when there need be no federal forestry. Their chief, Secretary McKay, has repeatedly said that he favors the disposal to private hands of various classes of public lands.

We called it corruption in Harding's time. It is not corruption when it is Administration policy. But it does show an intent, or perhaps only a willingness, to turn the clock back beyond Hoover, beyond the first Roosevelt, to the Old Stone Age of Republican domination by those to whom the infinite wisdom of Providence had entrusted the property interests of the country. Meanwhile the future of the United States is caught between the inexorable millstones. Population pressure steadily increases. The rivers fill with silt, the water table drops, the rains run off as floods. In the West, booms end because there is neither enough water nor enough electricity. The West too has had four years of drought, parts of it five years. Two dustbowls have formed: "The best place to get a Colorado farm is eastern Kansas." And the best place to get anything else you may want is the Department of the Interior.

Indirect damage such as the sacrifice of professionalism in the public service is manifest. But consider something else. If, for instance, the Central Valley Project should be sold to California, doubtless Mr. Hoover's evaluators could work out a price. (California utilities and the Department of the Interior co-operating.) What would be entirely beyond computation is the loss to the public in past investment, future waste, and future expense. Similarly with every other aspect of conservation — erosion control, flood control, watershed management, forestry, range improvement. Whatever is lost or weakened now will mean pyramiding loss in the future.

For it is the nature of the problems of land and water that damage done to either is cumulative. And it is also their nature, as the entire American experience has shown, that they can be grappled with effectively only by federal action.

Soil conservation districts, REA co-operatives, conservation organizations, browned-out areas of power consumers, towns and counties apprehensive about dust and drought — here are a lot of voters. One obvious giveaway is the presentation to the Democratic Party of a shining issue for 1954 and 1956. And if Schedule C proved to be a fine means for a quick cleanup in top administrative offices, it will remain one after the elections.

In the early fall of 1953 Washington birdwalkers reported a phenomenon which their amiable hobby could not explain. The number of turkey buzzards resident in and near the city had increased remarkably. The buzzard population continued to grow through the winter and the following spring. By now it has created a sizable problem at feeding time at the zoo.

Notes

Page 151

The only subject I have treated in the Easy Chair that had to be serialized is the one to which this piece and the one that follows it are devoted. They appeared at a time when *Harper's* was running the Easy Chair without a monthly title; so I have had to give them titles for this book. The title of the first one is the official designation of the war it discusses, and it is a more exact designation than the one we commonly use, the Civil War. The favorite euphemism of Southern newspapers, the War Between the States, is absurd, ungrammatical, and historically inaccurate. I note that it is also the designation commonly used by some of the historians discussed in this piece.

Page 159

One of the theses of this piece is developed at greater length in "The Century." It is the subject of my trilogy, *The Course of Empire, Across the Wide Missouri*, and *The Year of Decision.* The three books may be regarded as my solution of the problem of how to avoid writing a history of the Civil War, to the study of which I devoted my first years of historical research. I regard them as a treatise on the causes, outcome, and meaning of the Civil War.

Page 169

Obviously the FBI is an effective organization and obviously Mr. J. Edgar Hoover directs it effectively. He also has a genius for publicity; the government's gain was a memorable loss for the advertising agencies. Two kinds of occasion show his genius at its best, the annual return of appropriations hearings on Capitol Hill, and the publication of any article that criticizes the FBI. He has more pipes and louder swells than any pipe organ ever built, more fan clubs than Hollywood, and unlimited newspaper space, gratis. All anyone need do to set them off is to suggest that any employe of the FBI falls an inch short of Superman, that one of them may have momentarily forgotten the Golden Rule which is sewed into the hatbands of them all, or that the archepiscopal robes which Mr. Hoover keeps in his coat closet are showing signs of wear. Criticism of the FBI may not be treason at first glance but it is best to take no chances; the intellectuals whom he accuses of having betrayed us have no loudspeaker in a class with his.

When this article appeared, Mr. Hoover wrote to *Harper's*, saying that he would not "dignify Mr. DeVoto's half-truths, inaccuracies, distortions, and misstatements with a denial or an explanation." That is his habit; he maintains silence by the stickful on every front page. When he wrote to the magazine, he had already not dignified my "half-truths, inaccuracies, distortions, and misstatements" by denouncing me formally in an archepiscopal curse that was carried by every wire service and printed by every daily newspaper in the country. (Cost to me, nine cents a clipping.) He had not dignified them, as he always does, by neglecting to stipulate what, if anything, was erroneous in them. Not dignifying makes a neater game than answering criticism. It is also a form of loud-mouthed personal abuse, which has other names as well, by a man of great power and high public office.

Mr. Hoover's letter in no way answered my article and said nothing relevant about any part of it. It did, however, contain a laboratory specimen of what, not caring to dignify it as a misconception, I must call pure gall. He suggested that a person who is questioned by the FBI about his acquaintances is on the same basis as a witness who is testifying before a grand jury. He knows better. So do we.

Continuing to not dignify me by denials, Mr. Hoover said in another letter to *Harper's*, "Certainly questions of the nature alleged by Mr. DeVoto are not asked." I was writing about the Coplon case; the testimony shows that they were asked there. Does anyone care to score this as a fielder's choice?

Page 231

The articles in this group are arranged in chronological sequence, as those in the other groups are not, and I have made my selection to cover the most important events in the political contest they describe. They constitute more than half of the *Harper's* pieces I have written about the persistent attack on the Forest Service; I have not included any that discuss other aspects of the struggle for the public lands. My own and other publishers have occasionally suggested that I bring together in a book everything I have written on the subject, but I have thought it best to cover it by outline here, with these pieces. I am treating the whole subject in a book which I am writing as this one goes to press.

This group shows how the kind of journalism practiced in *Harper's* can do an essential job that journalism at large leaves undone. Here is a subject of national importance. Yet, as I say in "Number 241," no newspaper and no other magazine gave it anything like adequate coverage. No other is covering its current aspects now. I may therefore provide some annotation — and may add that I did not embark by original intention or desire on a course that has occupied so much of my time for eight years. My conception of my job required me to.

In 1946 plans for an attack on the Forest Service that had been carefully worked out by parties described in these articles were coming to a head. The immediate objective was to prevent reductions in the size of various grazing permits (not many all told, and not large reductions) in the national forests. Beyond that there were the objectives of discrediting the Forest Service and reducing or destroying its regulatory power. And the ultimate objectives were to destroy the Forest Service and the national forests. To make the Service merely the temporary custodian of cutover timberlands in process of reforestation, and to transfer the national forests, the most valuable of the public lands, to private ownership under forced sale and at bargain-counter prices. These are still the objectives of the same interests, of much more powerful interests that support them, and of their agents in Congress and in the Executive branch.

The decision was to develop a legislative program embodying these objectives, for introduction into Congress. How fast could such a program move? How many stages would be required and how much should be attempted with each step? These questions were debated for over a year. A program for the first stage was finally agreed on at a meeting in Salt Lake City, in August 1946, of the Joint Committee of the two national stock associations which my articles describe. The committee intended to launch it in the next session of Congress, at some date which it presently became my job to determine. They were counting on a Republican victory in the midterm elections, November 1946, and the event was to prove that they had calculated correctly. Their plans were bold; they were, in the literal meaning of the word, revolutionary. But success depended on two conditions: proper timing of the congressional assault and concealment of its specific details till it should be made.

What was planned *in general* was no secret. Historically, wealthy stockmen have tended to be loud-mouthed, boastful, and arrogant. Those adjectives describe their public utterances and those of their trade press during the spring and summer of 1946, and they talked even more arrogantly in private. Western conservationists therefore knew that something was going on. So did certain Western newspapermen but it is clear to me that they failed to understand its importance. If they had understood it, they would have tried harder to get the story; as I found out, it was not hard to get.

I was a newspaper reporter as a young man and, as other articles in this book also show, I have frequently written as a reporter for magazines. Furthermore, I have long devoted myself to historical research, which requires the same skills. I add that I have been acquainted with the Forest Service ever since I was in high school, though I had had no occasion to study its operations systematically until the events I am relating here. Also, as a historian I had a specialist's knowledge of the public-lands system, the history of the public reserves, the great land frauds, the conservation movement, and the psychology of the bronzed horseman and his politicians.

I had arranged to spend the summer of 1946 in the West, in order to work in the field on the book that was subsequently published as *The Course of Empire.* To finance the summer, I got commissions for articles on the West from *Life, Fortune,* and *Collier's.* When I headed west in June I knew nothing about the intended attack on the Forest Service but I began to pick up hints about it as soon as I crossed the Hundredth Meridian. I remember with pleasure that I got my first real tip by listening (I could have avoided listening only by going outside) to a very loud and very drunk cattleman in the Range Riders Café in Miles City. (A fine bar and it has a first-rate restaurant upstairs.) In the next few weeks I talked to a good many boastful and indiscreet stockmen, as well as to many other stockmen, most of them small operators, who bitterly resented the intention of the national associations. None of them of either persuasion knew any specific details. Neither did anyone else I talked to — for I soon realized that something important was being cooked up and I set out to learn what it was. By the first of August I had the whole story, except for the specific details of the legislative program. They were the heart of the matter. I decided that they could be obtained.

I have often been asked how I got them and it is an amusing story but the proper time to tell it has not yet come. Enough that every newspaperman knows quite positively that if plans are being kept secret, the plot includes at least one conspirator who is a captive, who opposes it but goes along because he is forced to. As a reporter, all I had to do was to find this man, and I found him. When I headed east again at the end of August, I knew as much as any member of the Joint Committee about the legislative program. Also, and this is what counts, I had a copy of a document which I will not describe but which no one except the committee and its employees had seen. I have not yet used all of it, which is one reason why the adversaries I promptly acquired have never used against me some measures they must have wanted to use. But I used enough of it in "The West Against Itself" to reveal to the Joint Committee that I had the facts that counted.

Here the nature of *Harper's* is again relevant. I had dug out a news story of national importance. By now, however, it was not a story that any newspaper could make a national story unless the *New York Times* or the St. Louis *Post-Dispatch* should assign a correspondent to it and give him his head. I could only assume that both papers had scouted the ground and decided that what they saw above ground did not justify the effort. It could become a national story only by means of a magazine — and what magazine was there? It was the sort of thing that George Horace Lorimer had loved; many times he put such writers as Emerson Hough and Stewart Edward White to work on just such jobs. But his era was over. As I was to find out later, his current successor on the *Post* would not touch such a subject with a ten-foot pole or anything else.

It was, that is, a *Harper's* story; by now, indeed, the danger was that some Western newspaper might get hold of some small part of what I had and publish it. I had certain knowledge that stockmen do get drunk in bars, and if the right one happened to say the right thing, the resulting partial publicity might enable the plotters to amend their strategy successfully. There remained a formidable editorial problem, when to break the story and how to break it most effectively.

Clearly the artificers of the program would keep it quiet till the bills were introduced in Congress. No one, not even the Congressmen and Senators who had agreed to introduce the bills, knew when that would be; they must be timed according to the necessities and opportunities of the coming session, which would begin in January 1947. On the basis of what I knew about Congress, I decided that the bills were not likely to be introduced before April. I also decided that my best timing would be to break the story about three months in advance. That would be roughly the first of January. The annual meetings of the two national stock associations were scheduled to be held in late December. I decided to use the story in the January issue of *Harper's*, which would be out in late December.

There were two decisions here. One of them was proved right; I am not sure that the other one was. I decided to tell the story of the landgrab — the word I applied to the operation, which has been used ever since — in the second of two lead articles I proposed to devote to my impressions of the West after spending a summer there for the first time since 1940. That is, I decided to unveil the landgrab in its social and historical setting, rather than to treat it by itself in a straight news story. My first article, to be published in the December *Harper's*, would be called "The Anxious West." (It is not reprinted in this book.) The second one would be called "The West Against Itself" and I would make the landgrab the climax of the argument it was to develop. This last is the decision that I now believe to have been mistaken. Publication of the story accomplished all that I had hoped it would, but I believe that it would have had even more impact if I had run it by itself, in its own terms, as news. As it was, we retired one Congressman and one Senator to private life, helped retire another Congressman, and made Praying Indians, for the time being, of the entire cowboy delegation. But we might have got another scalp, and not improbably two more, if I had foreseen the eight years of political maneuvering that followed. I knew enough to foresee them but the fact is that I did not.

I had expected "The West Against Itself" to be published while the first of the two stock association meetings was in session. But at 49 East 33rd Street publication day is a movable feast, and it appeared on the first day of the second meeting. Its disclosure of the plans made for Congress caused great consternation among the plotters, and even greater anger. (I am happy to say that the limited supply of *Harper's* in San Francisco forced the newsstand price up to five dollars.) And note this: monthly journalism had scored a news beat of national importance. The story should have been on the wires of all news services from Salt Lake City in the third week of August, but *Harper's* had an exclusive in December. Salt Lake *Tribune* and Ogden *Standard-Examiner* (edited by my old boss, Darrell Greenwell) please copy.

More to the point, my article fused an explosion. It provided the necessary information, the concrete details of the proposed steal. With that information in their hands, conservationists, Western newspapers, and Eastern news agencies and editorial writers could get to work. They got to work, and long before April, when I had calculated the program would be launched in Congress, they had roused public opinion to the point where it could not be launched at all. Of the bills prepared only one was introduced, the one discussed in "Sacred Cows and Public Lands." Its sponsors bitterly regretted introducing it and one of them paid for it with his public career; the Joint Committee and the cowboy lobby at large regretted the blunder even more vehemently. The proposed landgrab was stopped cold. The strategy of the attack on the Forest Service and on the public-lands system had to be completely changed. Everything had depended on hurrying the legislation through Congress before Congress itself and the public at large could find out what it was all about. There had been an excellent chance that the effort might succeed. A much better chance than the cowboys have ever had since.

The other articles in this group have been chosen to describe the principal developments from that time on. They analyze the changes in strategy and the crucial episodes in the continuing attack on the Forest Service. I reprint them with satisfaction as what the part title calls them, a treatise on one function of journalism. For they played a part in a decisive action. The reason why the landgrab did not succeed in 1947, and the reason why the continuing attack on the public lands system since then has not succeeded, is that journalism has kept the public informed about what was going on. *Harper's* and these articles have shared that public service — they have helped provide one of the reasons why the attack is not going to succeed even now, with a President in the White House who is ignorant of the situation and piously indifferent to it, the landgrabbers in control of the Department of the Interior, and the chambers of commerce in control of the Department of Agriculture.

Page 249

McCarran's three-year attack on the Grazing Service, a classic demonstration of how to assassinate a federal agency, had just succeeded when this article was written. The Grazing Service was abolished as such, being merged with the General Land Office, the historic (and often graft-ridden) custodian of the national domain, to form a new agency, the Bureau of Land Management, which took over its functions. BLM was so set up as to be entirely subservient to McCarran and the big stock interests he was stooging for, and from the beginning it was understaffed. The next year, 1947, he succeeded in getting its appropriations reduced to the point where it could not perform the functions originally assigned to the Grazing Service.

Page 329

This article brings the attack on the Forest Service down to the date of my preface, April 15, 1955. It also shows how the pieces of the attack on the public-lands system fit together. It was written before the election of 1954. In general the public power situation has bettered somewhat since then but everything else in the area of national conservation has worsened. It remains true, as the article says, that the Executive departments are much more inimical to our historic policies than Congress. SCS is nearer extinction than when I wrote and seems unlikely to survive. The article should be supplemented by one which would show the deterioration in the Department of Agriculture during the last six months.

Page 333

In April 1955 the top officials of the Forest Service are still under Civil Service protection; that is, they have not yet been put on Schedule C. But a shameful degradation of the public service, as bad as anything perpetrated by the Department of the Interior, has occurred. The supervisor of a national forest is the executive head. Never before has his been a political job but it now is. If it falls vacant, a successor cannot be named for a month and his name must be cleared with the Republican National Committee. Thus, while the Secretary of Agriculture formally adheres to the civil service regulations, he simultaneously applies the spoils system.

I get the above information from the Washington *Post and Times-Herald,* not from the Forest Service. I have been scrupulous not to ask the Service for any information, lest I expose someone there to suspicion. In all the federal bureaus I know anything about, the Eisenhower Administration has introduced a policy of tight-lipped secrecy. The citizen is no longer entitled to information about the workings of his government. Presumably the reduction of the Forest Service to the spoils system is on orders from the White House, at the direction of the National Committee.